RECORDED IN 1935

by Frederica de Laguna and Norman Reynolds

Edited by

FREDERICA de LAGUNA

Illustrated by

DALE DeARMOND

TALES FROM THE DENA

Indian Stories from the Tanana, Koyukuk, & Yukon Rivers

UNIVERSITY OF WASHINGTON PRESS

Seattle & London

Library of Congress Cataloging in Publication Data

Tales from the Dena : Indian stories from the Tanana, Koyukuk, and
Yukon rivers / recorded in 1935 by Frederica de Laguna and
Norman Reynolds ; edited by Frederica de Laguna ; illustrated by
Dale DeArmond.
p.   cm.
Includes bibliographical references.
ISBN 0-295-97429-X (alk. paper).
1. Koyukon Indians—Folklore.   2. Ingalik Indians—Folklore.
3. Tanana Indians—Folklore.   4. Tales—Alaska.   I. de Laguna,
Frederica, 1906–   .   II. Reynolds, Norman.   III. DeArmond, Dale.
E99.K79T35   1995
398.2'089'972'dc20   94-41285
CIP

This little volume is dedicated
to the memory of our predecessors
Father Jules Jetté and Dr. John W. Chapman,
who were the first to record tales from the Dena

CONTENTS

CONTENTS

TALES FROM THE DENA

IV / *Dena Storytelling* *73*

V / *Tales from Nenana* *81*

CONTENTS

COMMENTARY

X / *Myths and Characters* 285

XI / *The Building of Dena Myths* 301

CONTENTS

ILLUSTRATIONS

PREFACE

IN 1935 I ORGANIZED A SMALL PARTY TO MAKE AN AR-
chaeological reconnaissance of the middle and lower Yukon River
valley with the hope of discovering traces of PaleoIndian occupation.
The undertaking was made with the help and inspiration of the late
Dr. Edgar B. Howard, prehistorian at the University [of Pennsylva-
nia] Museum, and was financed by a grant from the Phillips Fund
of the American Philosophical Society to the University Museum.
Our hopes of finding traces of the "First Americans" remained un-
fulfilled, although Indian sites of much later date were located and
tested. (See de Laguna 1936a, b, c, d; 1947; and 1975b for the ethnological and archaeological results.) My companions on this trip were
the late A. J. Eardley (then assistant professor of geology at the University of Michigan), his graduate student assistant, Kenneth Gorton,
and my assistant, the late Norman Reynolds (then a graduate student
in anthropology at the University of Washington). Our search for
archaeological information, or for clues to places where "old things"
might be found, led us, of course, to the Native villages and fish
camps, where we took the opportunity of collecting ethnographic information as well as recording folk tales, although we were never long
enough in any one locality to do more than sampling.

The forty-one tales here assembled were recorded in handwrit-
ing by Norman Reynolds and myself, except for a few that had been
written down by Ella Vernetti of Koyukuk Station who generously
gave us her manuscript. This was long before the days of tape or even
of wire recorders, which were not to become available to anthropologists until about 1950. Although Dr. Chapman had recorded a few
Native songs on wax cylinders—now in the Folklore Division of the
Library of Congress, I believe—such fragile cylinders and their bulky

recording apparatus were hardly suitable for the trip down the Yukon in open skiffs which we were to make. These stories, therefore, were not recorded in 1935, as they would be now, by using a tape or cassette recorder to preserve the words of the storyteller in the Native language. Such a record also has its disadvantages, for it must be later transcribed and translated by, or with the help of, a gifted and specially trained bilingual speaker, a serious drawback for the non-resident anthropologist. Rather, we had to write down the words in English as the narrator was speaking. Whereas I tried to get down the exact words and colloquial expressions, Reynolds more frequently used standard English, except in his recording of Francis McGinty's autobiography. Since both of us often recorded the same story, what one missed the other generally caught, and the tales as given here combine our two versions. The recorder of each story is indicated if known. As will be seen, there are a number of instances where we deliberately substituted the more technical or polite word or phrase for the storyteller's more colloquial or graphic terms for body parts and functions, since sometimes the narrator would ask us for the English words. Many of our stories seem to be lacking in detail when compared with those published in the Native language. Norman Reynolds wondered if this were owing to a taboo against telling myths in the summer months—a widespread Indian concern—but I believe that the relative lack of detail was more likely due to the narrator's (or translator's) difficulty in using English. (See Tales 18 to 20, barely outlined by Chief Luke.)

I had originally titled this collection "Ten'a Tales," in memory of Father Jules Jetté, S.J., a pioneer in collecting Native mythology and ethnographic information from the people he called *Ten'a*. Jetté published Native stories from this area under the title of "On Ten'a Folk-Lore," in the *Journal of the Royal Anthropological Institute* (London), in 1908–1909. Although the Reverend Dr. John W. Chapman had published a few stories from Anvik in 1903 and 1907 in the *Journal of American Folk-Lore*, he also used the name *Ten'a* in tribute to Father Jetté when he published a large collection as "Ten'a Texts and Tales" in 1914 (volume 6 of the *Publications of the American Ethnological Society*). Father Jetté was a missionary at Kokrines and Nulato from 1898 till 1924, and, according to the Natives, "spoke their language better than they did themselves." Dr. Chapman founded the Episcopalian Christ Church Mission at Anvik in 1887 and served there until 1931. We experienced true Alaskan hospitality from Father MacElmeel and the Sisters at Nulato, and from Dr. Chapman's son, the Reverend Henry Chapman, and Mrs. Chapman during the week we spent at Anvik. We were, I believe, the first *anthropologists* to collect Native stories in the area.

While this volume remains dedicated to the memory of these pioneers, the name *Ten'a* has been abandoned in favor of *Dena,* which is the way the Natives themselves wish to spell their name, so that our title has become *Tales from the Dena.*

The designation *Ten'a,* as used by Jetté and Chapman, covered the Indians of the Yukon drainage from the Tanana River down to Holy Cross, including the Natives of the Koyukuk River. Anthropologists now designate the major part of this group as the *Koyukon,* but they draw the downstream line at Blackburn, 130 miles below Nulato, thereby recognizing as separate tribes the people of the Anvik area as *Ingalik,* and those of the Innoko River and Shageluk Slough as the *Holikachuk.* I also am using *Dena* in a loose manner by including the *Lower Tanana,* or Natives of the Tanana River from Nenana down to its confluence with the Yukon, among the Dena, as well as those of Anvik to Holy Cross. The *Ingalik* are called the *Deg Hit'an* by James M. Kari, in his *Athabaskan Stories from Anvik,* (Alaska Native Language Center, Fairbanks, 1981) consisting of the retranscribed texts of Dr. Chapman, but the name has not yet found general acceptance among anthropologists.

During our short stay at Nulato, Father MacElmeel, S.J., gave us every opportunity to study and make use of Jetté's unpublished "Dictionary of the Ten'a Language" (Koyukon), asking only that I should bring this encyclopedic manuscript to the attention of authorities or scholars Outside, who could better care for or publish it. The great fear in Alaska is of destruction by fire, due especially to faulty oil space-heaters. I fulfilled this charge by informing Father John M. Cooper, professor of anthropology at the Catholic University of America (Washington, D.C.), of the existence of the manuscript and of its ethnographic value, adding that I believed that a linguistically trained anthropologist should be sent to Alaska to check on the transcriptions of the unfinished portions, especially the place names. As a result, Robert J. Sullivan, S.J., was sent by Father Cooper to Nulato the following year (June 1936 to January 1937), and in 1942 he published the results of his fieldwork as *The Ten'a Food Quest*. Little was done with Jetté's "Dictionary" itself, however, until the 1970s, when a team of linguists at the Alaska Native Language Center in Fairbanks, under the leadership of Eliza Jones, began work on the "Dictionary," recognizing it as an extraordinary mine of ethnographic value, as well as a linguistic study.

Father Jetté would indeed have been happy to learn that Koyukuk Station had produced a Native scholar who could use his life's work and help to bring it into the world of modern scholarship. He would also have been proud that Miranda Wright, a Native of Nulato, is presently studying for an advanced graduate degree in anthropology at the University of Alaska Fairbanks, in order to become a professional in this field. Both of these Native scholars have critically read my manuscript version of these tales and have generously given valuable advice and insights, for which I wish to express my appreciation.

People like ourselves as we were then, young anthropologists and geologists unfamiliar with the country and with the languages of the Indian peoples, can hardly be expected to give a very full or accurate account of the Native cultures after only a few months spent in the country. We had not yet learned what questions to ask or what points to pursue. A number of isolated items scribbled in the notebooks I carried in my jeans pockets became really significant only when I recently reread them in the light of my studies of the Ahtna (Atna) Athabaskans of the Copper River in south central Alaska, made between 1954 and 1968, and my reading of recent publications on the Yukon Indians, not available in 1935.

It must also be remembered that we were in Alaska to make an archaeological reconnaissance rather than to undertake ethnographic work. Fortunately, my teacher Franz Boas had taught us to carry many strings to our bow, to be alert to all aspects of human existence, and to turn over every stone we could, for there might be unsuspected anthropological gold beneath it. Therefore, when not engaging in archaeological pursuits or questioning the Natives about old villages, we listened to what they had to say about old Indian ways, and we asked them to tell us stories. This collection of tales represents the fruit of "idle hours," the golden nuggets under the stones.

In preparing these stories for publication, I have consulted not only the published works of Fathers Jetté and Sullivan but also those of Dr. Chapman, Cornelius Osgood, Richard K. Nelson, Annette McFadyen Clark, and the stories translated by Eliza Jones, in addition to other works listed in the Sources. Eliza Jones has been kind enough to correct some of my efforts at spelling Native words, as well as to offer further information on the localization of some of the stories. Miranda Wright has painstakingly corrected errors in ethnographic detail and has brought me up to date on conditions among the Dena of today. I am also grateful for the help given me by Dr. Michael Krauss, director of the Alaska Native Language Center, and by others in this organization. Dr. Richard K. Nelson, whom I have never met but whose work I admire greatly, has seen parts of the manuscript and given helpful advice. Any mistakes concerning these topics are mine, not theirs.

The three volumes of Koyukuk stories told by Catherine Attla (1983, 1989, 1990), and translated by Eliza Jones, and the companion volume of analysis by Chad Thompson (1990), represent the latest presentation of this rich oral literature. The tales we recorded in 1935 languished for years in my files, and no one saw or made use of them except for one of my students at Bryn Mawr College, Anne Elizabeth Spillers, 1940 (Mrs. Donald S. Voorhees of Seattle, WA), who analyzed them in a Senior Honors thesis, and Celeste (daughter of the late archaeologist Richard Jordan), to whom I once told "the Owl story" (Tale 41) when she was three years old, and who for a year thereafter demanded it repeatedly.

Although these stories are not specially intended for children, it seems to me that they as well as older folk might enjoy them. To my delight, Dale DeArmond, who has illustrated so many Alaskan stories, expressed an interest in illustrating these and suggested that I write an Introduction. With this welcome collaboration, I knew that we should offer this book to the general public, and especially to anyone interested in Alaska, in its Native folklore, and in imaginative art. Not least among those who I hope will find enjoyment in the book are the children and grandchildren of our storytellers, who told us the *Tales from the Dena* so long ago.

Frederica de Laguna
Department of Anthropology
Bryn Mawr College, Pennsylvania

Postscript: Dale DeArmond and I have asked that twenty percent of the royalties from the sale of this book go to the Doyon Foundation, a Native organization in Fairbanks, Alaska, to be used for the benefit of the Dena children and young people.

F. de L.

Introduction

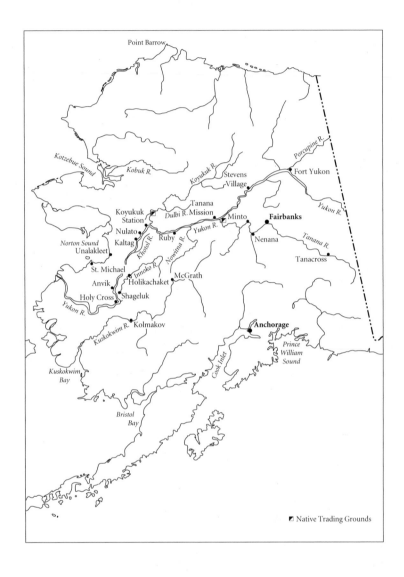

Point Barrow

Kotzebue Sound
Kobuk R.

Koyukuk R.

Porcupine R.

Stevens
Village
Fort Yukon

Yukon R.

Tanana
Koyukuk   Dulbi R. Mission
Station   Minto   **Fairbanks**

Nulato   Yukon R.
Norton Sound   Kaltag   Ruby   Nenana   Tanana R.
Unalakleet   Tanacross

St. Michael   Innoko R.   Khotol R.   Nowitna R.
Anvik   Holikachaket   McGrath

Holy Cross   Shageluk

Kuskokwim R.   Kolmakov

Yukon R.

Anchorage

Prince
William
Sound

Cook Inlet

Kuskokwim
Bay

Bristol
Bay

◪ Native Trading Grounds

Alaska: Native settlements in the middle and lower
Yukon River Valley, circa 1935

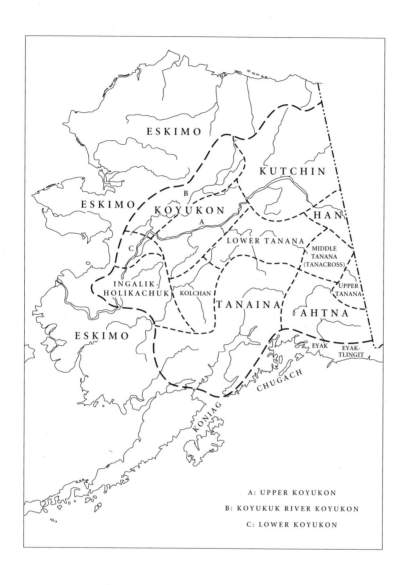

ESKIMO

KUTCHIN

ESKIMO

B

KOYUKON

A

HAN

LOWER TANANA

MIDDLE
TANANA
(TANACROSS)

C

INGALIK-
HOLIKACHUK

KOLCHAN

TANAINA

UPPER
TANANA

AHTNA

ESKIMO

EYAK

EYAK-
TLINGIT

CHUGACH

KONIAG

A: UPPER KOYUKON

B: KOYUKUK RIVER KOYUKON

C: LOWER KOYUKON

Alaska: Native tribal/linguistic groups

I

THE DENA
INDIANS

YOU WHO READ THE FOLLOWING STORIES MAY WONDER about the Native storytellers and how we came to hear these tales. Some of you may be the Dena of today, and you may wonder how your parents and grandparents were living in 1935. And others of you, perhaps not so familiar with Alaska, may be curious about it all. This section and the companion book, *Travels Among the Dena,* attempt to answer some of your questions.

THE BASES OF LIFE

If we were to visit again the small settlements of 1935 on the Tanana and Yukon Rivers, we would now find great changes. Some are deserted, others are grown to sizable towns, and still other sites, deserted when we saw them, are today repopulated. The rivers, too, have adjusted their courses to some extent, as the ice jams in the spring have dammed the floods and forced the water to seek new channels, and as the inexorable wearing away of the riverbanks has furnished silt for new sandbars. "We can never step twice into the same river" is true in more ways than one.

In 1935, the earlier semi-subterranean houses with pyramidal roofs and entrance passages, all heaped over with sod to retain the heat, with a hole in the roof above the central fire to let the smoke escape, had been entirely replaced by small log cabins or frame houses with conventional doors and windows. Skin or bark tents for the summer or for travel in fall and winter had also given way to the ordinary canvas wall tent. The Indian village then, as at present, looked like a settlement of white men, especially since the people were no longer wearing traditional Indian clothing.

5

Travel and Transportation

The greatest changes since 1935 in the lives of Natives and whites have come with improved transportation throughout Alaska's vast interior. The river sternwheelers, which in 1935 represented the height of luxurious travel on the rivers between Dawson City in Yukon Territory and St. Michael at the mouth of the Yukon, have been replaced by the airplane, no longer only those of bush pilots, as in 1935, but also of airlines flying more or less on regular schedules. At a period prior to our trip in 1935, the river steamboats were woodburning and had to stop at frequent intervals to take on more wood. There were, accordingly, many "woodyards" at appropriate intervals along the river, places where spruce logs, cut to the proper lengths, were piled up ready for the steamer. Not only did the Indians travel by steamer, especially children going to the mission schools, but the men earned money by supplying the wood, and some became river pilots. By 1935, however, wood had been replaced by gasoline or diesel oil and we saw no active woodyards. Now steamboat rides between Whitehorse and Dawson City, or from Fairbanks down the Tanana a short distance, survive only as attractions for tourists. Plane travel to Fairbanks and Anchorage, for shopping, for meetings, or for visits to the doctor, have brought Natives of many different tribes and languages together and fostered a cosmopolitan outlook that was just becoming noticeable in 1935.

Although we saw one or two canvas-covered Indian canoes, built like the traditional canoes of birchbark with slightly decked-over prows (none with decked-over prows *and* sterns), even these modern imitations were almost obsolete. Canoes were propelled with crutch-handled paddles or were poled upstream. They were ideal for traveling in the Kaiyuh Slough area because they were so light to carry over portages. The most common type of craft in 1935 was the long, narrow river boat with wooden ribs and planking, equipped with an outboard motor. Although not as steady as the shorter, broader skiffs that we were using, they seemed better able than ours to run upstream and could probably carry more passengers and baggage.

The seasonal round of the Dena in early days had always demanded movement of independent family units between the winter village and the spring, summer, and fall camps. When traveling on foot, it was usually the women who carried on their backs, with tumpline and shoulder harness, loads of fifty to seventy-five pounds, while the men with hunting weapons scouted for game. A family usually had a couple of dogs to guard the home, and, when changing camp, to carry packs that might weigh up to twenty-five pounds. Dogs were not used for traction until the practice was introduced by whites in the last century. The aboriginal-style sleds used by the Dena —for instance, to carry household possessions or to haul back meat that had been cached after the fall hunt—were short, double-ended, hand-drawn sleds, of the type known to ethnographers as "Kutchin." Personal clothing and bedding might be put into a large skin bag that was dragged over the snow like a toboggan, while some families had wooden toboggans for use in heavy snow. The dog team, hitched to a single trace in pairs behind the leader to a built-up single-ended sled with rear uprisers, similar to the modern Eskimo sled, was used by Russian parties exploring the Yukon and Kuskokwim area after 1830, and while this kind of sled was also used by the Ingalik and some Koyukon, the common method of hitching dogs in a single long line was the style used by the Hudson's Bay Company, and probably was brought to the lower Yukon by prospectors. Although the dog team facilitated winter travel, it increased the number of dogs owned by a family, sometimes enough for two teams, thereby demanding the catching and drying of more salmon to feed them. This last was made possible by the introduction of the fish wheel (see Hosley 1981a and b).

Since the "Snowmobile Revolution" of the 1960s, the dog team and sled have been displaced as the major form of transportation in the winter, although teams are still kept for visiting the trapline or for racing. The snowmobile to haul the sled is not only more expensive to run than the team but is more dangerous, since it can break down far from shelter and lacks the ability of the dogs to sense treacherous river ice under the snow. If the snowmobile falls through a hole, both driver and machine may be lost. If the dog team falls in, the driver sitting or running behind the sled is usually safe and can rescue his team. Many Indians and whites, however, use snowmobiles.

7

Fishing

Fish, the basic food for people and dogs, were formerly taken in fish traps of split spruce rods and hoops of willow, tied together with willow bark (sometimes with rawhide cord), with dip nets and with gill nets of willow bark. The trap and the fence leading to it were made and set in the stream by the men and usually tended by them, and the net was made and tended by women. Both were used chiefly in the clear-water tributaries, rather than in the Yukon. Dip nets were used by women for whitefish, and by men for the larger and heavier salmon. Men also took the large king salmon from the nets, killing the fish with a bone stiletto before taking it into the canoe. Fish spears or harpoons could not be used in the Yukon River and its major tributaries because one could not see more than an inch or two into their silty waters. The greater part of the summer's catch was dried for the winter.

The introduction of the fish wheel about 1910 was revolutionary, since its turning arms could scoop up fish ascending these opaque rivers and do so day and night. The wheel, however, did not entirely replace nets. Nets could be made and used by old people or women alone, while the fish wheel needed a man, preferably two, to make and position it. Also it was hardly worth constructing one without a wife and family to handle all the fish it caught. The people who had formerly lived along the side streams and sloughs during the fishing season now moved to the Yukon, where the major salmon runs could be directly exploited, and here were built the fish camps so characteristic of the Yukon in 1935.

At the camp of each independent family group would be a fish wheel, a dock or flat area at the bank where the fish were cut and prepared for curing, and usually a pot where the less desirable parts were cooked to feed the dogs tethered near by. On higher ground would be the tents or shacks where the people lived, and the smokehouse, usually a tall, square structure of poles and bark in which slow fires burned under the racks of sliced fish. Those seen on the lower Tanana River were of this type, but on the Koyukuk River, Eliza Jones informs me, the smokehouse was a long, low building of logs, roofed with poles, birchbark, and sod. One end of this structure, without

8

walls, contained the fireplace and served as a daytime living area for the family; the other, larger part, enclosed with walls of bark or willows, was where the fish were hung. Sometimes two families used the same smokehouse, each with their own fire. The fish were dried outdoors for a day on uncovered racks until they developed a dry crust. Then they were smoked indoors. But fish intended for the dogs were not necessarily dried in the smokehouse.

The enclosed smokehouse is not used among all Athabaskan groups. The Ahtna and Tagish, for example, smoke fish by hanging them on uncovered racks, or racks scantily covered with leafy branches, where they often grow moldy in the August rains and where the lack of a steadily burning smudge permits blowflies to lay their eggs in the fish.

The fish weir or fence of stakes had an opening in which was set the fish trap. The traps in 1935 were made of wire netting and were still used during the winter for a variety of fish, including whitefish, loche, grayling, trout, and blackfish, the last usually taken in the lakes. Though set by the husband, the fish trap was visited by his wife while he was away hunting and trapping.

Trapping and Hunting

Although the fish wheel still turns, the catch no longer means the difference between starvation and full bellies, for the Native who fishes for a living may have other sources of income to buy food, and public assistance is now available to all citizens of the state.

An important source of cash in 1935 was trapping—not primarily for meat but for furs to sell, although the meat of some of these animals was relished and eaten. A Native might have his or her own trapline or lines with exclusive rights to use that were respected by others, and this is still true today, despite the lower market for furs. Marten, mink, otter, lynx, beaver, muskrat, fox, wolverine, and wolf were taken formerly by deadfalls and snares, and a number of taboos and rituals had to be observed by the hunter and by the women of the household. A number of these religious precautions to ensure the goodwill of the animals hunted were, I believe, still being observed in 1935, and snares were still being used for rabbits. The snares were

9

usually set by the women near the winter dwelling. Larger animals, such as the caribou that provided both fur and meat, had usually been hunted by men in groups. The bear, highly valued for its fat in the autumn, was in earlier times confronted with the stone- or copper-headed spear, backed up by bows and arrows. In 1935 the bear was dispatched by a rifle shot, but it was still the most important adversary of the group of Dena hunters who usually attacked it during its fall denning or as it emerged from its den in springtime.

The social effects of several changes in basic subsistence and in wealth-seeking were observable in 1935. Guns, steel traps, and steel snares had taken the place of deadfalls, stone-headed hunting clubs, spears, and bow and arrow. Introduction of the rifle, which enabled the individual Indian to hunt caribou and even the solitary moose, meant the abandonment of the caribou fence traditionally overseen by the leader of the band; just as the fish wheel rendered unnecessary the large weirs supervised by the headman of the settlement. Both introductions weakened or changed the economic functions of the band leader. The development of the fur trade which led to trapping, and the various new jobs created by white activities (working for miners during the various gold rushes, woodcutting, river boat piloting, railroad and road building, even reindeer herding) brought wealth to individuals other than the traditional leader and enabled individual families to play a bigger role in feasts and potlatches. Use of firearms and steel traps also tended to merge the roles of husband and wife, since neither tool demanded the long practice of skills necessary for using a bow or a deadfall. Today many women have become as proficient with guns as men, and many women run their own traplines and do men's jobs. The self-sufficient woman who can carry her own load, manage her own team, feed herself in the wild, and contribute her own earnings (or catch) to the family, has been, I believe, always admired, as she is now.

Steel Blades and Other Useful Articles

Other introductions which must have made life much easier were iron and steel tools. The carving knife with long curved handle and short blade of beaver tooth became the crooked knife with curved steel blade, so deftly wielded by the maker of wooden plates and dishes, snowshoe frames, and the many other manufactures of the inland Athabaskans. Of even greater importance were the adze and the axe with steel blades, for it is hard to imagine how firewood could be cut with a stone blade. Yet procuring firewood was an essential chore throughout the year, for without fire one would freeze to death in winter and might be stung to death in summer by mosquitoes. The modern power saw, run by gasoline, was as great an improvement over the steel axe as the latter was over the stone blade, and it also could be used by women. Matches were long too precious for ordinary, everyday use, but by 1935 had replaced the fire drill, although older Natives were still familiar with the latter.

The Native garments of fur and tanned skin, with their decorations of porcupine quill work, later of dentalia and beads, are probably the Athabaskans' most beautiful manufactures, and were, aside from the canoe and snowshoe, almost the only form of wealth which a frequently moving family could carry. The woman took pride in fitting out the members of her family in their best furs, cut according to her own set of patterns, and lavishly decorated. This skilled work was originally done without the use of the eyed needle. Dena women had only awls of sharpened bone with which they made a hole in the skin through which was poked the sinew thread. The eyed steel needle, necessary for the fine beadwork characteristic of the Athabaskans today, did not reach the Dena women until early in the nineteenth century, although their Eskimo neighbors had used eyed needles of bird bone long before they obtained steel needles from trading posts and whalers, and had already developed the fine stitching, especially of waterproof seams, for which the Eskimo are noted. The introduction of the foot-driven sewing machine must have brought revolutionary changes for Yukon Athabaskan women, although I cannot document these.

Subsistence Living Today

A great deal of the old subsistence patterns of hunting, fishing, trapping, and berrying were still characteristic of the Dena culture in the 1930s, even though many necessities had to be purchased at the store.

11

As long as there was ample game and other natural resources to furnish the larger portion of food and warm winter clothing needed by the family, with extra furs and fish to convert to cash or credit at the stores, innovations could be adopted from the whites with relatively little disruption of the Native way of life. But the influx of whites, especially during and after World War II, and again after Alaska became a state (1958), meant more competition for limited natural resources. There has been concurrently a serious reduction of these resources, especially near the towns and settlements. Some formerly self-sufficient Native families have found themselves unable to live without assistance, as the economy has shifted from that of subsistence fishing, hunting, and gathering to one increasingly based on jobs, contracts, and cash—a new life for which they were not prepared.

Schooling

The introduction of schooling for the children was part of the missionary effort of the 1880s and 1890s. Although financial difficulties forced the mission schools to close or cut back in scope, a process already underway in 1935, public education has since then taken its place. The Indians are now literate, and many are sophisticated, competent teachers, business administrators, social workers, and politicians. In 1989 I was glad to find many Native women filling important positions in local organizations and in agencies of the tribal corporations. In 1935, however, very few Natives had had more than three or four years of schooling. These were the children of Native mothers and white fathers who saw to it that their offspring stayed long enough in school to become literate. A few were children with unusual abilities who had sought an education for themselves without parental encouragement. On the other hand, very few of the older people whom we met in 1935 spoke so little English as to require an interpreter. The exceptions were Old Blind Joe and his wife at Tanana Mission, and Andrew Pilot at Koyukuk. The children in 1935 usually spoke their own language as well as English, but perhaps neither as well as a monolingual speaker. Since the Athabaskan languages spoken by the

Tanana, Yukon, and Koyukuk Natives vary enough in vocabulary and pronunciation as to hinder mutual understanding, English has today become the common language.

All these changes have not been secured without paying a price. Because schools stressed reading and writing in English, in the 1880s and 1890s even forbidding the use of the Native tongue, the latter has been lost except by the older generation. The schools now (since the 1980s) are attempting to preserve the Native heritage through the use of bilingual texts. To this end the Alaska Native Language Center in Fairbanks has developed alphabets in which the Native languages may be written on the typewriter, and has published in these systems the stories recorded on tape by the elders in their own tongue, printing the Native texts along with their English translation (see those by Attla). But the old languages are foreign to the Native children, and once they are no longer used at home, their extinction is inevitable.

To give today's children a sense of older days and of their unique cultural heritage, the school districts in the Yukon drainage have published the autobiographies of quite a few noted elders. Arts and crafts classes at school teach the old skills in basketry, woodworking, and sewing, for example, using older Natives as teachers. But the skills that were necessary for survival in the Native world cannot be adequately transmitted except by actual use and practice; and there is no longer, as perhaps there was still in 1935, the chance of turning back the clock. Schooling is now necessary for success, even for survival, in today's world, but it eliminates the old seasonal round of activities, and may also separate children from their families. For some time the only choice was whether the family would live in town for nine months while their children were at school, with the father perhaps at intervals out in the bush on his trapline, or whether the children would be sent away to boarding school or left with a relative in town, while the family was away hunting and trapping—a hard choice indeed. At present the rapid transportation provided by airplane and snowmobile, and the special K–12 schools in most villages mean that children need no longer be separated from their families.

Health

The entry of the Russians into the Kuskokwim and Yukon River areas 150 years ago unintentionally brought tragedy to the Native peoples. In 1832–1833 the Russians established a trading post on the Kuskokwim, at the mouth of the Holitna River at the edge of Ingalik territory. The next year, Glazunov explored the Yukon from Anvik down to Holy Cross, and then up the Kuskokwim to the Stony River. This was enough to introduce the first great epidemic of smallpox which raged in 1838–1839, killing half of the Kuskokwim Eskimo and many Ingalik, although Zagoskin believed it was less severe among the Ingalik than among the Lower Koyukon on the Yukon River above them.

In later years scarlet fever, introduced from the Chilkat Tlingit, via their Athabaskan neighbors and the Han and Kutchin of the upper Yukon River, reached the Tanana about 1865. There was also a measles epidemic. These diseases, to which the Indians had not even the whites' limited immunity, were devastating in their effects. In 1919 and the 1920s, the deadly influenza which was so widespread in the United States also came to the Territory.

Tuberculosis, the scourge that was killing the Native population, was halted by the introduction of "new antituberculosis drugs, notably isoniazid," as both treatment and prevention (Fortuine 1992: 318); and in the recent figures indicating the increased life span of Alaska's Natives, we can see the effects of better and more available health care since 1935. Alaska's Native population today numbers more than it did in 1935, and the towns have grown. With the improvement in health facilities, we should also note the present greater need of them, for the traumas of American society in general that brought drugs into our cities have not spared the Indians, especially in the detribalized quarters of cities like Anchorage and Fairbanks.

INDIAN "TRIBAL" DIVISIONS

The Indians whom we met on our trip in the Yukon drainage area in 1935 belonged to three major divisions: the *Tanana*, the *Koyukon* (meaning those of the Koyukuk and middle Yukon Rivers), and

14

the *Ingalik* (a name originally applied to the downriver Yukon and Innoko River Indians by the adjacent Eskimo). There is, however, no sharp line to be drawn between these three, or between any of their subdivisions, for the customs, speech, and even the physical type, show gradations as one goes from one small group to the next. For this reason, it has been easy to include all we encountered on our voyage down the Yukon under the general term *Dena,* a name derived from their own word for "human being," *déné* (or variants), as Father Jetté and Dr. Chapman have done. Making finer distinctions, we should put the Indians of Nenana and, below them on the Tanana River, the Indians of Minto, Tolovana, and of the Kantishna, in one of the subgroups making up the *Lower Tanana.* Below that point, however, the Indians at Baker, Hot Springs, and Cosna on the Tanana have been classed among the *Koyukon.*

Subgroups

The name *Koyukon,* designating the main body of Dena, was introduced by Osgood (1936a) to eliminate the unnecessary multiplicity and confusion of earlier designations, especially the Russian ones. It combines the names *Koyukuk* and *Yukon* and also recalls the form *Co-Youkon,* used by Whymper in 1869 for the Indians from Koserefsky to Fort Yukon. The subgroup of Indians living on the Koyukuk River are properly called the *Koyukuk,* the Native name for the river referring to "willow country." The same subgroup lived at the village of Koyukuk Station and at camps on the Yukon near the mouth of the Koyukuk. We visited only Lower Koyukuk country; and I am not familiar with the Upper Koyukuk people, although there is a difference between them and those on the lower river.

The name *Yukon* is derived from the Native name *Yookana* for this river, and the Dena living along it also formed subgroups. Those of which I was aware were: the *Upper Yukon* bands: (1) from Rampart to the mouth of the Tanana, including Tanana Mission; (2) from Tanana Mission to the mouth of the Nowitna; (3) from the Nowitna to the mouth of the Koyukuk; and (4) the *Lower Yukon* band from Nulato to Blackburn, including the Indians of the Khotol-Kaiyuh drainage. The latter, as *Kkaayeh-Hʉt'aane* (Qayex-xot'ana) "Kaiyuh

People," or *Takayaksa* "Swamp People" (Zagoskin 1967:141, 144, etc.), are sometimes felt to be distinct. There were also the Indians called by an Eskimo name, *Ulukagmyut,* who lived or had lived at Ulukak ("Material for the Woman's Knife, *ulu*"), on the Unalakleet River which flows into Norton Sound. These last, related to the Lower Yukon band (4), were evidently a group that had moved over the divide from the Yukon, and in 1935 I ignored them. In fact, Francis McGinty (see his Autobiography in chap. IX), who had herded reindeer for some time at or near Unalakleet, mentioned only the Eskimo of that town and the immigrant Lapp herders, not Indians of Ulukak, although travel between Kaltag (on the Yukon below Nulato) and the Unalakleet River was relatively easy and followed a once-important trade route. (The benefits of this trade may have led the Indians to settle here.)

(In this and other sections, I follow the *Territorial Groups of West-Central Alaska Before 1898* of VanStone and Goddard, and the more detailed territorial groups of McKennan for the Tanana, A. M. Clark for the Koyukon, Snow for the Ingalik and Holikachuk, and Hosley for the Kolchan, all in the *Handbook of North American Indians,* vol. 6, 1981.)

The stories we recorded in 1935 came from the Lower Tanana of Nenana, the Upper Yukon Koyukon of Tanana Mission and Ruby, the Lower Koyukuk of Koyukuk Station, and the Lower Yukon Koyukon of Nulato. Our archaeological explorations, however, continued on below Holy Cross, and even though we recorded no stories from this lower stretch of the river, comparisons of our *Dena* (Lower Tanana and Koyukon) stories can be made with the *Ingalik* tales from Anvik collected by Dr. John W. Chapman between 1887 and 1905 (published in 1903, 1907, and 1914, and retranscribed and edited by James Kari in 1981), and also those collected by Cornelius Osgood in 1934, 1937, and 1956 (published in 1958 and 1959).

Jetté and Chapman included among their *Ten'a* the Indians on the Yukon from Blackburn to Holy Cross, those on the lower Innoko River, and those on the Thompson-Shageluk Slough. But today, following Osgood, these people are known as *Ingalik*. This name was originally derived from an unflattering Eskimo designation referring to the Indians' allegedly "lousy hair," and was the name used by the first Russian explorers who had come to them from Eskimo country in 1834. They call themselves the *Deg Hit'an* (people from here), but this name is not yet in common use. Ingalik also live on the lower Kuskokwim River, and on both the Yukon and Kuskokwim they are the immediate upstream neighbors of the Eskimo. They are distinguished from the Koyukon mainly in their language and their social and ceremonial life. They also show more traces of racial admixture with the Eskimo. Above the Ingalik on the Innoko was a related group, who moved down that river in the middle of the last century and established themselves at Holikachaket (or Hologochakat). It was these people, by then well mixed with the Yukon Ingalik, whom we met at Holikachaket, and who are now recognized as the *Holikachuk*. This village on the Innoko was abandoned some years after our visit, the people moving to the Yukon where they already had summer camps. The Ingalik of Anvik were also already mixed with the Holikachuk in 1935. (Miranda Wright informs me that the Nulato people can understand those from Holikachaket, but from Shageluk downstream it becomes increasingly difficult. It is impossible at Anvik.)

Population Estimates

The population of the Alaskan interior has never been large. In fact, we experienced the vast land in 1935 as largely empty of people, except at the small towns of Fairbanks and Nenana. Those who lived out of town, "in the bush," seemed to be strung out along the river courses, a house or a fish camp here, and then perhaps a long distance to the next habitation, with some stretches of the river, especially below Kaltag, practically empty. Census figures, when a count has been attempted, have usually been inaccurate. They reflect chiefly the guesses made by persons who have visited some but not all of the Native settlements in the given area. The lack of sharp distinctions between adjacent groups means that the lines between the major tribal divisions have been differently drawn by different investigators, so their figures are seldom completely comparable. Furthermore, the bands that represented the smallest population units (above the single family) were not stable, either in location or in composition, particularly during the last century. Thus, while the figures reported are inaccurate and inconsistent, they all indicate a sparse human occupation.

The Koyukon and Ingalik received their first white visitors of record: Andrey Glazunov, on the lower Yukon and Kuskokwim in 1833–34, and L. A. Zagoskin, who ten years later (1843–44) explored farther up these rivers. These two men furnished the earliest population estimates. Zagoskin in 1847–48 gave a total figure of 1,496 for the Koyukon, Ingalik, and Tlegon of the Upper Innoko, and the Kolchan of the Upper Kuskokwim (1967:306–8), but he complained about the exaggerated numbers of Natives claimed by his predecessor: "It was a serious error on the part of the first reporter to exaggerate the numbers of the native population, as it is impossible for those who come later to verify the data, and so they must believe on faith, and ascribe the shrinking of the numbers to disease or a change in the native way of life. There are records to show that the smallpox epidemic, which raged along the whole western shore of North America, did not destroy more than a fifth of the inhabitants of large settlements, and some villages were missed entirely by the epidemic."

Of the census counts and estimates only those given above are comparable. Zagoskin was probably accurate in counting the Natives he saw, but since he was unable to go above the mouth of the Nowitna (just above Ruby), his estimate of the total Koyukon falls short. Ivan Petroff furnished the figures for the Tenth U.S. Census of 1880, but he has been proven a source of dubious accuracy. In 1890, to which he also contributed data, the totals for the Koyukon and Ingalik on the lower Yukon are unfortunately lumped together. Later census counts also fail to distinguish between tribal groups. Thus the Thirteenth U.S. Census for 1910 (1915:122) reported a total of 3.916 Athabaskans in Alaska, but of these only 768 persons could be identified as Koyukon, Ingalik, and Tanana combined. Snow (1981:614) estimates for the Ingalik (including the Holikachuk) a steady decline in numbers from about 900 in Zagoskin's time, to 600 in 1900, to 500 in 1934, and with a slight increase to 530 in 1973–74, presumably counting only residents. The figures compiled and estimated by A. M. Clark (1981:585) offer a surer guide to what has been the general trend for

INDIAN "TRIBAL" DIVISIONS

POPULATION COUNTS AND ESTIMATES

YEAR	1845[a]	1880[b]	1973–74[c]
Upper Yukon Koyukon	56+	485	1,228 (902)[d]
Koyukuk River Koyukon	289	150[e]	645 (491)
Lower Yukon Koyukon	264	447	647 (503)
TOTAL KOYUKON	609+ 1,100?[f]	1,082	2,520 (1,896)
TOTAL INGALIK including Tlegon and Holikachuk	900[g]	(503)[h]	530[g]

[a]These are my calculations from Zagoskin 1967:306–8, based on his 1844 count.

[b]Calculations from Tenth U.S. Census (Petroff's figures, 1884:12; from A. M. Clark 1981:585).

[c]These figures are from the U.S. Department of the Interior (A. M. Clark 1981:585 for the Koyukon; and Snow 1981:614 for the Ingalik).

[d]Figures in parentheses are residents of the several areas; the totals include tribal members living elsewhere.

[e]In 1875 Allen (1877:141) estimated ca. 276 Koyukon on the Koyukuk River and its tributaries, including 164 on the river above Dulbi, 45 at Dulbi ("Red Shirt's village"), and 65 on the lower river. These figures are probably correct.

[f]A. M. Clark's estimate (1981:585).

[g]These figures are from Snow (1981:614).

[h]My estimate from the Tenth U.S. Census (Petroff 1884:12 and 16).

Alaska Natives. After steady and sometimes devastating declines from the days of first contact, chiefly from the spread of infectious diseases that neither Native "medicine people" nor the Russian medical facilities were able to halt, especially in the remote interior, this trend was finally reversed about the middle of the present century when the U.S. Public Health Service assumed responsibility for Native health. The results could already be seen by the 1973–74 figures for Natives, both for those resident in their tribal areas, and for totals that include those living elsewhere, usually in Fairbanks, Anchorage, and Seattle.

Chiefs and Leaders

We might be inclined to suspect that these groups, and the still more minutely delimited subgroups among them, had been defined only to satisfy the compulsive orderliness of anthropologists and linguists! The distinctions observed by these scholars were more easily recognized in the nineteenth century and even in 1935 than at present, I fancy. Yet the larger groupings: Lower Tanana, Koyukuk, Upper and Lower Yukon, and Ingalik, never formed tribes, if we mean by "tribe" a sociopolitical group led by a "chief" or a "chief and council." Men of wealth and influence were recognized as leaders (*kkuskkaa* [qusqa], "rich man" in Koyukon, and related forms in other Athabaskan languages, popularly translated as "chief"), but such leaders held no established position and no authority. They had to create their places in the local society by their abilities, and when these declined or the holder died, his position disappeared until another rich man of ability recreated it as his own. There was no native word for "chief," so the Dena adopted the Russian *toyon* (as *doyon, doyonh*), but it soon came to mean "insufferable, bossy person," for the Dena gloried in the fact that no one had power or authority over them (Jetté 1906:396).

The existence of the "band" as a recognized unit of Dena society depended, however, upon having one or more leaders or "big men" around whom the people could rally. Beyond the family or household, the village or "band" (numbering about 100 to 200 people) was the basic unit of Native society, although the influence of an able or charismatic leader might be felt among the neighboring settlements, drawing them closer together. There were no "real chiefs" before 1885, the Koyukuk River Indians said, for that was the year when Chief Moses united almost all the Koyukuk River bands. Before that date, the larger Koyukuk units, like those of the Lower Tanana, for example, were simply groups of bands, generally similar in speech and custom, that lived in much the same way in the same geographical area. Among the Ingalik, the "chief" and his family of several wives and children formed a temporary aristocracy, and the common people relied on his caches of food when hungry.

The notion of an elected chief was introduced by U.S. Government agents early in the present century, and the Council of the Tanana Chiefs in 1915 was formed largely under their guidance and that of the missionaries to mediate between the Natives and the whites and to deal with problems unheard of before. The Tanana Chiefs Conference was later reorganized as the nonprofit, cultural counterpart of Doyon Ltd., the largest of the twelve land-owning, for-profit Native corporations established under the Alaska Native Claims Settlement Act of 1971. The Conference and Doyon include not only all the Indians of the Tanana River but also all the Alaskan Athabaskans of the Yukon, Koyukuk, Kuskokwim, Chandalar, and Porcupine Rivers.

The functions of the aboriginal leader had been largely economic and ceremonial. Thus, he was someone who could gather together and direct the people of his band or settlement on hunts for a community feast, or in building and operating a caribou fence or a large fish weir. He was liberal (up to a point) with his supplies of preserved food. He was also the person who could sponsor the intervillage feasts or potlatches to honor the dead or the game animals slain that year. In addition to their religious functions, these ceremonies were formerly important for bringing people from different bands and larger groups together. On such occasions, gifts were exchanged, marriages were arranged, and trade partnerships were formed, usually between individuals of different bands who thereby extended their personal network of relatives or close friends. At the same time, these gatherings were opportunities to display the special characteristics and local distinction of each band, and to strengthen the prestige of its leader. These ceremonies were still being carried on in 1935, but we did not witness any because they took place in the winter months, and the ancient summer trade fairs had lapsed.

Clans

The Athabaskans of interior Alaska are organized by clans, membership in which is determined by that of the mother, descent and inheritance being matrilineal. Only the Ingalik of Alaska are without clans, having apparently shifted clan functions to the village under Eskimo influence. Matrilineal clans are found among all the tribes: Kutchin of the Upper Yukon, Ahtna of the Copper River, Tanacross and Nabesna of the upper Tanana, Nenana and Minto of the lower Tanana, Tanaina of Cook Inlet, the Koyukuk and Yukon Dena, as can readily be seen from the similarities of clan names among these diverse peoples. Similarly named clans in different tribal groups are recognized by the Natives as being "the same, but a little bit different." The Ahtna, Upper Tanana, and Tanaina were alike in possessing two exogamous, matrilineal moieties that functioned like clans, but which were actually groups of clans.

Clans (and moieties) regulated marriages; that is, a Caribou clan man was not supposed to marry a Caribou clan woman, but was free to select a wife from any other clan, perhaps from his father's clan or from one in which he had no relatives. There was, however, a strong tendency for two clans in the same settlement or in neighboring ones to become linked in marriages, since unions between cross-cousins (children of a brother and a sister) were favored, and two such clans formed the basis of the settlement. In addition, in each band there was always a third or "middle" clan whose members married into both of the other two, although the identity of the middle clan varied from group to group. This third clan in any community originated in a group of strangers from another band who had moved in, searching for spouses. But as time passed and more unions were made with the residents, the middle clan would gradually become identified with one or the other of the two local clans, for the basic structure of the society was dual. Because the numbers of individuals involved were so small, there were frequently some persons in a band who could not find mates in the clan traditionally "opposite" to their own, so they might move to another village as married-in spouses, thus forming the nucleus of another "middle" clan. I do not believe that the system was fundamentally a tripartite one, even though each band seemed to have a "middle" clan.

The clans of each group were (see Tale 23, and de Laguna 1975b, plus personal communications from Catharine McClellan, Robert McKennan, and Edward H. Hosley. The dates given below refer to the years in which the field observations were made, not to publications):

Lower Tanana, Nenana: (FdeL 1935, CMcC 1960)
1. Caribou people
2. Fish Tail people
3. Middle people (name indicates "Red Paint people")

Lower Tanana, Minto: (CMcC 1960, RMcK 1969, two sets of answers)
1. Caribou Horn or Caribou people. Came over the hills from the Yukon, or possibly the Kuskokwim. "Top clan"
2. Fish Tail. "Came up the river"
3. Nultsina, "Rabbit Tail." Came from "Cordova area," i.e., the mouth of the Copper River

1. Beaver people. "Almost the same as the Caribou Horn. Came from down river"
2. Red Paint people
3. "Middle people, related to both sides, similar to Nultsina"

(The reason there are so many clan names for the Minto people is because so many persons have moved here from other areas.)

Yukon, Tanana Mission (FdeL 1935, RMcK 1962)
1. Caribou people
2. Noltsina, "Maggot people" (probably a mistranslation)
3. *Toneedze Gheltseelne* (Tonidza ʀaltsiɫna) "being continually formed in midstream," meaning "Middle people," but called "Fish Tail people"

Yukon, Ruby-Lowden-Galena (FdeL 1935)
1. Caribou people, "from the north, high class"

2. Noltsina, "Black Bear people, from the other side, the poor man's side"
3. "Middle of the River people" or "Middle people" (identified as Brown Bear people or Fish people)

Yukon, Galena (RMcK 1940s)
1. Caribou people, "lighter colored"
2. Nultsina, "Other people, Brown Bear people"
3. Middle of the River people, "came from a fish"

Koyukuk Station, and Lower Koyukuk River (FdeL 1935)
1. "From among the Caribou people"
2. Noltsina, "Black Bear or Copper people, from underground"
3. (Tonidza ʀaltsiɫna) "From Out-of-the-Water people" or Marten people, associated with dentalia and fish

Koyukuk River (four bands, 1970s) (Clark 1975:172–73)
1. "People who live among the Caribou"
2. Nulchena or "Iron" people (probably Bear or Copper). Most important clan
3. "In the Middle of the Water." Have most friends. Formerly important because of association with dentalia, so called *Gitlina,* "Dentalium people"

Yukon, Nulato (RMcK 1940s)
1. Caribou people, "good people, lighter colored" [light-footed, agile, tireless walkers] *
2. Neltsina, Bear people, "bad people"
3. Middle people (not otherwise identified) [associated with beaver, salmon, water animals] *
   *[Information from Miranda Wright, of Nulato, who questions the assignment of "good" and "bad" to the Caribou and *Noltsin,* but knows little about the latter.]

Yukon, Stevens Village, mixed Kutchin and Upper Koyukuk (CMcC 1950s)
1. Caribou people
2. Naltcina, "Multipliers"
3. "Middle Race"

Upper Kuskokwim, Kolchan (EHH 1960s)
1. Caribou people or "people who live in caribou country"
2. Fish [tail?] people, associated with lower Kuskokwim and Innoko Rivers
3. People in the Middle, middle kind
4. Nalchin (mentioned by some, but belong to Lake Minchumina and Birch Creek of lower Tanana)

The name *Naltsina* or *Noltsina* (and variants) means "Came Down from Above (the Sky)" in Ahtna of the Copper River, where I suspect the clan originated, but I do not know how it is interpreted in other languages. The sky origin, however, is assigned by the Upper Tanana people to a different clan, also from the Copper River and related to the Naltsina, but who among the Ahtna claim a coastal origin.

Jetté wrote (1906:402) that the Dena told him that they were divided into the three clans: *medzihterotana*, *tonitserotana*, and *noletsina* (our Caribou, Middle, and Noltsina), but that the distinctions were meaningless, and he could find no one to explain them. Later, however (1911:253), he wrote that the *Medzih-te-rotana* (Caribou people) were "under the special protection of Dzada," the Spirit of Cold, so that to obtain cold weather for traveling, one beats the snow on the grave of a member of this clan, and *Dzada* will hasten to bring cold and a snowstorm to cover the grave. Despite Jetté's failure to learn anything more about the Dena clans, in 1935 I was told how they originated (see Tale 24), although not all the Indians were then following the rules of clan exogamy. I was also told (de Laguna, 1947:102; 1975:119–20) that leaders of the clans from different villages had "something like a debating contest," in which the challenger would make a speech full of obscure allusions to some object symbolic of his clan, or to an event in their history, the meaning of which the opposing clan (and its village leader) had to guess and counter with a similar speech. This was the way in which misunderstandings or quarrels could be settled at potlatches without directly speaking about them. It also indicates that there may have been an association of a clan with a village, probably that to which the village leader belonged. Unfortunately I did not pursue this further in 1935.

McKennan also learned about the clans when he was stationed

on the middle Yukon during World War II, and in 1961 and 1968–1971. Older natives among the Koyukuk River people gave A. M. Clark fuller information about clans ("matrilineages") and their functions, although young people up to the age of thirty then did not even know to what group they belonged. She reported (1975:172–75) that, in former days, the clan affiliation of a stranger from another band or "tribe" was always ascertained, and his clanmates gave him hospitality and safe-conduct within the territory of their band. It was also the rule in the old days to marry outside of the band, as well as the clan, and for the son-in-law to live with the wife's parents, at least for a year, working for them, just as he had worked for them when courting to show that he was an eligible husband for their daughter. In their old age, the parents would live with a married daughter (or sometimes a married son) and be cared for by the younger couple.

I believe that sometime in the past, the local members of a clan played a role in preparing for and giving the memorial potlatch (Feast for the Dead) for their deceased clanmates (see also Loyens 1964:138). Persons of another clan (the major "opposite" one in the community? or that of the decedent's spouse? or father?) had attended to the disposal of the corpse, and now had to be paid at the ceremony. Sometimes they even "helped" with the give-away, making it more important by privately adding to the wealth that was to be distributed to the guests, although I suspect they were also among the guests, getting it back again. Such a custom was and is common among the Tlingit.

Miranda Wright offered a somewhat different interpretation: Everyone attending the feast was supposed to bring a "gift" to be "given to the spirits" (of the dead). These offerings were redistributed, so that each person attending the ceremony would receive a gift (as a surrogate for a particular dead relative of the giver), and no one would leave without such a "blessing." This rule of the ceremony has been ignored in recent years by those who do not understand its meaning. Rather than insult the spirits by omitting some of them from these benefits, contemporary natives who would follow the protocol of ancient times supply the necessary extra gifts, but clan membership, even if known, is not involved. (The Feast of the Dead is further explained in chap. III, pp. 52–55.)

The old system of partnership linked brothers-in-law (who were also cross-cousins in the old days) through exchanges of gifts (formal trading) and reciprocal hospitality. There were still partnerships in 1935, although they were not necessarily based on kinship ties, but might involve simply sharing in assets and work. This was the case with a partnership we encountered in 1935 between a white man and a Koyukuk Indian at Koyukuk Station.

II

THE DENA
ANNUAL CYCLE

IT IS NOT POSSIBLE, OF COURSE, TO RECONSTRUCT NATIVE
life in the past before the first direct contact with the white man,
but we can make an attempt to sketch some aspects of the aboriginal Native economy, even though much will always remain hidden.
In making this attempt, however, we must remember that the Dena
yearly round of subsistence activities during the eighteenth or early
nineteenth century was not simply like that of the early twentieth
century minus the use of fish wheels, steel traps, firearms, outboard
motors, and steel axes and knives. The adoption by the Natives of
these inventions meant more than additions to the existing Native
culture; their use produced revolutionary cultural changes, as I have
attempted to indicate. Nor were the early Athabaskan cultures of the
Yukon drainage all alike, and, because of cultural differences among
them, the new inventions produced differing effects.

For these reasons it is not really possible to encompass with
a single description the annual cycles of all the groups here called
Dena, because the seasons and their activities, as well as the differing foreign contacts affecting them, varied greatly as we pass from
the Lower Tanana or the Upper Koyukon to the Ingalik. In any given
locality, the seasonal weather, the fish runs, the caribou migrations,
and the cycle of rabbits (snowshoe hares) were liable to change from
year to year. Even within the general cultural pattern for a particular
band, there were usually several alternative activities for a given season from among which an individual family could choose.

On the whole, the upriver Indians relied mainly upon hunting
for their subsistence, and so they had to travel a good deal during
the year. They lived therefore in temporary camps or semiperma-
nent settlements of hastily built homes, even in winter. By contrast,

the Indians on the lower Yukon, had richer and more regular sources of food not available to the upriver hunters; so not only did they more-or-less regularly occupy summer settlements, but in their winter villages they built substantial underground houses and ceremonial houses (*kkuskuno*), not unlike the *kashim* of the Eskimo neighbors. Since the greatest contrasts were likely to have been between the Tanana and the Ingalik-Holikachuk, these groups are not included in our present consideration, which will focus on the Koyukon.

The following sketch of the annual cycle (in which you will note my obligations to Richard K. Nelson, 1983, and to A. McFadyen Clark, 1975) does not pretend to fit accurately the life of any one band. It attempts to give only a picture of the "average" seasonal round as might have been lived by an "average" group of Koyukon in the early nineteenth century, before the introduction of western commercial traders and their wares, gold seekers, and river steamers made possible new subsistence patterns. In this I am using, in addition to printed sources, the information given by Johnny Dayton, a Native of Koyukuk Station who acted as our guide on a ninety-mile trip up the Koyukuk River, and the corrections and suggestions made by Miranda Wright and Eliza Jones.

The year for the peoples of the Yukon River and its tributaries is marked by a succession of "moons," during which different sources of food become available or disappear. It is divided most sharply into two major seasons, the short summer and the long winter, defined not so much by the apparent movement of the slugish sun as by the condition of the lakes and rivers along which the people live. The Indians also recognize and name the spring and fall as the transitional periods between the two major seasons.

The rivers may begin to freeze in late September. The first ice cakes that float past the villages, and the first icy crust forming on the swamps and lakes of the floodplain, are signs that travel by canoe must soon stop, although the lowlands are still too spongy to encourage travel on foot, and there is no snow yet for the sled. (Even today, as we observed in 1935, natives and traders with skiffs and outboard motors, as well as the captains of river steamers, all hasten to reach their wintering places before the end of September, for sometime in

October the freeze-up will imprison them wherever they may be.) In September, one is finally free of the late-summer plague of tiny biting gnats that supplant the mosquitoes in August, and some brilliant golden days may break the late-summer cycle of rain and wind. There is frost every night, and a tang in the air at noon, so that work out of doors is undertaken with zest. Driftwood on the bars and standing dead trees are cut for firewood and left stacked to be brought in by sled when the snow comes. The migratory birds have been winging southward in giant straggling Vs across the sky, and hibernating creatures from the great brown bear to the tasty little ground squirrel of the uplands have fattened on the last berries and are readying their snug dens. Any fresh meat or fish that may be obtained by the people can now be frozen and hung in the cache; but late berries in covered birchbark containers are put in underground pits against the frost. (After the adoption of the dog team for traction, sleds and dog harness would be checked, mended, or replaced with new items, while dogs and people alike would eagerly await the liberation to be brought by the ice and snow.)

More dramatic than the first silent descent of snow or the cessation of the running rivers and streams in the fall is the breakup of these same rivers in the spring. This may come in April or May. It starts near the headwaters, so that cakes of ice begin to move downstream before the ice on the lower reaches has melted. This huge, noisy shoving of ice blocks upon ice blocks may create vast dams in the river that hold back the water until the river rises and overflows its usual banks. These spring floods, ranging up to ten or twenty feet above normal water level, spread across the lowlands on the south and east of the Yukon, cutting new channels and, in old channels, forming new lakes to be left when the waters subside. The floating ice and floodwaters may also damage boats (and later fish wheels) that have not been secured well above the river, and will sometimes knock down or carry away houses. This menace of floating ice and flooding waters usually lasts for at least two weeks at any given place. Yet there may be some sections where the river has managed to freeze over again at night or where the ice has not yet broken, and here travel may be possible until the end of May. The river ice has become spongy and soft, however, slowing down snowshoes (and sled runners), and, since ice in melting first becomes detached from the banks, the traveler runs the risk of finding himself (and his team) stranded on an ice island until someone comes out by boat to rescue him. Even when the ice is gone, upstream travel may be impossible for a week or more because the river will be so full of meltwater that it covers the sandbars or small islands that usually offer the eddies needed for paddling or poling upstream, or drowns the paths beside the river used for towing canoes against the current.

(Because the breakup is of such critical importance, and because the times of its occurrence vary from year to year [recorded from April 26 to May 15], it is not surprising that, since 1917, Alaskans have been wagering on the day, hour, and minute of the breakup at Nenana, the exact moment being determined when a metal spike in the ice moves far enough to touch a wire across the river that is connected to an electric clock. Only Alaskan residents are permitted to wager in the Nenana pool.)

For the Natives in times past, the breakup was signaled by the first flights of migratory waterfowl, honking, quacking, and cackling on their way to the breeding grounds in the river bottoms or tundra marshes. As the snow melts and bare patches of soggy ground appear, so do the first mosquitoes. The meltwater drips into the entranceways of the winter houses, and the people scramble out to live in summer or spring dwellings above the wet. Resident birds and beasts, like the ptarmigan, spruce hen, snowshoe hare, and weasel, begin to shed their winter white for the first ragtag patches of summer brown. The many small singing birds of summer signal their arrival in the thickets where they will nest and fatten their offspring on the abundance of insects. For people, however, spring is the season when the winter's supplies of food for men and dogs are exhausted, the summer's bounty is not yet come, and it is still hard to get provisions. Rabbits (hares) and grouse snared by the women near home, or porcupines trapped by the men, may be all that is at hand to fill empty food bowls.

Before the breakup, and before the beginning of May, people have taken advantage of the warmer weather and longer days of spring to travel. "The Koyukon are passionate travelers, and spring is the traditional season for long journeys" (R. K. Nelson 1983:9). Some go to visit other settlements, some move to their spring camps, but all hunt what they can on the way: caribou moving north, a moose if its trail is fresh and there are many hungry mouths, and sometimes a bear just out of its winter den. Parties of men may even visit a den where a bear is known to be still hibernating, and there may attack and kill it. A moose or bear kill causes a halt in the journey, for the party will camp until the meat is eaten or properly cached.

At the spring camps some families erect birchbark lodges or shelters of spruce branches, but most live in tents of dehaired hides of caribou or moose. These are tipis about fifteen feet in diameter, with a fireplace in the center of the circle, a hole above for the smoke, and a skin door. Spring also brings a welcome change in diet. The arriving geese and ducks are hunted with bow and arrow. They are also taken in rectangular nets of willow bark, which are stretched between two trees, one on each side of the slough along which the birds are flying. People stand at the ends of the nets with disk-shaped pieces of birchbark which they throw like frisbees above the flying birds. Mistaking the sailing bark disks for hawks, the ducks or geese dive to escape but fall into the net. People pick cranberries after the melting snow has uncovered them, to mix with pike and whitefish roe, and a little fresh snow.

The mainstay at this time, however, are fish. Grayling, whitefish, pike, loche, and suckers are caught in rectangular nets of willow bark or sinew, twenty to twenty-five feet long and eight feet deep, equipped with floats of cottonwood bark and stone sinkers. Such nets have been set across the narrow sloughs under the ice during the winter, and are now used in open water after the breakup and throughout the summer, being moved as needed to intercept the various species. These nets are intended to catch the fish by the gills; therefore, nets with meshes of different sizes to fit the various species are made by the women, the size of the mesh being measured by a special tool, which in historic times was the ordinary mesh gauge familiar to white and Eskimo fishermen. Fish are also caught in large traps, made like openwork baskets, with a funnel-shaped entrance inserted at one end. This permits the fish to enter but prevents their escape. These traps are set in openings along a fence or weir built across a stream or slough, the open ends pointing downstream, and like the set nets are repositioned as needed to take the different kinds of fish. During the breakup, traps and set nets have to be taken from the water, but dip nets can be used in eddies along the shore. The dip net is held in the water with the mouth downstream and is lifted when shaken by a fish trying to swim through it. Men and women usually have their own tasks in making and setting weirs, fish traps, gill nets, and dip nets, although a single person of either sex can tend these alone if necessary.

At the spring camps, an important task is the repair of canoes and the making of new ones, for boats are necessary for fishing as well as for summer travel. Spring is the best time for gathering the bark needed for canoes, baskets, roofing, and other essentials. Men make the canoe frame; women sew on the bark cover. Then all the seams must be made tight by pitching with spruce gum. As soon as open water permits, parties of three or four men, each in his hunting canoe and armed with bows and arrows, may go out at night to a nearby lake to hunt muskrats, calling them with a "sucking" or "kissing" noise produced by a sharp intake of breath through puckered lips.

In early June, before the salmon runs begin and when the main rivers are still too high for setting out traps and nets, groups of men, less often accompanied by their wives and children in the mid-nineteenth century than in later times, may go on a trading trip to some traditionally neutral location where they meet with similar groups from other regions. There may be feasting and dancing, as well as trading, at these meetings. In the Lower Koyukuk River area, whole families moved to central locations for the spring celebrations, according to Eliza Jones.

(The most famous of these trading centers, where the Koyukon, Kutchin, and Tanana used to meet, before trading posts were established and even for some time later, was Nuklukayet Point (*Noocheloghoyet*) at the junction of the Tanana and Yukon Rivers. Another place was at the confluence of the Nowitna River and the Yukon, east of the present town of Ruby, where Indians from the Koyukuk River, and from the swampy lowlands of the Kaiyuh-Khotol region and the upper Innoko, east of the Yukon, met with the local Koyukons. So, apparently was Kateel on the lower Koyukuk, to which the Kotzebue Eskimo came to trade with the Koyukon, although the latter and the Ingalik also made trips to visit their trading partners in Norton Sound.)

Summer comes with the warmth and the endless days of June and the appearance of the first salmon. The first to arrive are the kings (spring or Chinook), the run beginning in the middle of June or the first of July and lasting about three weeks. These especially prized salmon are taken in the women's nets, which are set out as soon as the river is low enough. A woman may visit her net two or three times a day, her husband often accompanying her to help in subduing a fish too large to be safely taken into the canoe while struggling. It is clubbed with a wooden maul or stabbed with a bone-pointed stiletto. Some men, however, prefer to fish alone with a dip net. (Today, of course, the fish wheel supplies virtually all the salmon). The major run is that of the dog salmon (chum), which comes in July, followed by that of the silvers (coho) in August, but since there are both early fish and stragglers, the catch at any time is likely to include more than one species.

Cutting the fish with a semilunar knife (*ulu* or *ulo*), formerly with a slate blade, now preferably with one of steel made from the blade of a hand saw), requires the skill and speed of the experienced woman, and such a woman is greatly admired. She is also in charge of drying and smoking the fish that must be put up to feed people and dogs through the winter. The women will string salmon heads on a long willow withe to let them "ripen" for a couple of weeks in the running water, then will boil them to extract the oil. Fish oil is used in cooking, for light in the small clay lamps, and to grease the skin canoes made of moosehide or the kayaks which some Indians trade from the Eskimo.

Salmon eggs are stored in baskets in the underground cache until "ripe," when they and the "ripe" salmon heads are boiled and eaten like cheese, supplying much-needed nutrients. Bear fat and moose or caribou tallow (and often some seal oil) are heated and melted together. The mixture is constantly stirred as it cools. Some fresh snow, or a dry powder made of fish flakes (whitefish boiled, squeezed, and dried) or, later, of crushed hardtack is added at this time, and bear berries are scattered through it. Another dish is of whitefish or salmon roe mashed with cranberries (and sugar), sometimes with snow, and there are other recipes for dishes so prized at winter feasts. Although all these preparations are especially the affairs of the women, their

34

menfolk also help with the heavy work of getting the fresh fish to the camp and of hanging those that are cut and ready to be dried.

The men have also built the fish racks and the smokehouse and have supplied most of the wood for smoking the fish, but when much of this work is done, they can take off for a few days to hunt bears, small animals, or waterfowl, bringing home meat that makes a welcome change from the fish diet. Ducks in particular are taken when they are moulting and cannot fly, and a successful duck hunt is the occasion for a community feast. Such hunts and feasts are coordinated by the village leader. Beaver are shot from the canoe or while feeding on the beach. All this time the women are continually busy at the fish camps, for upon their skill and diligence depend the lives of their family members.

The house occupied in the summer is usually a small dome-shape lodge of birchbark with a tightly fitting door to keep out the mosquitoes. It is used primarily for sleeping, for all cooking is done out of doors over an open fire. Before retiring for the night, people may build a smudge inside the lodge to kill off the mosquitoes indoors, or the smudge may be in front of the door, so that the mosquitoes still clinging to the people are not taken inside. In addition to mosquitoes, large deer flies in July torment animals and people; in August, as the mosquito clouds begin to thin out, the savage stinging gnats or "no-see-'ums" are ready to take their place.

As summer wanes and the salmon runs dwindle, the dried fish are bundled and carried back to the winter village where they can be stored in the tall caches (little log cabins set on high posts that marauding animals cannot climb), and the equipment at the summer fish camp is stored for another season. Prudent families begin to cut or gather as much firewood as possible, to be later taken to the winter camp by sled. Ducks and geese are hunted as they begin to gather on the ponds for their fall migration to the south. The slopes above the Yukon are bright with blueberries. Also ripe for picking are mossberries, rose hips, salmonberries, blackberries, and cranberries, but berry-pickers must be alert to the bears that also seek out the best berry patches. Women and children usually go out together in a party for a whole day of berry-picking as soon as the salmon runs have dwindled.

By mid-September, most people have moved to their fall camping places. The days have shortened, and the nights are dark because the snow has not yet come. The fall houses are the same size and shape as the winter houses but are entirely above ground and are less solidly built, although both are constructed of moss, bark, logs, and earth piled on a framework of poles. It is now necessary to conserve heat at night, so the smokehole in the center of the roof has a gut skin cover that is put in place at bedtime, when the coals are taken from the fireplace.

In the fall, before the freeze-up, river fishing is almost at an end, although gill nets are left in the river as long as possible to catch sheefish and the last straggling salmon. In the sloughs and lakes, a bountiful harvest of pike, burbot, and especially whitefish can be netted.

Early fall is the season for moose hunting, for the animals are in rut and the largest bulls can be found in the brush along the river bottoms. This is also the time when the men leave on their annual fall hunting expeditions to the hills. Caribou are the principle quarry, and the hunters go to the caribou trails at the heads of the side creeks where caribou fences or corrals have been built. Here the migrating animals are taken by snares set in the fence, or are dispatched inside the enclosure by bow and arrow. Or animals swimming across a river or lake may be stabbed with the copper dagger by men in canoes. The men also shoot any other game that they encounter. They are especially on the outlook for bear, now fattened for hibernation. Most of the meat procured is covered with skins and cached on tree platforms, the locations marked by blazes (scars) cut in the bark. No shelters of any kind are taken along, but the hunters may build a temporary brush lean-to if overtaken by bad weather, keeping warm by the fire that burns across the open front.

Meanwhile the women have been snaring rabbits, spruce grouse, willow grouse, and ptarmigan, and have picked the last berries.

By mid-November most of the Koyukon families are established in their semi-subterranean houses at the winter villages. These are very different from the big, but only semi-permanent, dome-shape lodges of eighteen to twenty moose skins used by most of the Tanana and Kutchin. Such domed shelters of skin or bark may have been the original Athabaskan house type, and the semi-subterranean house a form adapted long ago from a widespread coastal type. The Koyukon, and especially the Ingalik of the lower Yukon, build substantial structures, excavated to a depth of about four feet, with walls and roof of stout beams and split poles, covered with birchbark and turf. The entrance, traditionally toward the river or lake, is a tunnel from six to eighteen feet long which one enters through a shed built above ground (to protect the entry from drifting snow?). There is a sunken antechamber at the outer end, and the tunnel opens at or below floor level in the house itself. The tunnel is so narrow and low that one must crawl through it on hands and knees, and while it serves as a cold trap in winter, it is "in wet mild weather nothing but a sewer" (Whymper 1869:176). The walls of the tunnel extend into the single room of the house, which may vary from a rectangular space about ten by sixteen feet up to eighteen by twenty-five feet, in the center of which is the fireplace. The roof above is shaped like a truncated pyramid, about seven and a half feet high at the square smokehole in the center. This is closed by a gut skin cover after the fire has been extinguished for the night. Around the walls are benches or platforms on which the occupants sit and sleep, their heads toward the center of the room. Such a house may shelter two families, and the biggest houses even more. As described by Jetté (1908–9:305–8, 344–45), the two benches at the sides are occupied by the active adults, the husband sitting in the middle between his two wives (if he has two), the first (or a single wife) on his river side, since she must often go in and out and it would be impolite for her to pass in front of a man; and the second wife on his inland side, "As she was of inferior rank, her passing in front of her husband was not considered to matter, she herself being of secondary importance" (Jetté "Dictionary," quoted in de Laguna 1947:96). The benches at the front are occupied by the children, and that across the back of the house is for those of lowest status: the aged, unmarried, or widowed. But Jetté (1908–9:298) described the ten to fifteen occupants of the Dena winter house as sleeping on the floor all around the house, wrapped in blankets, their heads to the walls. (The sleeping benches seem to be found only in houses of the Dena and Ingalik who had contact with the Eskimo.) The largest house in the settlement serves as the meeting house (Jetté 1908–9:305, *koskonon*) for dances and celebrations, and is big enough to accommodate the entire population, plus as many more visitors. Among the Ingalik and Holikachuk, the *kashim* (ceremonial house) serves as a club house for men, to whom the women bring the evening meal, and where the unmarried youths sleep. (See E. W. Nelson 1899:241-63 for similar Eskimo houses and kashims.)

After the freeze-up, nets and fish traps are set under the winter ice through holes that must be kept open during the winter. Holes for drinking water are also kept open, for to melt ice would take too much fuel, and to drink meltwater from snow is known to be unhealthy. (Derived from snow, it is practically distilled water, lacking essential minerals.)

In the early winter, after the first snowfall, family parties go up into the hills to bring home the meat that has been cached by the hunters, dragging it back on hand-drawn sleds. Some have toboggans for use on soft snow or to carry small children. Men wear snowshoes to hunt moose, for the animals are at a disadvantage in the deep, soft snow. The reflection of starshine and moonlight by the snow is what makes travel possible in these dark months when the sun lags below the horizon most of the day.

Now that the winter's supplies of food are safely in, everyone again begins to gather wood, and the piles that have been cut and left at various places are fetched in sleds. Since it must be so difficult to cut living trees with stone-bladed adzes, and since seasoned firewood is needed, the people probably make full use of the quantities of driftwood deposited on the river bars. Firewood is piled on the roof of the house and beside it. Wood, game, fish, and pelts are not carried into the houses by the entrance tunnel, but are passed in through the smokehole. (This seems to be a matter of convenience, but some Athabaskans feel that the ordinary doorway is profane, and not to be used for valued things, such as fur pelts, lest it offend the animal spirits. Even at the present time, goods to be given away are passed into the potlatch house through a rear window by the Tanana and Ahtna, for to do otherwise would destroy the giver's luck, and he would never recover their value in the gifts he would receive at subsequent potlatches.)

In November, if they have accumulated a sufficient supply of wood for the household, the men trap for furs; and the meat of some of the furbearers is also eaten. (Although furs not needed for their own use are now sold to commercial traders, in earlier days they were traded by the Indians to the Eskimo for seal skins, whale or walrus gut skins, Siberian reindeer skins, or for finished garments and other native manufactures.) Visiting the trapline may involve trips of several days away from the winter village and the caribou or mooseskin tent may be used, as in the spring. Nearer the village, snares are set for hares, and grouse are hunted. But in the most bitter cold of December and early January little fishing or hunting is attempted, and in the cramped quarters of the winter houses, illuminated during the long dark hours only by the open fire and the small clay lamps of fish oil, the Koyukon wait for spring, or, with the lights extinguished, listen while some storyteller "bites off a piece of the winter" with a myth of "Distant Time" (to use Richard K. Nelson's felicitous phrase for "Myth Time").

After the winter solstice, when the increase of daylight has become noticeable, the time arrives for potlatches and feasts. Still later, in the last part of winter, food supplies will usually be running low and hunters must make special efforts to replenish them. The sweet meat of beavers is especially relished, for late winter and beginning spring is when they are taken by deadfall or by the barbed arrow.

The ice is still firm, but the days are rapidly lengthening, and the April sun both takes the bite from the cold and invites the Dena to travel or go on long hunting trips.

The year has run full cycle.

The above sketch is definitely an optimistic one, perhaps giving undue emphasis to the happier times in Dena life, for it fails to indicate that the fish runs may be uncertain and the caribou migrations disappointing. We have also supposed that the moose at that imaginary period in the past frequented the middle and lower Yukon valley as they do now, although moose are notorious for drastically changing their ranges. Thus, Whymper (1869:245) reported of the Yukon above the Ramparts: "This part of the river abounds with moose . . . [and] is therefore a favorite part of the Yukon for the Indian hunter. The moose are scarce below Nuclukayette [at the mouth of the Tanana] and never known as low as Nulato. They must, however, be abundant

39

on the smaller rivers, as, for example, on the Newicargut [Nowitna River, near Ruby], where the meat obtained was nearly all of this animal."

Yet Sullivan reported successful moose hunts in the Nulato area in 1936, and wrote [1942:68]: "Moose are more important than caribou for the food supply of the Ten'a of our study, for, though there is by no means an abundance of them in this section, they are much more numerous than the caribou."

But when the fishing and the hunt fail, and when the snares for rabbit and ptarmigan are empty, the people and dogs go hungry. I do not believe that the Indians have ever been driven by expedience to eat their dogs, nor forced into cannibalism. Rather, the women surrender their small shares to their children, and especially to their husbands, on whose strength to hunt all depend for their survival. Little babies and old people are the first to die: the nursling because the mother's breast is dry, and the old because they are too weak to follow when the family moves camp, hoping for better luck elsewhere. No doubt the Dena, like the Copper River Ahtna, have suffered the loss of whole settlements through starvation. Fear of starvation is always in the backs of their minds.

A NOTE ON CLOTHING

It is difficult to know exactly what the Dena Indians wore before they were influenced by the earliest traders. We know that sometime in the nineteenth century their style of clothing underwent a change when they adopted Eskimo styles, especially for wear in winter. It would seem that before this change, the Koyukon and Ingalik were wearing costumes much like those of the contemporary Tanana and Kutchin tribes. Unfortunately, most of the sketches of such garments were made in the summertime, so we do not know in detail what the Dena wore in winter.

There was little difference between the cut of men's and women's garments. The furs and skins used for clothing were (depending upon the availability in different places): marten, caribou, moose, mountain sheep, muskrat, ground squirrel, rabbit, and bird skin. Beaver, otter, wolf, and wolverine were used for trim. In addition, Siberian reindeer skins, various kinds of seal skin, and walrus hide were traded from the Eskimo. For waterproof clothing, dehaired seal skin, fish skin, and gut skin were used. The Indians wore their best clothing when hunting, visiting, attending cermonials, or when preparing for death at home or on a raid.

The Eskimo-style winter parka worn in the 1930s was illustrated by the garments that Madeline Dayton of Koyukuk Station had made for her husband, their children, and herself, and which she generously let us study. The parka, with attached hood, was of caribou skin, fur side turned out. There was a ruff around the face made of a wide strip of wolf fur on the outer edge and of wolverine fur next the face, for the Natives claim that the breath will not freeze on wolverine fur. There were also strips of wolverine fur at the wrist, to be tucked inside the mittens. The woman's parka came down to the middle of the calf and was slit up on the sides to the middle of the thigh, forming two graceful, U-shape flaps of the same length, one in front and one behind. Around the bottom was a mosaic band of little triangles or squares of different-colored caribou fur with a wolverine fringe at the very bottom. The man's winter parka came to just above the knee and was cut off straight, with a border of caribou skin mosaic and a fringe of wolverine fur. It was also ornamented on the chest by two long pointed strips of contrasting fur that came down from each shoulder to the breast. In winter, both men and women might wear an undershirt of squirrel fur or of "knitted" rabbit-fur cord.

Fur boots, with a firm sole like those of the Eskimo, were worn in winter by both men and women. These were made of six strips of caribou leg skin (amounting to one and a half caribou per pair), the fur outside, sewn to a sole of heavy moose skin, and trimmed with a band of beaver or river otter fur at the top. Some boots came to the knees, others to the thigh. Inside the boot, a stocking of young caribou fur, cut like an Eskimo boot, was worn, the fur inside. For traveling on snowshoes, however, only soft-soled moccasins could be used. There was also some kind of skin or fur pants, but about these there is little information, unless those described by Osgood (1940:261–62) for the Ingalik were typical of tribes farther up the river. These were the winter "under trousers" of fur, worn by men around the house and under an Eskimo style of trouser when outdoors; the Ingalik woman wore fur trousers as underwear only when outside; in the house she wore the combination moccasin-pants. Miranda Wright of Nulato tells me that her grandfather had leggings of wolf skin, the fur outside, that covered his legs from ankle to mid-thigh, or just above the bottom of his parka. Wolf skin leggings were worn by Raven in Tale 23, and therefore are probably an old-style garment.

The aboriginal style of shirt or tunic, anciently worn by the Koyukon and Ingalik, and indeed by most Northern Athabaskans, is illustrated by a few specimens collected from the Dena and their neighbors. (See J. Thompson 1990, figs. 51, 52, 54, 102, 106, 114; Fitzhugh and Crowell 1988, figs. 67, 68, 298.) This shirt was of caribou skin, worn with the fur inside in the winter, and of tanned hairless skin in the summer. That for both sexes was made with a shoulder piece, or yoke, to which the front and back pieces were sewn. The man's tunic fell almost to the knee, but with deep cuts up to the waist at the sides, making a pronounced point in front and in back. The bottom was trimmed with fringes and porcupine quill (or bead) work. The woman's tunic reached to the mid-calf, and was cut with a less pronounced dip behind, and in general was less elaborately fringed and embroidered.

In very cold weather, an undershirt of rabbit fur might be worn. This was made by cutting a rabbit fur spirally into a single long cord, twisting this so that all sides of the resultant cord were furry, and lengthening it as needed by sewing on a similar cord at the end of the first. This was then fashioned into a looped fabric, either by a twining technique, or by a technique called "knotless netting." Undershirts were also made of ground squirrel furs stitched together.

Johnny Dayton said that in summer, women and some men might wear a separate skin hood as protection against the mosquitoes. The hood had a drawstring around the face that was pulled tight and tied under the chin; and the bottom was tucked into the neck of the frock or shirt. He also described a man's hat of grass, made by a coiling technique, on which were painted pictures of his prowess as a hunter, but I have been unable to find any other reference to such a summer hat.

In winter, separate fur hoods were worn. These were big enough at the bottom to cover the shoulders, and probably, like modern parka hoods, had ruffs of wolf and wolverine hair around the face. Some men wore a fur cap. Anyone out in the bitter cold, especially if there were any wind, had a strip of wolverine fur that could be drawn across the face. This had a hole for the mouth and covered the nose, cheeks, and chin. In winter and spring, snow goggles, made of wood with narrow horizontal slits for the eyes, were worn as a protection against the glare, which could cause snow blindness. These goggles were like those of the Eskimo.

The old-style lower garment for both sexes was the typical Northern Athabaskan combination moccasin-pants (or "trouse-boots"), in which the covering of the feet, legs, and the lower part of the body was all in one piece, held up by a belt. In some cases, the belt supported a genital covering of skin and two separate legging-moccasins. In winter, these garments were of caribou or mountain sheep skin, worn with the fur side turned inside; in summer they were of tanned, dehaired skins. The decoration was the same on both. The foot and leg covering was made of a single piece, seamed up the back of the leg, and stitched directly to a sole of dehaired moose hide at the heel and to a triangular inset over the instep. In later years, a false "apron" was sewn over the top of the whole foot, in order to display fancy beadwork. On a man's trousers, there was a decorative band of quill (or bead) work running vertically down the front of the leg and splitting in two at the ankle to encircle the foot. There is a similar decorative band around the leg at the knee. A woman's moccasin-pants were similarly decorated, but lacked the vertical strip. Not only was the combination garment a protection against the cold winds, but in summer it kept out the mosquitoes. When Eskimo-type clothing was introduced, the Ingalik woman still wore the combination moccasin-pants indoors in winter, while the men adopted the Eskimo-style trousers, to be worn with the stiff-soled Eskimo-style boot. A stocking, worn inside the combination suit, was cut like an archaic type of Athabaskan moccasin. It was made of one piece of skin pulled up over the foot and seamed for a short distance up the front and back, making a pointed toe. Sometimes a narrow piece was sewn in to cover the instep. A moccasin of this type, but usually with a wide strip or flap sewn to the top and wrapped around the ankle or calf, was worn as a summer moccasin by the Koyukon and many other Athabaskan tribes. In winter, the Indians wrapped their feet loosely in a rabbit skin or other piece of fur as duffel, and put dried grass in the feet of the combination suit as insulation.

Of great importance in winter were the mittens. These were of beaver, fox, and lynx fur, and came up to just below the elbow. The fur was on the outside, the hair pointing toward the finger tips. The palm was of dehaired moose skin. The cuff was of fur. Sometimes the whole mitten was of moose hide, with a band of beaver fur around the wrist at the edge of the cuff. In winter, mittens with the fur inside might be worn, or the hand might be loosely wrapped in a piece of fur as duffel. Some mittens "for fancy dress" were decorated with porcupine quill (later bead) work. Because their loss might be catastrophic, mittens were connected by thongs sewed on at the wrist, just above the thumb, the cord going around the back of the wearer, and fastened to a connecting piece across the chest. This would prevent loss if the mittens had to be removed for work demanding dexterity.

In rainy weather or when working in wet places, as in setting out the stakes for the fish weir, the Koyukon wore waterproof garments of fish skin, those of the king and silver salmon being especially saved and treated for this purpose. While such garments were made in pre-contact times, we do not know how they were cut. In more recent years the upper garment has been a parka, cut like that of the Eskimo, with a hood that can be tightened around the face with a drawstring. The woman's rain coat was longer than the man's. The lower garment, however, was cut like the aboriginal moccasin-pants and was probably the ancient form. Later, the Indians purchased the full Eskimo outfit of a parka made of beluga (white whale) gut skins for two beaver pelts, plus waterproof pants of the same for four beaver pelts, and seal skin "water boots" with soles of bearded seal skin. The price of the boots varied from one to two beaver pelts, depending on whether they came to the knee or hip. The Indians also made boots of fish skin with soles of tough seal skin. The Ingalik even had over-mittens of fish skin, worn over the warmer mitten when working in the water.

In addition to preparing the skins—and tanning moose hide is a hard job—cutting out the skins and furs, sewing them together and decorating these garments for her family, and making extra ones to give away at potlatches, the Dena woman also made the bedding. The sleeping bag for husband and wife was made of four caribou skins, with the fur inside, and was seamed up the sides with a flap to cover the face. Pillows were of young caribou skin, stuffed with duck or goose feathers. Whereas Johnny Dayton said that husband and wife had separate pillows, Osgood (1940:277–80) reported that the Ingalik couple used the same pillow, and, as an informant remarked, since it was never washed, "It is so dirty it shines and you can smell it about a mile." Under the sleeping furs on the benches in the old-style winter house, and around its walls, were twined grass mats.

From moccasins to dwellings, from skin-working tools to hunting gear, and from fish traps to water craft, the Dena exhibit in their technology that ingenuity and adaptability to make the most of what they have, or to borrow from others and transform it to meet their own needs, that distinguishes the Athabaskan. The rapidity of their adjustment to the opportunities and demands of late-twentieth-century Alaska, without losing their pride in their identity, is witness to the strength of Athabaskan culture, which, like their incomparable snowshoe, may bend and at times slip, yet can swiftly cover the miles without breaking.

III
DENA
RELIGION

MISSIONARIES

CHRISTIANITY CAME TO THE DENA AT THE SAME TIME AS
the first traders and trading posts, beginning with the Russians during the first half of the last century. The Russian posts of most importance to the Dena were (with their founding dates): Kolmakov just
inside Ingalik territory on the lower Kuskokwim (1832), St. Michael
at the mouth of the Yukon (1833), Russian Mission at Ikogmiut on the
Lower Yukon (1836), and Nulato (1839). Only the last was well inside
Dena territory, and was apparently established to intercept the trade
in furs of the Koyukuk River people with the Norton Sound Eskimo.
The Russians had few Orthodox priests in Alaska, and although the
priests visited St. Michael in 1844, and lay members of the Orthodox
faith were encouraged to proselytize and thus to build up for themselves "families" of baptized converts, it is unlikely that the Dena
received from them any clear ideas of the Christian faith. Evidently
some Dena were baptized, as we could tell from the names in the
graveyard at Koyukuk Station. In 1847 the Hudson's Bay Company
established Fort Yukon (later taken over by the Alaskan Commercial
Company) at the confluence of the Porcupine and the Yukon in western Kutchin territory, and its influence reached the Dena and Tanana
because of the long-established intertribal trading that was carried
out at Nuklukayet, a meeting ground on the point between the Tanana
and the Yukon Rivers. It was in this way that the Indians obtained
their first guns, because the Russians would not trade them firearms.
But intensive missionary efforts were not undertaken until the period
of the gold rushes, beginning in 1887, the year when so many missions
were established: the Roman Catholic Mission at Nulato, the Episco-

pal Mission and school at Anvik, and St. James Mission and school at Tanana (founded by the London Missionary Society but transferred to the Episcopal church in 1891–92). Although the first missionary, Reverend V. C. Sim, had visited the Tanana River Indians in 1884, St. Marks (Episcopal) Mission and school were not established at Nenana until 1907; others on the Tanana River date from 1908 to 1929.

Missionaries did not all preach the same religion. The Indians were exposed, in varying degrees, to Russian Orthodox, Roman Catholic, Episcopalian, Presbyterian, and Moravian versions of Christianity, and were undoubtedly puzzled by the differences. Thus, Dr. Chapman, returning to Anvik with his new wife, had to make a formal explanation to some of his parishioners who were disturbed because the Natives at Holy Cross (Catholic) had averred that he could not be a real priest since he was married (Chapman 1948:82–83). After an initial competition for souls among the representatives of different churches, the proselytizers wisely agreed to divide up the territory so that no two denominations would missionize in the same Native settlement or band.

Despite the fact that probably all the Natives we met in 1935 would have believed themselves good Christians, I think that a considerable number of the old shamanistic beliefs and practices still held, especially since these were not felt to be in conflict with the new faith. Indeed, the old myths would be cited as dealing with the same incidents as the familiar Bible stories (Noah and the Flood, for example, where Raven takes the place of Noah and builds a raft [Attla 1983:127–38].) Some of the old practices could also be continued—for luck, just to be on the safe side, or because it felt awkward or risky not to observe the old rules. For this reason, I will sketch a few of the most important aspects of Native religion, since this may lead to a better understanding of the Dena myths, just as the latter explicate in narrative form the fundamental nature of man, the animals, and the spirits.

SPIRITS AND HUMAN SOULS

"In the beginning all animals were man," the Indian will say, for in the stories of Distant Time the characters combined both human and animal features, sometimes shifting from one to the other. Charac-

47

ters that appeared to be human usually became animals or birds at the conclusion of the story. Of greater importance was the belief that animals in Distant Time could speak. There are still animals that can understand Athabaskan—that is why one avoids the use of their names in connection with hunting—but they have lost the power of changing their shapes, and of speaking. An exception to the last is the horned owl, whose hooting predicts the weather, and who speaks in excellent Athabaskan to warn the shamans (medicine men and women) of impending catastrophe, which the latter then use their powers to avert.

The world of the Dena and of other Alaskan Athabaskan tribes is an *animate* one. (In explaining this point of view, I shall first sketch the beliefs and practices of the Koyukuk River and the Yukon Koyukon at Nulato, relying upon Jetté, Sullivan, A. M. Clark, and R. K. Nelson, and later mention those of the Ingalik of Anvik, according to Chapman and Osgood.)

In an animate universe, there is really nothing like blind chance or impersonal forces; events occur because some Being has acted. As might be expected, the world is full of such beings—they are the spirits, and because they are "fierce and cruel" (Jetté 1911:97), men have to propitiate them, and bargain for their help. (Jetté, I feel, paints a bleaker picture of man's relation to the spirits than do later authors, probably because of his profession and his times. Richard Nelson points out that the spirits could also be benign and helpful at other times and on other occasions.) In Koyukon thought, according to Jetté, among the most powerful beings are the Spirits of Cold, of Heat, and of the Wind, and these are responsible, of course, for the seasonal weather which so controls Dena life as well as death. The most dreaded of the major spirits is the *Ten'a-ranide* (*denaaghe-neede,* DenaRanidƏ), the "Thing for Man," that is the "Thing That Kills People." It is also known under other names, as the "Spreader of Disease" or the "Evil Spirit."

Among the lesser spirits are those associated with living beings. It was the general belief among the Koyukon that humans have two kinds of "spirits" or "souls." The primary "soul," which animates and remains in the human body until death, is the *nokabeedza* (Clark) or *nokōbëdza* (Jetté), or *nɯkk'ɯbedze.* (noq'obidza). The outer or secondary "spirit" is the *yega*, "picture," or "shadow." Man has a *yega*, but so do animals, plants, and even some (all?) inanimate objects; but only man has the (*nʉkk'ʉbedze*). The Disease-Spreader, *Ten'a-ranide* (Dena-ʀanida) kills by sending "earth-sickness" in the form of a phantom that prowls the settlement at night. It is assisted by innumerable lesser malignant spirits *nękędzaltara* (Jetté), *nek'etsaałdaaghe* (nek'etsałdaʀa), visible only to shamans (medicine men) as monstrous animal forms that are also abroad in the dark. That is why people are loath to venture outdoors at night. Almost all the performances of the shamans are directed against the Disease-Spreader or one of the lesser assistant demons, for these spirits cause death by *eating human souls*. The human shadow soul or spirit (*yega*) can be eaten, or lost through fright, and the person does not die immediately, but when the soul (*nʉkk'ʉbeze*) is devoured, the person dies. Such a death comes to every person. All are victims of the monstrous appetites of evil spirits.

The Ingalik give the name *yeg* to souls and spirits, also to the shadow. The *Giyeg* is the evil spirit that kills men by separating the victim's *yeg* from his body and then eats his corpse. All human beings are so eaten. The *Giyeg* sends disease simply by thinking about his intended victims. This is just as if he were setting traps to catch them, and they will die in a day or two, to be cooked and eaten, unless the *Giyeg* can be distracted. Other spirits help *Giyeg* to trap human beings. While the person is alive, his *yeg* or shadow is called his *dena-yeg* (person's spirit); the *yeg* of a living animal, like a bear, would be called its "bear-*yeg*." The *Giyeg* is both singular and plural: It (They) send(s) disease, and is (are) attracted by noise; therefore, people try to be quiet, especially at night. The *Giyeg* send(s) dreams, and that is when the *denayeg* leaves the human body to wander during sleep. The cannibal women in the myths are said to be manifestations of *Giyeg*, and bad medicine men are his assistants, killing people they dislike for *Giyeg* to eat. The medicine man dies only when another practitioner with a stronger *denayeg* overcomes his and gives it to the *Giyeg* (Osgood 1959:106–10). The word for spirit is clearly the same in these related Alaskan languages: *yega* (Koyukon), *yeg* (Ingalik), *yegi* (Ahtna), and *yeik, yeigi* (Tlingit).

The Fate of the Human Soul

Yet the human soul (nʉkk'ʉbedze) is immortal, according to the Koyukon. It lingers by the body and the grave, then journeys up the Yukon River to the afterworld, where it waits to be reincarnated in a human child. Such a soul is called *Na-redǫniłna* (Jetté), (*naaghedeneełne*, naʀedeniłna) "Those Who Are Becoming Again," and the afterworld where they wait is exactly where the town of Dawson was built! (Jetté 1911:100). The souls of shamans also go up the Yukon when they die, but they travel in a tunnel under the river and go to a separate place to wait. A few may be reincarnated in the form of the animal which they assumed when making their shamanic journeys, but most return as human babies. Jetté (MS Dictionary) wrote that this human "inner soul" so longed for reincarnation that it might enter the body of its clan animal (caribou, bear, or fish), while waiting for a human baby to become available, and then it might have to battle other souls, also wanting to be reincarnated.

In these afterworlds, the souls continue the kind of occupations they would pursue if alive. They hunt, but the animals they kill are of species unknown to us, as can be seen from the bones which the ghosts neglected to burn. These are the fossil Pleistocene remains, "Bones of the Underground Game," that we find in the frozen silts. Thus, on the south bank of the Yukon, about thirty miles below Tanana, near the "Boneyard" or "Palisades," Jetté noted a great collection of mammoth tusks and other fossil bones, which the Indians called "The cut bank of the *Na-radǫniłna* (souls awaiting reincarnation)." The bank there has since caved away, but it must have been part of the same formation that we visited in 1935.

The human soul is not only immortal but sexless, according to the Koyukon, so that the soul of a man may return in the body of a girl. People may recognize the returned soul by birthmarks or character traits retained from its former incarnation. Reincarnation may or may not be connected with giving the name of a long-dead relative to the new baby.

The Ingalik believed that a person had three parts: a body, a soul (or shadow, *denayeg*), and breath or speech, the last becoming a kind of ghost that inhabits the graveyard after death. The soul might go to one of four afterworlds, depending on the manner of death, but it is uncertain whether the *denayeg* was ever reincarnated, for each baby was said to receive its own new soul.

Death and Funeral Ceremonies

Death, and the ceremonies associated with it, form the central social and religious events in the lives of the natives.

All of the Dena believed that the soul (ghost) of the recently deceased is dangerous to those who have been close to it in life, for it may try to take a relative or friend with it on the journey to the Land of the Dead. For this reason, the Koyukon used to carry a dying person outdoors and, after the death, would build a fire in front of the door, or would ring the dwelling with a line of charcoal, barriers which the ghost could not cross. Next morning, while the women and children in the settlement stayed indoors, the men would try to "run the ghost out of town" and start it on its way upriver. While the close relatives and members of the deceased's clan mourned, members of another clan took charge of the body, washing and dressing it in the clothing saved for that purpose. Grease was put on the hands of the corpse before they were encased in mittens to prevent the ghost from seizing another soul. Jetté (1911:706–7) reported that the Dena individual who was dying would claim that he or she had been warned by an omen, and, accepting the inevitable, would even cheerfully anticipate lying in a fine coffin and wearing new clothing, articles which caring relatives would place where the invalid could see them.

The Koyukon formerly bundled up the body and put it up in a tree or on an elevated platform. Sometimes it was placed, erect, inside a number of poles stacked up to form a tipilike or casklike receptacle. Only where no trees were available would the body have been left on the ground. For ten days or so, food would be given to the dead by burning it in a fire at the grave, until the deceased was judged to have become accustomed to the food of the ghosts.

The Ingalik of Anvik and the people of Holikachaket put food and water beside the body while it was still in the house. They did not take the body out until the shaman had given the signal, for they wanted the ghost trapped inside, not free to roam. A four-day funeral was held in the kashim (the community hall), where the corpse was propped up to witness the dancing and singing in its honor. Food and water were placed beside the dead, and renewed frequently, but it was some old person who consumed them. These down-river Indians put the bodies in wooden coffins, and further offerings of food were made while the coffin was still on the rack awaiting burial. In former days a slow fire was kept smoldering below the rack to dry the corpse. Later, the coffin, sometimes double-planked and, for an important man, painted with images of the animals he had hunted, was placed in a grave house or on an elevated stage. The poor, lacking coffins, were simply interred, wrapped in bed skins or matting. Those who died violent deaths (by suicide, or war) were cremated.

The Tanana, like the Ahtna and Tanaina, cremated the dead, and later disposed of the bones and ashes in trees, or in the ground.

Among all the tribes, people who had been in close association or physical contact with the deceased had to observe rites of purification before they could resume normal life. These were often more stringent for the widow than for the widower. Mourning might last a full year before she remarried.

After contact with whites, all these peoples began to inter their dead in cemeteries. The missionaries, of course, encouraged inhumation. Usually a little house would later be built over the grave, and sometimes the individual grave plot was enclosed by a fence. Articles used in transporting the body or in digging the grave, and objects that the deceased had used or treasured were often left at the grave. In the 1890s at Anvik, according to Chapman, grave goods were "killed" (broken, pierced by a stake), so the deceased could use them. Jetté (1911:708), however, denied that objects left at graves were for the dead, arguing that the dead could receive something only if it were burned. Things were left at the grave because they were painful mementoes of the deceased, he believed.

The best possessions of the deceased, along with many additional gifts, would be distributed, months later, by the relatives or clanmates at a potlatch to those who had worked on the body or the grave. This is the *Feast for the Dead*, given by the community every year or two to memorialize those who have died since the last celebration. Formerly held in midwinter, it is still observed in March or April at Nulato and Kaltag as a "truly religious ceremony" (Renner 1993:2). It is certainly the most important one of the Dena, for through it the Native cultural identity and values are reaffirmed, and the bonds of society are strengthened. While it may have been something of an interclan ceremony in the past, it now has become clearly an intervillage one.

Since many guests will come from other settlements, and this ceremony can not be held until the hosts have accumulated sufficient wealth and food, it may not take place till more than a year after the funeral. For example, in 1907 at Kokrines on the Yukon above Ruby, one man alone is estimated to have given away goods worth $1,600, and at Kaltag one man gave complete sets of fur clothing to seventeen persons at one feast (Jetté 1911:716–17). Therefore, two settlements, like Anvik and Shageluk, or Nulato and Kaltag, or even Nulato and the Eskimo of Unalakleet, might host the ceremony in alternate years (Loyens 1964:134). The host village, and especially the persons who "dress" the special guests (see below) gain prestige through their generosity, and Jetté (1911:716) reported that a man rarely impoverished himself to gain such prestige.

The functions of the Feast for the Dead are to memorialize the recently deceased and to supply the spirits of the dead with food, clothing, and trade goods. These they receive when the living, who have worked on their graves and who now represent them, enjoy the actual gifts and food given to them as payment for their services. Always one or more of the relatives of the deceased will "dress" in a complete suit of winter clothing those who have been most helpful at the time of the death or funeral. These are the special guests, who in their own persons become symbolically the dead being memorialized. The rites also allow the grieving relatives to express fully their sorrow during the week-long singing of special eulogies composed for the dead, and of similar songs from previous occasions. Each relative of those memorialized is supposed to compose his or her own eulogy for the whole group to sing, but those unskilled may have another "put the song in his [or her] mouth"; as many as thirty songs have been composed for one celebration (Loyens 1964:138). To these mourning songs, sung by a chorus of men, the women dance in place, their movements symbolizing the catching of tears in the kerchiefs they hold in both hands. It is said that this dancing and singing make the dead "walk again on the earth" (Loyens 1964:138), thereby hastening their reincarnation (Jetté 1911:100). The ceremony finally enables the mourners to put their grief behind them in the last joyous night of feasting, dancing, and gift-giving.

This final part of the ceremony is called the "Stick Dance" (*heeyo*, hi'o), being named for the decorated pole or "stick" that is carried through the village and set up in the center of a large house or in the community hall. While the pole is being danced though the village, those in the hall sing the twelve sacred "Stick Dance Songs." These must be rendered in the correct order and are tabooed on any other occasion. When the pole is installed, the entire assembly begins to dance around it clockwise, to the rhythmic repetition of the syllables "*hee-yo*," with musical variations. Such dancing continues in festive mood throughout the night and well into the next day, when the pole is taken outdoors and broken. At one point, the gifts to be distributed, including bolts of cloth, are brought in, all tied together to form a long garland, and all dance this around the pole. Finally, the exhausted dancers reach a "trance-like inner peace" (Renner 1993:3).

That last evening, after an elaborate and bountiful feast (called "potlatch" by the Koyukon), with plenty of leftovers to be taken home, the surrogates for the deceased put on the beautiful new furs with which they have been "dressed" from head to toe. They are careful to pull the hoods of their parkas over their faces (so that they will not look at anyone and thereby take that person's soul into the next world). Others who have helped with the funeral, or have come from a distance, receive special gifts, but everyone attending gets a small present, like a handkerchief, "as a souvenir" of the Stick Dance (Loyens 1964:136), or as a "blessing" (Miranda Wright). The new winter furs and the other gifts are left in the porch of the hall overnight so that the spirits of the dead may take possession of them. The next morning before the visitors leave, the newly "dressed" persons walk about introducing themselves by the names of those whom they have represented, shaking hands with their relatives and friends, symbolizing the last good-byes of the dead (Renner 1993:4).

For the Lower Koyukon, the decorated pole was the symbol of the Feast for the Dead. Farther up the Yukon, at Kokrines, for example, there was no pole and the ceremony would be held within a large area enclosed by a fence (*nootseł, nutsił*). The feast was not eaten there, but the food was distributed to each family to be eaten at home, after some bits had been put in the fire for the deceased. Singing, dancing, and distributions of gifts seem to have been much like those at Nulato. In former times, among the Koyukon, young widows might make a brief appearance, stark naked, to indicate that they were ready to remarry (Jetté 1911:717; Loyens 1964:140). Also in the past, there used to be races, games, and wrestling matches out of doors; now the Upper Koyukon play cards indoors.

At Anvik, still farther down the Yukon, the dead were also remembered by the Ingalik at the *Partner's Potlatch,* and especially at the *Potlatch for the Dead.* This ceremony, sponsored by a single rich man *for* a relative who had died, was given *to* honored guests, among whom the most important was a man selected from another village (treated symbolically as the Village of the Dead) who acted as a stand-in or representative of the deceased. Thus, the new garments given to him supposedly went to the dead person, and the food offered to the guests was ritually offered to the dead but was actually consumed by the guests and old people. On the last night, the *Hot Dance* might be performed; this is the Ingalik equivalent of the Nulato "Stick Dance" (*heeyo*), but it also included the Eskimo game of "Putting Out the Lights," permitting sexual play.

The souls of the deceased were now satisfied by these feasts, and would stay in the Land of the Dead until reincarnated. The ghosts of shamans, and of those for whom no *heeyo* had been held, might still linger about the village, to do good or harm as they chose.

Because the upriver direction is associated with death, cemeteries are usually located on the upstream side of the village, and (in 1935) no one willingly traveled upstream for several days after a death, for fear that his own soul would be taken away by that of the deceased. I believe that when a village was moved because of misfortunes it was usually relocated downstream from its earlier site (there are exceptions), although still later the original village site might be reoccupied, or an upstream location settled.

THE SHADOW SOUL OR SPIRIT

The spirit, or *yega* (*yeege'*, yiga'), "shadow soul," of each Koyukon (and of each animal) is a protector, in the sense that it would avenge the injury or death of its ward. The Dena, however, debated philosophically whether the white people possessed *yegas*, because if they did not, they could be killed with impunity, provided no one knew about it (Jetté 1911:602–3). Other Dena believed that the white people (especially Russians and Creoles) were the Indians' actual ancestors returned from the Land of the Dead; therefore they were simply returned souls and had no *yegas*, all of which came to the same thing.

According to Jetté (1911:603), if a person with a *yega* were killed, the *yega's* inevitable revenge could be avoided only by cutting open the victim's body and eating a bit of his liver or fat. Jetté goes on to explain that this was apparently what was done when the Koyukuk Indians murdered the Russian, Iván Bulégin, on their way to attack their Native enemies at Nulato in 1851. Dall's account of this act (1870:49), however, Jetté criticized as exaggerated, probably because the witness did not understand it. A similar belief and practice in the case of manslaughter were described to me by the Copper River Ahtna. It was not an instance of gustatory cannibalism, but a gruesome precaution. For many days after this terrible act, the Ahtna killer would have to live apart, observing stringent taboos and rituals. But he usually came to a bad end, anyway, going crazy before he died. The Peel River Kutchin also practiced such ceremonial cannibalism after slaying one's first victim, and this was corroborated by the Crow River Kutchin, in both cases, as among the Dena and Ahtna, to prevent a serious illness, described as involving convulsions (Osgood 1936b:87–88). This belief and practice may possibly have been more widespread among the ancient Alaskan Athabaskans than has been recorded. An Ingalik warrior may eat the eye of an enemy he has killed, in order to obtain the latter's power, but this is a different affair (Osgood 1958:65).

CREATURES OF THE WOOD AND WILD

Jetté (1911:105–8) described a number of "goblins" or mythical creatures which the Koyukon believed inhabit the woods or water. The first of these are transformed persons ("goblins" or "bugbears"), usually women, who become wild during times of famine, forsaking ordinary human contact, but hanging around fish camps so they can steal food from the drying racks. They have long arms, clawlike nails, and are hairy all over. They are called *Nenle'in, Nenele'in,* or *Nedoron.* Jetté (1908–9:315–20) published the story of such a woman from Kateel on the lower Koyukuk, who was finally captured and tamed, way down at Holy Cross, where she married and produced many children. If such a wild, transformed person touches a child, that child will become a shaman, but it is bad luck for an adult to encounter one. Some men have killed a wild person, but have then had to eat a bit of its liver to save themselves (Jetté 1911:105). Osgood (1959:110–13) described the *Nakani* of the Ingalik, usually called "the woods man," or "the bad Indian," that are dangerous only in summer when they steal children. Since they are said to be people who went crazy during a period of starvation and became lost, they are probably the same as Jetté's *Nenele'in.* (See also R. K. Nelson 1983:194–99, "Woodsmen.")

Another creature is the "Man of Fire" or *Kun-Ten'a* (*kkun' denaa,* Qun'-Dena) that pursues travelers, trying to burn them. They can escape if they throw stuff behind them, and he will stop to burn it up. Or he will come just at sundown on a winter's day, when the eyes of travelers are tired, appearing on the darkening horizon as a flash that can be mistaken for a house. In this way he may lure his victims to him. Jetté's story, "The Canoe" (1908–9:347–54), includes an escape from the Man of Fire, who was finally scared away by the yelping of a bitch when her ear was bitten—the standard Athabaskan practice to drive away Thunder. The Ingalik also believe in such a Man of Fire. He kills people for the *Giyeg* to eat, usually in the kashim after a sweat bath (by a stroke?).

Somewhat similar to the last are the Spirit of Cold or "Man of Cold," the Spirit of Heat or "Man of Heat," and the Spirit of Wind or "Man of Wind," already mentioned among the spirits. The Man of Heat killed his victims by making them feel so hot that they would remove their furs, and so freeze to death on the trail.

"People of the Rocks," *Tson-te-rotana* (Tson-te-xut'ane), are wild men who are kidnappers of children and the very old. "People of the Air," *Yo-rotana* (Yo-xut'ane), bring nightmares.

Monsters may live in or under cut banks, according to both the Koyukon and Ingalik. One has the shape of an otter. It lives with the beaver in an unusual house built only of mud and moss. One man who attacked such a beaver house was killed by the water monster. The *Netsinot'an* live under the caving banks of the river, into which the current and wind may drive a Native canoe, where it is in great danger of being crushed by falling earth and trees. *Torega* (Toxige, Toheege) are water monsters who lie in wait in the sloughs and side channels to prey on those who venture into their domain (Jetté 1911:107). Foggy Man, who was defeated by Raven according to the myths we collected, was one of these water monsters (see Tales 2 and 32).

Osgood (1959:114) told about two monsters who were supposed to live just above the narrow place where the Anvik River finally cut through to the Yukon in the late 1930s. The Indians avoided this place, even though it made a handy portage between the rivers. After two boys were lost there, two old women routed the monsters by walking down the beach on the Yukon side, sticking their awls into the cut bank at intervals and singing the "bad song" that kills. Even after the narrow earth wall between the two rivers was washed away, and a shaman had declared the monsters gone, Indians passing by might still throw a small offering into the water—just to be safe.

A very small creature, "Your Grandma's Needle," is often the disease object that is extracted from the body of a patient by the Koyukon shaman.

We may note the belief also in giants and in tiny dwarfs, about whom stories are told.

ANIMAL SPIRITS

Animals lacked souls (*nʉkk'ʉbedze*) like those of men, having apparently lost them along with their ability to assume human form, according to Koyukon belief. They had only their *yega*, but these spirits served as their protectors and enforced the taboos and rituals which should be observed when the animals were killed. Jetté (1911:604) discussed whether there were both individual *yega* for each individual animal, and/or a *yega* for the whole species or class (like fish). This second kind of *yega* would be like the Bosses or Masters of Game of other tribes. Failure to treat the slain animal with proper respect might mean that the hunter could never kill another of its kind, for the creatures would hold aloof from him. In other cases, the offender, or some member of his family, would suffer fits or seizures. Killing for no reason, wasting any part of the animal, or laughing at it, are punished. The Dena did not like to talk about these matters, Jetté reported, for fear that the *yega* might hear and be displeased.

Men out hunting sing their hunting songs (different ones for different kinds of animals) which they believe please the *yega* of the animals. One old Nulato man in 1936–1937 gave Sullivan a caribou song. Since the Canada jay or "camp robber" was always around when they killed a caribou, the natives sang the jay song to elicit the help of its *yega* in hunting. Later they would reward the bird with scraps.

The Ingalik also had "animal songs," short magical spells that would lure the animals to the hunters. These songs were supposed to be the ones sung by the animals themselves in their own kashims, and were learned by humans before animals and men became separate beings. In theory, a song could now be acquired only by purchase (plus instruction) from a person, usually a relative too old to use or need it. The Ingalik had such songs (usually spoken spells) for almost everything, from eclipses to luck in general, or to kill (Osgood 1959:118–25). A song was represented by or associated with an amulet. The *Animals' Ceremony,* the longest and most liked ceremony of the Ingalik, was intended to lure animals, birds, and fish to the village by performing the same ceremonies that these animals (or their spirits) performed in their own kashims under the mountains.

The most important animals, demanding special treatment by the Koyukon, are the four predators: the bear (black and cinnamon alike), wolf, wolverine, and lynx, and their *yegas* are most to be dreaded. A. M. Clark (1970:81) reported that the Koyukuk Indians believed that these four animals had souls like those of human beings. Jetté mentioned important furbearers that are likewise treated with special care after death. In general, the proper names of these animals must not be used, but they may be referred to by circumlocutions. Their flesh and bones must not be given to dogs, and the bones or other discarded parts must be disposed of in special ways: burned in the case of most land animals, or put back in the water for fish and beaver. Animal remains must never be left where people might walk over them, or dogs gnaw them, so the important parts of some species are cached in trees.

When a bear is killed, its eyeballs are slit and its paws cut off, so that its spirit cannot see or run away. The men eat the head and paws at a special feast, which the women do not attend. The flesh of bears is forbidden to women, except that old women are now permitted to eat the hindquarters of the black bear. No use at all is made of a bear skin by the Upper Koyukuk River people. It is hung up near where it had been killed for the chickadees to peck at it. The Yukon Dena men can use it, but the women are forbidden to wear or sleep on bear fur, and women must never mention the bear's true name. For this reason, the men never sing the bear song where women can hear it. They keep even the existence of the song a secret from them. Bears, however, understand human speech and, in consequence, an Indian planning to hunt one must never voice his intention. (Although our sources are silent on this point, I had wondered whether Dena (Koyukon and Ingalik) women, like women in other tribes, can also talk to a bear if they encounter one, and successfully plead not to be harmed, the belief and practice now confirmed by Miranda Wright.)

The Koyukon say a woman must be chaste and busily employed while her husband is hunting beaver, and when he brings home his catch no one in the house may sleep until it is all skinned. When a wolverine is killed, the animal is reverently carried back to camp with the cries "The great one is coming! The chief has arrived!" The carcass is laid on a blanket in the hunter's house, and the finest food is offered to it by each family in camp; there are songs and stories about it, and the people feast on the offerings—as at a potlatch for a dead person. The Upper Dena, who no longer carried out these observances in Jetté's time, would simply burn the whole carcass after taking the pelt. The same was done for the wolf, although a fish was always put in the animal's mouth, as was done for all carnivores. Places where these animals were cremated were taboo, especially to women, and one who had walked near such a spot became lame.

The large meat animals, caribou and moose, and fish also, must be treated with respect. The first king salmon caught by the Koyukon was laid out on some fresh clean willow leaves, everyone in camp sprinkled it with fresh water from a willow branch, saying "Draw up your canoe here!" to attract more fish. Everyone ate a piece of the salmon, and the women wore cords of twisted willow bark about the neck and wrists.

The Ingalik observed a similar feast for the first salmon, and for the wolverine, and a ceremonial skinning of the wolf when these animals were killed, but curiously enough they lacked a bear ceremony, although this is all but universal among circumpolar peoples of the northern forests in Eurasia and North America (Hallowell 1926).

In general, the Indians were careful not to leave any bits of animal flesh, skin, bones, tufts of hair, or even blood around camp where someone might step on them. In our excavations we found very few animal or bird bones that had not been made into tools, or were not partially shaped with that intention. People were also careful to bundle up their own hair combings, nail parings, the afterbirth, and even old clothes and they cached these in trees outside the village to avoid contamination. Especially dangerous to the hunting success of a man was contact with a menstruant or pubescent girl, and for this reason the latter was secluded in a corner of the house for a full year (shortened if necessary), while the menstruating woman, like the new mother, also avoided contact with a man and his possessions.

Eventually, as the rules for honoring the dead game were relaxed, the Koyukon limited their precautions to freshly killed game, about which presumably the *yega* still lingered, while the flesh and bones of animals or fish a few days old could safely be given to dogs. Women, who formerly were excluded from eating certain parts, were now free to do so, although in 1935 many of the older rules were still being observed.

SHAMANISM

Koyukon shamans (*deyenenh, teyenen,* "one who conjures"), both male and female, owed their powers to their familiar spirits, called *sën, senh* (sin) and/or *ałtaa, ełt'aa'e.* These spirits resembled a special kind of *yega,* and with their help the shaman performed extraordinary feats. Jetté (1907), our best source on Dena shamans, although an openly biased one, thought that some shamans were sincerely convinced of their own ability to help the sick, while four others, whom he knew personally, acknowledged that they were impostors. Jetté himself believed that in general the shamans consciously worked on the credulity of their clients for their own profit. One in six of the practitioners known to Jetté was a woman.

Although it is the spirit that chooses its shaman, some persons are naturally predestined to be called. These are the cross-eyed, the crippled or lame, the deformed, and women who are unable to bear children. The shaman will have only one familiar spirit, but several shamans (and their spirits) may collaborate to perform some extraordinary task. It is said that building the Kaiyuh Slough, undertaken to make travel to the various camps easier, was the work of a team of shamans (Jetté 1907:162–63).

The familiar spirit first appears in human form to the future shaman in a dream. The next day, the dreamer will go out into the woods, led to the place seen in the dream. There he (or she) will see a spot, covered by a blue flame, in which are about twelve to twenty small round objects, like beads of all colors and as big as a salmon egg (or a pea), that are dancing around the blue flame. This is the *karunih* (*k'aahooneyh*, "action, power"). Here he may renounce the spirit's call, and go away. But the future shaman will pick up a bead, and, wishing for a certain specified power, look for a sign that the wish has been granted. If it was not (since not all spirits have all powers), he will ask for another desired power. In this way the shaman will acquire all of the beads for his amulet bag or box, and with them all the powers linked to them, and also his familiar spirit. When he is to use one of the powers granted, the shaman will pick out the special bead and swallow it. He will never lose the beads, for they are always in the box when needed. It is quite possible that this explanation of how a shaman obtains his power was true only of a particular Nulato shaman, or line of shamans, for I suspect that for the Koyukon, like the Ingalik, "shamanism was a highly individualistic growth," and that "everyone," especially the older people, "does a little shamanizing" (Osgood 1958:269). The shaman can utilize his power only after he has been given a present, and there are many occasions for this, as in prophesying and averting evil. This becomes, as Jetté describes it, a kind of blackmail, especially when a wealthy man, who has something the shaman wants, is willing to give it in order to escape the fate prophesied.

The shaman also cures the sick. All disease is caused by the entry of an evil spirit into the body, the Koyukons believed. The help of the shaman is solicited by a request phrased obliquely, along with a gift. The latter is rejected or returned if the shaman is unwilling to try, or if he fails to effect a cure. A shaman can also cause sickness and death.

A curing séance was accidentally witnessed by Father Ragaru, who happened to be outside an open window. The patient was in bed in a corner. The audience, sitting along the walls, were singing the shaman's spirit song led by the shaman. The shaman then pulled a blanket over himself. He began to dance, still singing, and finally worked himself into a frantic state, his face bathed in sweat, distorted, with saliva dripping, and his voice hoarse from yelling. Typically, this would have gone on for one to three hours, until the shaman felt able to extract with his hands the evil spirit that had entered the patient's body. This dangerous entity would then be disposed of by being taken into the body of another. No one volunteering, the shaman would take it into himself; or he might throw it into the fire or out of doors. It was in attempting to do the last that the shaman discovered Father Ragaru outside the window, which brought on a panic and an immediate end to the performance. (Jetté 1907:170–71)

Other cures might be effected simply by the shaman's wish, or by his giving the patient a cup of water to drink.

The Ingalik attributed sickness to the thoughts of the *Giyeg*, or to the theft of the patient's *denayeg* by an evil spirit. The shaman could effect a cure by sending one of his spirit animals to obtain the release of the patient's *denayeg*. When the latter was free, the shaman would scold it for leaving its "partner" and would send it back to the patient. If the *Giyeg* should attempt to recover the escaped *denayeg*, the shaman would thwart it by making a thick smoke through which the evil spirit could not see. The shaman accomplished the cure by singing his magic songs, blowing on his hands and rubbing the patient, sometimes sucking part of the latter's body. He might tell the recovered patient never to eat a certain kind of food on pain of death, because this was the food with which the *Giyeg* had lured

63

away hi *denayeg,* and that now the spirit of the food in question had become dangerous to this person.

At Anvik in 1935 there was a man named Ralph who was *berdache* (a transvestite who does the work of the opposite sex). His brother told us that Ralph had been sick as a boy and that when the shaman treated him, he imposed this kind of life upon him as part of the cure. Ralph dressed in an old-fashioned hooded parka like a woman's dress, had the gentle manners of a Dena woman, and was a skilled basketmaker. Osgood (1958:261–62), who also knew him, denied that Ralph was a homosexual.

The Ingalik shaman might also be called upon to protect a house in which children had died. He would beat the upper walls and floor with wild roses, making it difficult for an evil spirit to find, and would tell the father to put dried dog-salmon heads in the corners, so that their bark (?) would scare away any spirits.

The most powerful Koyukon shamans could summon the fish that the people were to catch, or the game they would kill, but the shaman could do this only four times during his life. Sullivan (1942:21–23) described the visit of the shaman to the home of the Fish to secure the promise of good runs. This was done in winter and involved his apparent immersion in the river all night, wearing his waterproof outfit. Meanwhile, two youths kept watch for his return to the water hole in the ice, while the rest of the community sang his spirit songs vigorously all night long in the lighted house. When the medicine man reappeared miraculously at dawn, wet and shivering, and reported there would be plenty of fish the next summer, the grateful people showered him with gifts. The two assistants also received a share of these, which Jetté (1907:174) suggests were considerations that prevented them from any "indiscreet revelation that might have brought suspicion on the genuineness of the venture."

A famous Ingalik shaman could also call the fish as part of a four-day séance during which he went into the river from a little platform between two canoes lashed together. He finally disappeared from sight, and the men in the canoes paddled back to shore. On this occasion, as in the case of the Koyukon shaman, all the people were supposed to sing and drum all night long while the shaman was away. When loons were heard in the morning, the shaman appeared, perfectly dry, made medicine in the kashim, and sent the people out fishing. At each fish taken, the catcher cried like a loon. They say that some fish had feathers in their mouths, and one had a piece of the shaman's stick. They caught so many fish and gave so many to reward the shaman, it didn't matter that he and his wife secured only a few by their own efforts (Osgood 1958:60).

Sullivan also described the calling of caribou before a hunt (1942: 79–80). The hunters would gather at night in a house. The shaman danced around the room, singing, and soon the hunters took up the song, while the shaman's spirit (*senh*) communicated with the *yega* of the caribou. The shaman would usually announce that his spirit had told him the hunt would be good. At times he would interrupt the singing and inform individuals about their personal hunting luck. Those whose luck he said would be poor, would attempt to better it by paying him for private ceremonies.

In former days, a Koyukon medicine man went with the hunting party so that, in case of bad luck, he could see the caribou *yega* in his dream and next day tell the hunters where to find the animals. Or he might encircle the caribou with an invisible ring during his sleep, singing the "ring song," and the hunters next day would kill many caribou in one place. The Koyukon shaman made medicine for a bear hunt in much the same way as described above.

Since the Dena are very generous in sharing their catch with all the camp, it goes without saying that the shaman who assisted in the hunt would receive a suitable reward of meat when the results of his efforts were successful.

Another function of the shaman was to entertain people by a display of his powers. Such displays were rewarded by a shower of gifts. One shaman could fly through the air, but only if no woman were watching him. Another permitted himself to be hanged in such a way that he was decapitated; then his head and body would rejoin of themselves. On his last display, this failed to occur. Others could be shot with a gun and, unscathed, cough up the bullet; or they could take down the stars from the sky, lay them out on the cabin floor, and then carefully put them all back in their proper places. "[T]he medicinemen in the old times were skilful performers, a qualification which their actual successors lack conspicuously" (Jetté 1907:175). But the natives of Jetté's day, though becoming skeptical, were loath to give up faith in shamanism. They admitted, however, that their shamans could not compare with those of the past. A few persons in 1935 were credited with medicine powers.

An Ingalik shaman established his reputation, and thereby what he would be paid by his clients, through demonstrations of his powers. One shaman, whose familiar was the "fire man," had a big fire built in the kashim. He was reputed to sit directly on the fire, but first he sent the audience out of the kashim since they would be blinded by any demonstration of power. When they returned he was sitting away from the fire in his usual place on the bench, unharmed. A young man on becoming a shaman would be tested in the kashim. Someone would bind him with a babiche line, doubling up his arms and legs, and covering him with a mat. All would leave, and when they returned he would be lying out straight, the knotted babiche line beside him. He might repeat this act, and if he could escape from his bonds while everyone in the kashim watched the mat that covered him, then he would be hailed as a great medicine man. Such an Ingalik shaman would hang the skin of his most powerful medicine animal on a post behind the kashim. When he died, the roof boards of his coffin would be painted with an image of his medicine animal, and would be kept loose (enabling his ghost to go in and out). (Osgood 1959:131; de Laguna 1947:81–82)

Jetté (1911:719) mentioned three great shamans among the Dena whom he knew. There was the medicine man, *Otsioza*, of Nulato; the medicine woman, *Noidola'an*, of Koyukuk; and *Kedzaludla*, the medicine man of the Kokrines-Tanana Mission group. The Dena of their "congregations" were very proud of their shamans, although these "doctors" were also hated and feared because of their powers. They were able to do anything they wanted, because no one could oppose them.

The misfortunes and accidents that the Ten'a could not explain as due to some transgression against a *yega* (breaking a taboo), were believed due to the ill will of a shaman. Some had the power of the Evil Eye—"Their eye-fire is strong" (Jetté 1911:718). Others used their "familiar demon" to injure or kill. They were continually fighting one another, and their relatives often suffered in consequence. The ordinary Dena who was afraid to kill or injure a personal enemy could hire a shaman to do the deed. He could then blame the shaman, while still believing in his own innocence.

After death, the shaman appeared even more powerful than in life. People would pray to him for help, offering small "token" gifts of buds and weeds that represented wealth, as well as real beaver pelts and other valuables, which they burned so that the dead shaman could receive them.

CEREMONIES OF THE INGALIK AND HOLIKACHAKET INDIANS

Elaborate ceremonies, including masked dances, lasting for days or even weeks, and often involving guests invited from another village, are or were celebrated in the kashim, providing fun for participants and audience. The guests of the Anvik people were likely to be those from Shageluk, and the reverse, since their villages were of about the same size. The purposes seemed to be to honor the dead and provide them with food and clothing, and to increase the numbers of game animals and the size of the fish runs. These ceremonies were occasions on which persons increased their prestige as generous hosts, young people might be recognized for their accomplishments or stages of development (a boy's first kill, a girl's finishing her puberty seclusion, for example), and everyone had a good time. The kashim structure itself, the types of wooden masks used, as well as certain specific cere-monies, all show strong resemblances to those of the neighboring Eskimo. Such ceremonies were still being observed at Holikachaket in 1935.

MODERN BELIEFS

The accommodation of the early Catholic Fathers to Native practices, as well as the Dena accommodation to the teachings and demands of the Church, have been described by Madeline Solomon, who was the young wife of Johnny Dayton when we met her in 1935. In her autobiography (1981:26–27) she reports that the first Roman Catholic priests, Father Jetté, Father Ragaru, and Father Rossi, "used to go along with the people," seeing no harm in the Stick Dance (Feast for the Dead), whereas the later Fathers Prangey and Baud "used to be really against it because they thought there was a superstition in there. But there wasn't. These Fathers that are here now they find out there's no superstition in there so they join in too." When Father Baud said that "anyone going to Stickdance, no sacraments given out to you," the Natives felt really hurt. So they just went to Communion first, and then to the Stick Dance. "They thought it was all fun and that was their custom anyway for paying the people for working at their dead people. They were just paying them off with stuff. They make a dance out of it before they distribute the things to the people. White people pay with money but the Indian people don't. They like to have fun with it. Like their dancing around with the things they're going to pay out with. That's what this Stickdance potlatch is all about. . . .

"Father Ragaru used to really like lynx meat. One time when he traveled way up the Koyukuk River one of those hunters gave him a piece of lynx meat to take home. They told him after you get through eating it, gather all the bones and throw them in the fire. Don't throw it anyplace on the road or anything because that will give us bad luck. After Father finished eating the meat, he used to gather up the bones and send them back up the Koyukuk River to the person who gave it to him. Let them throw it away or do anything they want with it. That way he got along with people."

We also were impressed by the great tolerance shown by the Indians in matters of religious belief and practice, as exhibited in the few instances we encountered.

By the early 1960s, when the Second Vatican Council was held and the Church was becoming more liberal in recognizing other ways of worship, the Jesuit missionaries in Alaska also began to change their attitude toward the Stick Dance. Quoting from a document in the Oregon Province Archives of the Society of Jesus, Father Renner (1993:8–9) explained how this change came about. In January 1952, Father James C. Spils, S.J., who had served on the middle Yukon for almost a decade, came down to Nulato for a visit. He did not support the efforts of the local priest, Father Baud, to suppress the Stick Dance. Spils argued instead: "We are killing the spirit of our natives by trying to abolish their old customs and make white people out of these natives." Renner adds that Spils "was ahead of his time." It was Father William J. Loyens, S.J., whom Renner credits as "the catalyst that brought about the changed attitude of the Jesuits toward the Stickdance that began thirty years ago" (1993:11).

In 1963, Loyens, then a student of anthropology at the University of Alaska in Fairbanks, with the anthropologist's appreciation of other cultures, visited Kaltag. There he and Father Jules M. Convert, S.J., already open-minded, discussed the meaning of the Stick Dance and sanctioned the dance by their attendance. Loyens's doctoral dissertation on the Stick Dance won the Bobbs-Merrill Award, and the prestige that this brought him, as well as his attendance at the ceremonies, did much to establish the respectability of the Stick Dance in the eyes of his fellow priests and of the Koyukon themselves. Finally in 1985, Father James A. Sabesta was formally "dressed" by Virginia Kalland to represent her dead husband, Edgar, because Sabesta had eased her husband's last hours by giving him oxygen from the mission plane. Both Virginia Kalland and her husband were Natives, and Father Renner remarked as follows upon the occasion: "This dressing of a Catholic priest by an Alaskan Native for an Alaskan Native, in the presence of Michael J. Kaniecki, S.J., Bishop of Fairbanks, and in keeping with the age-old rites of the Koyukon Feast for the Dead, dramatically signaled the end of a century of misunderstanding, periods of alienation, tension, pain. After those ceremonies the Koyukon people have reason to be convinced that their time-honored, sacred mortuary feast will never again meet with clerical opposition." (Renner 1993:12)

Tales from the Dena

I V

DENA

STORYTELLING

ABOUT THE STORIES

AMONG THE NATIVE PEOPLE OF THE TANANA, KOYUKUK, and Yukon valleys, the person who could tell stories well has always been admired. Before adequate lighting made it possible to work indoors at night, storytelling was a way of passing the long winter evenings. When all the occupants of the house had wrapped themselves warm in their fur sacks or sleeping skins, and when the last feeble flame of the earthenware lamp had been extinguished, someone would call for a story, and anyone who had one might volunteer it. The narrator would pause politely after the first sentence, until encouraged by the cries of "*Anni!*" from the audience. As Jetté wrote (1908–9:298–99):

The story-teller speaks slowly, in a sort of mysterious undertone, which contributes, together with the darkness and the wonderful character of the facts presented, to cast a sort of awe on the audience. As the story develops, the interest increases; peals of laughter, exclamations of commiseration or disgust, reflections on the characters and actions described, conjectures as to what is going to follow, soon cross each other from all quarters. The intense interest and excitement then displayed I cannot better compare than to the impressions manifested by the audience in our theaters [*especially at a Western in a movie theater in the era of silent films*—FdeL].

But the darkness had to be absolute. When Jetté struck a match, the better to write down a story, the effect was disastrous: everyone was paralyzed and not a further word from the narrator or audience could be elicited that night. (Fortunately for us, the rule that stories

73

could be told only in total darkness had long since been abandoned, and Eliza Jones informs me that she, also, heard many stories in broad daylight.)

We must remember that the stories had been heard many times before, and the audience therefore knew what was going to happen. For this reason, I suspect, it was possible for the narrator to skip over some details and to elaborate on others. It would not be necessary, for example, to identify the principle actor as Raven or Crow, because his identity would soon be revealed by his gluttony, especially in eating dog's flesh (which would be abhorrent to a Dena), or in leaving his three-toed track.

As Jetté puts it (1908–9:289): "They may have heard the legend scores of times, they may be able to tell it themselves; their interest is not the less for their knowledge of it. The stories are never stale to them, never old or tiresome." Something of the same effect—that of knowing in advance what the action will be, the better to savor the details peculiar to each version—may perhaps be gained by reading the several versions of the "same" story in the following pages. Furthermore, we must not underestimate the importance of the audience in enlivening the narration. Each telling, even by the same narrator, would have been different because the audience would always be different in some way, though composed of the "same" persons. Comments on the actors and their doings would vary, just as the moods of the individuals in the audience would never be absolutely the same.

Unable to take notes in the dark house, Jetté was forced to memorize the main features of the story and then try to induce the narrator to give him the details the next day. Although he was thus able to record a correct text in the Native language, many of the rich details of the oral renditions were lost. Many years later, when I was tape-recording some of the favorite stories of an excellent Ahtna storyteller, I found that if I did not respond freely with interjections and laughter, the recording was technically better, but for interesting detail it could not compare wih the livelier versions in which I did not try to suppress my comments or expressions of interest.

Miranda Wright further explains that repetition of the tale by the same narrator serves to fix it in the memory of the listeners, and that the ability of the young people to repeat the story accurately, and honestly (without help or hints), would be tested later by their elders. (Jetté, who had to rely on the written word, had obviously failed.)

Entertaining and exciting as these Dena tales may have been to their old-time audiences, they were not just amusing fairy tales about animals and men with extraordinary magical powers. They had more important functions than to entertain. Without writing, the only method of preserving and communicating the wisdom of the elders was through oral discourse. Tales that embodied knowledge or moral precepts were more easily remembered by impressionable young people than direct admonitions by their parents, or long expositions. Therefore, in these stories we will find the looks and behavior of animals explained in terms of their origins. For example, the Wolverine girl, whose man-eating family have been killed, retaliates by taunting: "I'll fix you yet. I'll get even. I'm going to rob you. I'm going to steal from your cache. I'm going to bother you all your lifetime. . . . You watch out for me!" (Tale 5). Or, when a woman's husband turned into a Caribou, he "ran as far as the river. The Caribou man heard his wife talking so he went back up a little ways. Even now, when you chase a caribou, he beats it, but then he stops and starts to come back again a little, to find out what's the matter. This story is the reason why they do it" (Tale 12). And again, "That is why loons are heavy and can't walk, and why they have no tails. That is why they dive under the water and come up and hide under the edge of the grass. That is why they kill all their eggs but one" (Tale 40). These are tidbits of knowledge interesting to hunters, young and old. The stories instruct as well as amuse.

But these myths are certainly more than "Just So" stories, and conversely, the animal traits they "explain" are often trivial. Many of the stories told to us contained no such explanations. The morals to be drawn from them are never obvious. For example, Crow (Raven) embodies all the vices and very few of the virtues stressed by the Indians, so that while they laughed at him, even the laziest and most greedy could recognize that he was not to be emulated. These tales instruct because they illustrate the consequences of particular actions. Repetition of the tale helps the listener to ponder the lesson therein

75

illustrated. (I am indebted to Miranda Wright for the insights in the last two sentences.)

According to Jetté, the Dena have no chiefs with the power to command, no authorities to tell people what they ought to do. Each may, or rather *must,* choose for himself or herself what actions to take, and with this freedom goes the responsibility for the consequences. He is like the Protestant, who, free of papal authority, is alone responsible for his own salvation. It is for this reason that the Dena individual, when contemplating some important step, will seek out others and endeavor to gain their advice. If the action is one he wants to take, he may even elicit their demand that he do so. The Dena are very sensitive to what others may say. In this way, the individual feels secure against possible criticism of the act, since it was urged by another, and the unwritten laws of the people are enforced through the strength of public opinion (Jetté 1906–7:395–99).

Catherine Attla, the Koyukuk narrator, characterized and entitled one of her published collections (1989) as "the stories we live by." As in the Bible, "people did things differently in *kk'adonts'idnee* (Q'adonts'edni)," a name that covers both Myth Time (Distant Time) and the stories of events in that time. This was a period so remote that its realities are not those of today, and are not to be believed or judged in the ordinary terms of the present. That was when all Animals were Men, with the power of human speech, and the stories about them are intended as true stories of events that actually occurred then, although they could not occur now.

So the myths are treated as seriously as the devout Fundamentalist among us would treat stories in the Bible. Miraculous events really happened then: patriarchs might live six hundred years, a whale could swallow a man, waters might part to leave a dry road for the deserving, and a dead man could rise from his grave. But we do not expect such things to happen now. And like ourselves, there are those among the Dena who only half-believe in these miracles, or do not believe in them at all. But just as reading from the Holy Bible may be felt to be sanctifying, so telling these myths, as Catherine Attla has explained, was for the older natives "their way of praying" (1983:3). "They prayed to the spirits for a better life. Praying to the spirits is the same as praying in the Christian sense" (1989:4).

The very act of telling the myths shortens the winter itself. That is why the stories were told only during "the first part of winter, until the celebrations of the mid-winter festivals are passed, *i.e.,* for about six weeks, from the beginning of December to the middle of January" (Jetté 1908-9:298); before the winter solstice in mid-December, and the mid-winter ceremonies (Miranda Wright), or from roughly mid-September to mid-December, before the mid-winter ceremonies celebrating the solstice (Eliza Jones). (Storytelling time evidently now is begun and ended earlier than in Jetté's days.) The latter part of the winter, when the lengthening hours of daylight became apparent, was the time for riddling; and riddles could be told at any time of day, in daylight as well as dark. In ending a myth, the teller should use a set phrase (peculiar to each locality) to the effect that he or she had shortened the winter. "A part of the winter is become short" (Jetté 1908-9:470). Or, "I thought the winter had just begun and now I've chewed off part of it" (Attla 1989:4). Or again, "Water is dripping from the roof." Other narrators in different villages might use different endings, but the meaning was the same.

In the following collection, the tales told by each storyteller are arranged in the same order: First come those about Crow, since he figures almost as a Creator. (This character is actually the Raven, *Dotson,* though he is universally called "Crow" in English, despite the fact that there are no crows in the Alaskan interior.) Next follow the episodes of the Traveler Cycle, "The Man Who Went Through Everything," as one of our narrators phrased it in English. He was responsible for introducing some of the changes that separate the world of Distant Time from that of the present, and therefore it would seem (to whites, at least) as if his activities had taken place later than most of Crow's. Last come the miscellaneous stories about other characters. The titles, except those specially designated, are ones that may either have been used by the tellers in speaking English or are handy ones we coined for identification. Only very late in our trip did I discover that the stories had Indian titles. Where known, such titles are given. The subheadings are mine, intended as aids to analyzing the stories. Words or phrases in parentheses are those which the Native narrator (or interpreter) has introduced into the stories to clarify the meaning, or are words that we believe were spoken although we could

77

not be sure. My remarks are in italics, and those within the tales themselves are also in brackets.

A NOTE ABOUT SPELLING NATIVE WORDS

Only a few Native words appear in this book, but the astute reader will certainly have noticed by this time that we are dealing with at least three Athabaskan languages, each with its own system of spelling. The modern systems have been worked out and established by the Alaska Native Language Center (ANLC) at the University of Alaska Fairbanks. Both Norman Reynolds and I, of course, attempted to write down Native words, but we used the more universal system of phonetic transcription employed by anthropologists and linguists of that time (Franz Boas and Edward Sapir, for example). I thank Dr. Michael Krauss for correcting our efforts. Since the ANLC system for the Lower Tanana is different from that used for the Koyukon language—for example, Lower Tanana uses **k** and Koyukon **kk** for the same sound, one I would write as **q** (a **k** pronounced back in the throat). The **gh** for these languages sounds to us like an **r,** and I have used **r** to designate it, since it is not really our **r.** There are also sound shifts in which **ch'** at Nenana is replaced by **k'** by our Koyukon informant and translator, Blind Joe and Joe John, at Tanana Mission. (Eliza Jones informs me that the people now living at Tanana Station speak the Upper Koyukon dialect, in which **ch'** should appear instead of **k',** but this is not shown in my original notes of 1935.) For the **h** of Koyukon and of Lower Tanana I use **x,** because it is pronounced back in the throat. The **nh** of both Lower Tanana and Koyukon is a voiceless **n** (blown through the nose, which I did not hear). The apostrophe mark (') after the **ch, k** and **kk** indicates that the sound is made with an explosive release of breath.

Jetté used a still different system of spelling, an elaborate one of his own which he was refining over the course of years, and which I have attempted to simplify. In this he used many diacritical marks, most of which I have omitted, although an ogonek or hook (ͺ) under a vowel indicates that it is nasalized (spoken through the nose), and he used signs (‾) and (˘) over vowels to indicate their length (long or short), which I have not copied. His **r** is the same as the ANLC **gh** or my **R,** although I have not always changed his spelling. Some words I had to write as I heard them, and these may have **x** where others might have written **h.** The **h** is like our sound, just breathing, while the **x** is a harsher sound like that produced if you try to prolong a **k.**

McFadyen Clark used a similar but simplified system of spelling, which I have retained for the few words quoted from her work.

It is not my intention, however, to offer a lesson in Athabaskan linguistics—even if I could!—but only to point out that these different usages are not mistakes in spelling. No one should pretend that Athabaskan is easy!

V

TALES FROM NENANA

Twelve stories, counting different versions of the "same" story as different tales, were told by two men, Titus Bedes, and John Silas. There is some uncertainty in the first name of Bedes, since Reynolds consistently identified as "Paul" the man I called "Titus" Bedes. I believe that there was a small Native audience for most of these stories, so it is possible that "Paul" was among them, and that this led to our confusion of names.

It was June in Nenana, with pleasant weather, and the Indians were living in tents, not in their winter houses. Because the salmon runs had not yet arrived, it was a restful time, and everyone was out of doors most of the day. Although I have always felt a bit anxious when approaching a new group of people, wondering how they will receive me and my inevitable questions and notebook, it was easy to meet the friendly Natives of Nenana. Neither shy in giving information about old customs nor reluctant to let us take their pictures, they posed with some of their best costumes and heirloom weapons. I was introduced to Titus Bedes, said to be the best storyteller. Bedes was reportedly born in 1847, the year that Fort Yukon was founded, which would have made him eighty-eight years old! According to a letter I wrote home, I asked him if he knew the story about Raven and Magpie, thinking of a Chugach (or Alutiiq) version, in which Raven induced the little birds to make a pretend war in order to divert attention from his tricks. But Bedes said it was not birds who made war, but "men" that Crow made from pine cones, and he launched into the story of Crow and Willow Grouse woman (Tale 4). That broke down any reticence, and he went on to tell other stories, as did John Silas, in that session and later ones. At the first visit I had been alone, later Norman Reynolds accompanied me and also went by himself one day when I had a bad cold. John Silas was not quite as old as Titus Bedes, but other than that, I have no impression of him.

1 / Crow and the Beginning of Things

TOLD BY TITUS BEDES

Recorded by FdeL

Crow Gets Fire

LONG TIME AGO, THE INDIANS DIDN'T KNOW HOW TO MAKE fire. Somebody thinks it was too much hot. All the people stayed together and talked about it. They had seen a fire but didn't know what it was.

"Why do you think it's hot?" someone said.

Crow, he said, "*I* know how to build a fire. *You* can't get the fire. You get a chicken (grouse) or a rabbit. Put them on a spit to cook them."

The people tried all day but couldn't make a fire. Hundreds of people try to make a fire. They couldn't do it.

Crow, he laugh. "Me, I done it! I got it easy!"

Then he took a long stick and made a hook on the end. He threw it in the water and hooked up fire. He hooked up burning coals. The people had never thought of that before. Crow took a little grass. Pretty soon he had a fire. He roasted the chicken and the rabbit.

After that, the people talked about how to keep the fire. All the Alaska people wanted to make another fire. Everybody tried, but they couldn't do it.

One Indian boy said, "I know what to do!"

He took a white rock and a black rock and struck them together. He made a spark. He took light, shiny sand grass. The spark caught in it. It burned. He shook the grass. But it was no good yet. Another fellow thought. He took rotten stuff (punk) from a birch. He made a string drill, a bow drill. He took the spark off with a bone knife. That fire worked.

Crow Makes Women

There were no women, only men. One place there was a girl, sitting down. Everybody tried to talk to the girl. She wouldn't say anything. Crow went after her. He was the boss. He tried to talk to her. She said nothing.

He built a fire. Crow said, "I'm sick."

The girl went to get wood (for a fire to keep him warm). Crow was just fooling. He saw a big sack of caribou skin. He grabbed the sack and put it in his canoe. The woman hollered and tried to locate (stop) him. She couldn't do it.

Crow went home to his own village. He had some women's clothes (that were in the sack). He had a whole suit. He dressed some of the men in women's clothes. Next day they turned into women.

There were still no children. The women didn't know how to get a baby. [*Crow evidently taught them.*] The women started to get pregnant. They thought they were sick. The baby was moving inside. The woman wanted to cut her belly open and take out the child.

Crow said, "Don't cut it! That's not the way."

The women were alone. One woman held up another woman. Crow told them how. In half an hour the babies were born.

They wondered how to feed them. The babies couldn't eat.

Crow said, "Babies can't eat. Babies must suck on mother's breast." The babies suck(ed) their mothers.

Crow told them what to do when the mother goes away. They asked what Crow said, "Take fat. Put the fat on a long sharp stick. Baby is going to suck on the fat."

That's the way the Indians do today.

The narrator told us that there were pictures of men and women, painted on rocks "near the Chena River," at the very place where Crow made women. We did not have an opportunity to search out this site. For a description and a copy of the pictures made by Louis Giddings, see the Commentary, page 303, and Fig. 1 on page 304.

2 / [Crow and] the Foggy Man

TOLD BY TITUS BEDES

Recorded by FdeL and NR

IT WAS SUMMER, ABOUT THE MIDDLE OF AUGUST. IT was in the ducks' country. The people were going out on the lakes to hunt ducks. As soon as the people went, a big fog came up and they never came back. People were getting lost all the time in the fog.

The people next to that place said, "I don't know what's the matter."

Old Crow said, "Take me." He said, "I'll find out."

He went to work and made a canoe out of sand stuck together with pitch. And the paddle was made the same way. He studied about making an arrow. "I've got to make it fancy," he said. He made it out of pitch. "Let me go. I'll fix them!"

He went out and around the lakes. He saw a man paddling in the lakes, and said to himself, "No wonder all the men are missing. There's the man that caused it. That's why the men get lost."

He paddled close to him. The man was called Foggy Man (*Ok dena;* Oq dena).

He told the Crow, "What do you want? You looking for trouble?"

"No, dear friend, I never look for trouble. Let's be friends together all our life time."

"What for? I don't want to be friend," said Foggy Man.

Crow said, "That's no trouble to make friends."

"Let's have a race in our canoes."

Crow said, "All right. I'll take you on."

Old Crow win it.

"What do you say? Shall we be good friends and trade our canoes?" asked old Crow. [*Special friends among the Dena would exchange some of their possessions.*]

"No," said Foggy Man. "I won't stand for it. You are trying to fool me, or something?"

Crow said, "No, mister, I never did. I don't want to fool you. I just want to be good friends with you."

"Well, let's trade canoes."

The Crow said, "We'll trade everything we have, just the way she stands."

"All right, I'll take you on."

The Foggy Man paddled right into the middle of a big lake like an ocean. He was in Crow's canoe in the middle of the lake.

Crow said, "I'm going to make that man disappear. Let the canoe return to ashes."

That's the end of it. The canoe turned to ashes. That's how Crow killed the man that way.

Crow, he came back and as he paddled home, he sang, "You ought to do that long time ago. Leave it to me!"

He told the people, "You could go out to hunt ducks any time now. You needn't be afraid. I got rid of that man. No danger now. Go out and kill anything you want to."

K'uda (Q'uda) — The end.

Foggy Man lived in the water. I don't know why he killed the people that got lost. The Foggy Men lived below the water. Whenever they came up it was foggy.

Titus Bedes must surely have known that Foggy Man was a man-eater.

We have three versions of this story, including Tales 32 and 34. The Nenana version suggests that there are several Foggy Men, ready to kill and eat the hunters "who venture into their domain," as Jetté wrote about the water-monsters (Toxige, Torega) (1911:107). In the stories from Koyukuk Station and Nulato, there would appear to be only the single Foggy Man called "Grandma's Needle" (see also Attla 1989:133–47).

3 / About a Brown Bear
[Crow and Brown Bear]

TOLD BY TITUS BEDES

Recorded by FdeL and NR

BROWN BEAR PUT OUT A FISH TRAP. ABOVE IT (UP-stream on the river) was old Crow's fish camp, and different tribes and other fish camps. But Brown Bear caught all of the fish so that not one passed. All the people above were starving.

Old Crow studied about it. He caught a big whitefish and scaled it in his canoe. He figured that way he would fool that Brown Bear.

He went down to Brown Bear's fish camp. "Partner," he said. "What's the matter? There are lots of fish, all kinds of fish up above you. How is that? Come take a look in my canoe."

Brown Bear said, "I don't know what's wrong. I thought not one of them pass." He thought he was getting all of the fish.

Mr. Crow said, "Well, I'm going to help your tribe. Let's look over your fish trap and see what's wrong."

They went to the trap. They went in the water, Crow was leading and Brown Bear was behind. Crow lifted up the fish trap fence with his foot, all the way across. Brown Bear didn't see what he was doing.

Crow said, "That's why you don't get any fish." [*The fish all went under the fish trap fence and not into the trap, was what he meant.*]

Brown Bear pushed his fence down tight again so that nothing could get by.

Crow said, "Well, that's fixed. That's good now. You go ahead, I'll come behind you." Crow was lifting the fence up high again with his foot [*as he followed Brown Bear.*]

89

"Well, friend," Crow said, "I'm going to go home."

"All right."

Crow went up to the other fish camps and said, "You ought to have done that long ago. I fix him. I fool him. Watch for fish tonight."

He got all the fish and Brown Bear got nothing.

Then Crow said, "Leave it to me. You ought to do that long ago."

K'uda—The end.

Attla (1989:115–31) recorded the same story from the Koyukuk under the title, "The Baby Who, According to His Aunt, Resembled His Uncle."

4 / Crow and Willow Grouse Woman

TOLD BY TITUS BEDES

Recorded by FdeL

EVERYBODY WAS STUCK ON THAT GIRL. THEY CAME from all the tribes. Nobody ever made up with that girl. Her old folks wouldn't stand for it. They were looking for a rich man.

Old Crow said, "I'll go to that place. I'll fix them."

They said, "You go."

He went a little ways. About three-quarters of a mile from this girl's camp, he sent the boys on ahead.

"I'll wait a little ways behind you," he said. He wanted to dress. He had a dress all hung with dentalium shells.

The girl's brother was a kid. He ran out. All the others were sitting in front of the house.

The kid said, "Oh, Mother, someone is coming to be my brother-in-law!"

Old Crow went over to sit on the wood [*a log in front of the house?*]. He didn't see the girl. He waited and waited there. He sat.

"When are you coming in?" said the old folks.

The young fellow (the girl's brother) said, "He can't come in on bare ground."

The old woman grabbed caribou skins from the bed and made a carpet for him to come in on. He came in.

He sat alongside that young girl. Everybody was eating. The old woman had cooked some kind of meat. It was a first-class eat, but old Crow can't eat and can't talk. He was thinking.

His father-in-law (to be) said, "Why doesn't he eat?"

[*It would have been very rude to have complained directly to his prospective son-in-law. Such remarks may only be made about*

92

someone, not to that person, even though the individual mentioned is supposed to hear.]

An old mangy dog came in and lay down inside.

Old Crow said, "I can't eat on account of that old dog."

The old woman chased the dog out and hanged him with a rope in the woods.

The old man ate and old Crow ate, too. He finished his meal. He stayed with the girl all night. He gave her a dress with dentalium shells.

Crow Betrays Himself, Loses and Regains His Beak

Next morning every man cut wood. Old Crow had taken the eye out of the dog (to eat). The chief could see that a man with three claws had taken the eye. He ordered, "Everybody take your moccasins off and show up your foot!"

Everybody did it. Crow did it fast, but they could see he had only three toes.

His brother-in-law pulled the beak off his face. Old Crow was out of luck. He went home, but he couldn't eat any more.

"I got to do something. I can't live without my beak."

He pulled the cones off the spruce tree. He made forty men out of them. He made these men (come) alive.

Old Crow ran back to his in-laws.

"I see a war coming!" he told them. "You pack your stuff away."

(In the confusion) he grabbed the sack that the beak was in. He ran a ways back, opened the sack, and put his beak back on. He set it on crooked. That's why crows' beaks are on crooked.

He spoiled that girl. Got her head all dirty. Her sister washed it for a week, but couldn't get it clean.

Although not stated, it is probable, by analogy with similar tales, that Crow's fine clothes had been made magically from rubbish. The narrator seems to have been ashamed to tell how Crow got the girl so dirty.

Even if the Crow had not been named, any Indian would have guessed who the protagonist was as soon as he got the dog's eye to eat—food that no Indian would touch.

Titus Bedes also knew other stories about Crow, although he did not tell them.

5 / The Man Who Went Through Everything

TOLD BY TITUS BEDES

Recorded by FdeL and NR

This was the title given in English by narrators in Nenana, although Eliza Jones said that she knew it by its Koyukuk title as "The One Who Paddled Among the Animals and People." It is the Saga of the Traveler, the Culture Hero who traveled from the headwaters of the Yukon down to—we cannot say, for we never heard the end of this long complex story. It is analyzed in the Commentary, page 326. As told by Bedes, the story lacks its traditional beginning, which tells how the Traveler left his home.

Making the Canoe

CH'ETEETAALKANE (CH'ETITALQANI) WAS A BRAVE MAN and a great man. He was studying how to make a birchbark canoe. "I wonder how I'm going to make a birchbark canoe." He killed a spruce chicken (grouse). He took out the breastbone. He fitted the bones together to make a frame for the canoe. He sized up the bone to make a frame for his canoe out of it. He took birchbark and cut it up. There were no women around him.

He went out and said, "My goodness." He called, "I wonder who is going to sew up my canoe." He talked loud like that.

Well, way back in the woods someplace, a girl said, "Well, take me to sew your canoe."

The man went right back to his house, lay down and pretended to sleep. The girls, those Spruce Chickens, came down and sewed up his canoe for him. He went out to look at it and was tickled to death. It was all sewed up good. The next job was to put on the pitch.

But he took a look at his canoe and said, "My, my, that canoe is no good! I wouldn't use a canoe that's sewed up like that." So he ripped it all apart.

Then he hollered the same way as before, "I want somebody to sew my canoe!"

He Fails to Get a Wife

Five or six girls came up from under the water. He pretended to sleep and watched them sew it (the canoe). He wanted to catch one young and good girl; he wanted to catch the prettiest one. He jumped up and ran down and grabbed her. All the rest ran away into the water. The one he caught hollered and began to scratch him.

He thought, "She won't do for me." So he let her go. He couldn't make that young girl stick to him at all. "Well," he said, "I'm no good for women anyway. I'll get through with my business first."

He came to the Yukon River. He started to paddle down river in his canoe. He found lots of animals living like people.

He Visits the Mink and Mice

He first found some Mink that looked just like people. He wanted to marry one of the Mink girls, but they wouldn't pay any attention to him. So he kept on going.

The next camp he came to was the Mice's camp. They had nice clean houses, and what they were eating looked good to him.

He said, "I'm hungry. I want something to eat."

So the Mice said, "All right, I'll give you something to eat."

So he ate until he got through, and then he said, "Thank you." And then he went on again.

The Mice said, "You come along again?"

But the man said "No, I don't think I'll be back again." He went on down.

He Visits Rabbit

That evening he found another camp—the Rabbit's camp. He studied to see how Rabbit killed men. He had a sharp point on the end of his tail. The man was afraid he was going to kill him. The man studied about it.

He thought, "I'm going to get a big flat rock. When I go to bed, I'm going to leave it on my chest, to protect my heart, and see what he does to me."

He lay down and pretended to sleep. He (Rabbit) was coming closer and closer to him all the time. Rabbit got on top of him easy and tried to stab him with his tail. He started to poke him with his tail and kill him. The Rabbit broke off his tail. He started to holler.

The man got up quick and said, "You be Rabbit!" He made good animals out of rabbits that time. ("Now people will eat *you!*")

"Well, I'll keep on going," he said. The Rabbits were ashamed and didn't talk to him. The man went on.

Wolverine's Trap

He paddled way down to the point. He saw something moving. Two rocks were opening and closing, coming together, automatic like a machine, so no one could pass.

That was Wolverine's trap. That's the way he killed people.

"I don't know how I'm going to pass," he thought. "Well, I could get off, and pack my canoe around," he thought. "But I couldn't get rid of that thing that way. That wouldn't do."

He took out his bow and arrow. He shot a big-pointed arrow through and it hit the trap just a little bit.

He thought, "I'm going to fool him, and see what he does."

He went right through between those rocks. But his shirt was sticking out, and he touched the rock with a little bit of his shirt. It brushed one side, and he got caught on the rock (between the rocks) by his shirt. His canoe floated on down a ways and came ashore.

Wolverine said, "Well, I'm going out to my trap and see if there's anything in it."

He saw a man hanging down from the trap. Wolverine said, "Ha! I catch smart people that way. I fool somebody."

He put the man in his canoe and called for his kids. "I got a good feed for you kids. Come on, take him ashore."

The kids were glad. They thought he was dead. They fooled around with him for a long time. The man pretended to be dead. He let the Wolverine do anything, even take off his pants. He peek out of his eye, just a little.

One kid said, "Papa, he don't die. He's alive!"

Wolverine said, "Oh, you kids are crazy! He's dead. Bring the butcher knife."

He started to work to make it sharp on a stone. He was pleased and smiling all the time as he sharpened the knife on a stone. He told the children, "Go back home now."

He started to go around, and the man jumped quick and grabbed a stone axe. He knocked out Wolverine with the stone axe (and killed him). The kids ran away up in the trees.

The young Wolverine girl, about sixteen years old, was all alone back in the woods and didn't know anything about it. [*She was in puberty seclusion and, therefore, had the power to spoil a man's weapons.*]

The man said, "I'm going to kill that woman first." He ran to her camp.

She said, "Don't kill me first. Kill me last. Kill my brothers one at a time." She climbed a tree.

The man killed the boys first, and then the girls—cleaned up the family. He went back to the girl in the tree.

"I'm going to clean you up. You're bad people and no good. I might just as well kill you all."

He got a bow and arrow. He tried to hit the girl, but his arrow went the wrong way as if it had no power. It hit, but it didn't seem to hit in the right place. He shot all his arrows.

Then he lit a fire around the tree. "I'm going to burn down

that tree with you." But when he tried to set the fire, the Wolverine woman started to urinate down and so there was no way he could set the fire.

The man said, "Well, I'll let you go, but you be good!" The man was tired. He had been fooling around for three or four hours trying to kill her. He went back to his canoe.

The Wolverine woman yelled, "I'll fix you yet. I'll get even. I'm going to rob you. I'm going to steal from your cache. I'm going to bother you all your lifetime. I'll get even with you that way. You watch out for me!"

He said, "Well, I'll chop down that tree." He started to chop down the tree, and that woman threw up all over his shirt and on his head; it was just like she had taken a physic; she defecated down his shirt and on his neck.

So he had to let her go. "One of you got to live. I should have killed you first. I have got to leave one of you." It was only the woman that could beat him.

He Visits the Otters

He went to the Otter camp. There was a nice-looking girl there. He looked at the bed where they (the Otters) slept. It didn't look good, and neither did the food. He tried to eat, but he couldn't. He could only eat a little.

The Otter girl was stuck on him. She said, "You could go to sleep."

He said, "Yes," but he thought they would kill him. He thought, "I've got to fix them; no use to let them go. I see how they kill men." He wanted to kill them all, so they couldn't get him.

The girl pretended to get sleepy. The man was sleepy, but they (the Otter girls) bothered him so much he couldn't sleep. One of the girls went to sleep with her head on a log.

"That's a good chance to kill one right here. I can't kill them all," he thought.

He had a bone club and he clubbed her head against the log,

and killed her that way. Then the rest of them weren't wild any more. He tamed them.

He Visits the Gnats

Next he went to the Gnats' camp. They were the smallest people he ever saw. He waited there. Those people had a canoe made out of dry leaves. He sat down and talked with them; he ate with them. They were good people, so he stayed a little while.

There was a mouse swimming across the lake.

The people yelled, "There's a moose coming!" Everybody went to their canoes. About fifteen of them tried to spear it with porcupine quill spears. But the waves were too big.

So the man went out in his canoe and picked up the mouse. Lots of people got killed from his waves. So he picked up the mouse alive in his canoe, and he picked up the rest of those Gnat people and took them ashore.

He said, "Now I'm going to go. You remember me, my Old Testament, when I leave you people." He saved them.

Before he died, *Ch'eteetaalkane* (Ch'etitalqani) told the people, "My story has got to be a long story. It has to take eight days' time. When you start you have to tell the whole thing. You can't pick around."

That is, the whole story must be told with all of the episodes in proper sequence.

A discussion of this complex tale and its variations will be found in the Commentary, pages 326–33.

6 / Thunder

TOLD BY TITUS BEDES

Recorded by FdeL and NR

THUNDER WAS A BIG MAN, A WILD MAN, A STRONG MAN. He was a good wrestler and killed people when he wrestled with them. He had sharp stones like razor blades in his house and when he wrestled he used to kill men by throwing them on the sharp stones that cut them.

Two young brothers were studying about it. They exercised three times a day. They were wrestling early in the morning, and they broke sticks before they built a fire. They were quick, too.

The younger said, "Well, it's about the best time to tackle him."

The older one said, "No, we got to take a long time before we do it. We got to study other things."

He watched all the birds that fly and picked out the fastest ones of all. "We got to make a canoe that way—like that duck—that will travel just as fast and can keep up with those ducks."

Well, they made a canoe, using the duck's breastbone [*as a model for the bow?*].

He said, "We got to make a nice stone house, all underground, with five or six different roofs of logs and stones and sand mixed up together. We better be prepared, because we're going to tackle him right now."

(So they made the house.) "Now we are prepared to tackle him!" So they went right up to Thunder's house.

Thunder said, "Hello, boys, hello." He wasn't angry but talked just fine. He said, "Here's where I'm going to have my fun."

The boys said, "Sure, it's better just to have more fun. Let's have lots of fun."

There were lots of people there to watch them, too. Some grown-up boys were there to study wrestling. The grown-up boys started to wrestle.

Thunder said, "What's the matter? You don't wrestle?"

"Well, we don't know how. We never seen people do it before."

The younger brother asked his brother, "Shall I tackle him first?"

The older said, "No, leave it to me. If he beats me, you will be the last one."

Thunder said, "If I get killed there will be bad damage." He told the people, "I make flames. It will blind and kill people, and it will destroy the houses and everything. The only way you could stop me is with a female dog. Pinch her ear and scold her and make her holler all you can. That's the only way I could stop." The young fellows heard that.

He started to wrestle. The older brother wrestled, and he pretended to fall down once in a while. Then the boy lifted Thunder up in the air and threw him on the rock and cut him in two and killed him that way. He told his brother, "Beat it!"

So they ran out as fast as they could and started to paddle as fast as they could to their home at top speed. They ran right underground into their own house. Thunder was right up to them already. He hit that place awfully hard, like gunpowder, with flames and lights and everything. He broke through all but the last roof.

The brothers said, "By golly, I don't think we live!"

But they had a female dog with them, so they pinched her ear, and she started to holler and squeal. The Thunder stopped.

People in Alaska still pinch a female dog's ear to make the thunder stop.

Jetté (1908-9:347-54) published a story not unlike this, at least in its latter part when the protagonist flees from the Man of Fire. Our tale, however, has two brothers fleeing from and defeating Thunder. Are these two brothers the prototypes of the twin heroes that the Athabaskans took with them to the Southwest? Jetté indicates that the Man of Fire is frightened away by the yelp of a female dog whose ear has been pinched, and "disappears amid the thunder and lightning." In our tale, the yelp drives away Thunder. Both the Man of Fire and Thunder are accustomed to kill their victims in a wrestling match. Are they one and the same mythological character?

7 / The Owl

TOLD BY TITUS BEDES

Recorded by FdeL

The Owl was identified by Eliza Jones as the Great Horned Owl.

OWL WAS MARRIED TO A WOMAN. THEY HAD TWELVE CHIL-dren. Owl could not support them all. Everything he caught was just enough for himself. He could not feed his wife and children. They were all hungry. Sometimes he would catch twelve (spruce) chickens in one day and eat them all himself. Sometimes he would give only the gizzard to his wife. She got sore.

He went off for some time. The wife caught a brown bear in its den. She killed it. She studied it.

"I'll fix that old man with how much he could eat!"

She brought snowshoes and tied them for a chairback (back rest). She made thirty pounds of lard from that bear. She roasted all the tallow. She made the Owl eat it. After he got through, he drank up all the grease. The Owl got sick. He couldn't walk any more. That's why his eyes turned to yellow.

Attla's story (1989:191–211), "The Woodpecker Who Starved His Wife," deals with a similar theme of wife abuse but in much greater and more subtle detail. Whereas the Owl's wife was independent enough to kill a bear by herself, the Woodpecker's wife, in her complete subjection to her husband, should be taken as a horrible example of over-submissiveness, because she was unable to take from his sled the food she needed for survival, until her brothers appeared. But Dena women, alone in the camp with an unloving, mean husband, are known to have been driven to suicide by hanging.

8 / Crow and the Goose Woman

TOLD BY JOHN SILAS

Since this version has clearly been made up of incidents from other stories, with shifts of interest, I have divided it up into five parts, "Tale 8a" to "Tale 8e," which will facilitate later analysis. This stringing together of virtually unrelated episodes illustrates one way in which stories are modified and epic cycles are formed.

Crow Marries the Goose Woman [Tale 8a]

CROW WAS STUCK ON THAT WOMAN, A GOOSE WOMAN, AND wanted to marry her).

But she told him, "You can't fly across the ocean," (which he geese had to do when they migrate).

He said, "Why not? I can fly upside down on the ocean."

"Well, if you can fly that way, you can try."

He was over here (on the Tanana River) when he got stuck on that woman. They stayed here after the Geese came in the spring, and all summer. In the fall, the Geese said they were all going back to where they belonged. Crow was going to go with his wife. Of course, Crow couldn't swim, but the Geese—they could swim any place when they got tired. Crow thought he could make it over there, but the Geese said No.

Crow Gets Tired

They started over the ocean. The Geese told Crow that there was no land any more; they couldn't stop, except on the water. Finally,

Crow told his wife he couldn't make it, he was too tired, he was flying too long.

Well, his wife tried to help him. She got too tired, so she got her brother to help. Every one of them tried to pack [*carry*] him, but they gave up. Finally they got tired of him.

They told him, "We can't do nothing with you. Might just as well drop you in the water."

Down they went in the water with him. They all landed in the water. They told him, "We are tired of you. We like you all right, but we can't carry you over there to where the Geese go to."

There was one little piece of driftwood. Crow sat on that, on the water, after the Geese left him.

Crow Makes Ground

One little piece of driftwood came along, and Crow told it, "Come along. Come on! Come on!" And that piece came to the one he was sitting on. Poor Crow had an awfully hard time, sitting there. Finally all the pieces of driftwood came together and he made just like a ground out of driftwood. He stayed there for a long time. By luck he was living; he got something to eat.

He made ground after all, a big ground he could sit on. He didn't know which way he was going to start (to go home). He didn't know which way he came from. All together sky, water, ground. He didn't know which way to start; he didn't know where his Alaska was — lost his head. He stayed there pretty near a year, I guess.

Crow Makes a Canoe [Tale 8b]

[*At this point the story begins to shift its focus, and what follows is not part of the original story of Crow and the Goose woman.*]

Next year he was just like a man. [*He had changed his shape from that of a bird to that of a man.*] He thought to himself he could make a canoe. He could fly over the ground but he didn't

know where he he was going to fly to. He made a raft, but he didn't go very fast on that.

He started to think about a canoe. He find out how to make it. He killed a duck. He thought a duck's breastbone would make a canoe [*be a model for the bow?*]. He thought, "I don't see why I don't go as fast as the ducks. Ducks have wings (and I used to have them, too)."

Then he got birchbark. He got to ground where birch grew. Birch grew on that ground, and spruce grew, and cottonwood grew on that ground, too. He wanted to make the canoe out of bark. He took some spruce bark off first. He took it down to the water. He put it in the water, but it drew too much water, pretty nearly sank. He took that spruce bark back. He went to the birch tree and took that birchbark off, a little piece. He put it in the water, and it didn't sink as much as the spruce bark.

Then he got something to sew with. He got a tree and started to cut lumber. He started cutting pieces for a frame. He didn't know which way to start to set it. He thought and thought, "Which way am I going to set it and sew that bark on?"

He made the canoe finally, but he didn't know about using pitch to stick around. He tried sand. He pitched with that when he sewed. Soon as he put the canoe in the water, it all came off the canoe, and everything came out. Then he went in the woods. He saw pitch on the spruce trees. He put his hand against it and it stuck to his hand. So he took that pitch for his canoe. He started on that, and no water in his canoe after he used that.

Crow Gets Lost in the Fog

Well, he had a canoe, but he didn't know where to go. He went every day a little way and came back. He didn't know where he belonged.

Finally another Goose came back. He asked him, "Where's your wife?" That other Goose must have known about his wife.

Crow said, "Well, they left me here. I couldn't make it."

115

"Are you going to stay here?"

"Well, I don't know. I don't know which is my way. I can't fly any more, but I can paddle."

"Well, if you want to go back to your place, just follow me," the Goose said.

He started to fly and Crow started to paddle. Finally a fog came along; they went into a fog. Crow was paddling, and he lost the Goose, because the Goose was flying in the air. He paddled around. He didn't know where he was going, but he paddled anyway. He felt awfully sorry. He didn't know where he was.

Crow is Captured by Fish People [Tale 8c]

[*The interest will now shift from the original Crow to a shaman Crow.*]

Then he found a hill. It was sticking out of the middle of the ocean. There was nothing in there. There was no current. It was just like a lake. He went around that hill to see what he could see. Finally as he went around, he saw a young woman come out of that rock.

[*Apparently she lured Crow back into the hill.*]

He had gotten inside the hill, but he didn't know how he did it. Then he lost his nerve and paddled. He was sitting in his canoe right in the middle (of a house). Poor Crow! He thought to himself that he didn't know where he belonged now.

All the people in the house told him, "You get off that canoe!"

He got off. They took that canoe under their pillow, so he couldn't get at it. He thought those people were going to kill him.

They told him, "Go over there in that corner. Don't move around."

He thought he could sneak out, but he didn't see a door—it had disappeared—or which way to go out.

So he started to think about another Crow, "I hope my partner helps me."

The Crow Medicine Man

His partner was in another village. The Crows start to work on that — that one of their men was missing. All the Crows came together in one place, because their best man was lost — that is, Mr. Crow.

There was a great medicine man there. They all paid him and asked him where Crow was. All the village knew that he knew better (than anyone else). They all went to that village where the old Crow lived.

They told him, "Can you find that man, where he is?"

He said, "Yes. If you want me to get that man, you make me a box that I can lie inside."

Two of them cut a tree, split it open, and hollowed out both sides with crooked knives, so that he could get inside.

He said, "Make teeth and a big mouth in one end to look like something going to bite."

They had teeth and a big mouth at one end of the box. He went in altogether. He got a rope, a long rope leading back to those people, and that stretched to where he was going.

He said, "If I pull that rope, you pull me back!"

The Medicine Man Rescues Crow

He went down to the lake, by the water. He took that water up [*lifted the surface*] and went under it. Nobody knew where he went to, but he went to that house where Crow was. He went inside where the people were. When he hollered inside that coffin, it talked loud.

He came by the door and said, "Where is the man you people took?"

Well, everybody was afraid. Poor Crow, he was still sitting there in one corner. He was awfully skinny. That big teeth look like danger. That big mouth looked like it moved, was talking, when that medicine man was talking inside. The people gave the Crow to him.

117

Then he said, "Where's the canoe?"

They grabbed the canoe and gave it to him.

Then he said, "Where's the clothes you took away? Quick before I eat you up!"

So they brought everything that belonged to Crow. They were all like men inside (their home), but they were really Fish. That's why Crow didn't know how to get back.

So Crow got back everything that belonged to him. Then the other pulled (jerked) that line. He was all ready now. Then the people started to pull that line back. The water was still up there, where he pulled it up when he went under it. It never went down. He came out with that man.

That fellow, Crow, had an uncle, he had a father, he had lots of family. They paid the Crow medicine man a lot, all they could.

After that, the water raised.

The Crow Medicine Man Gets Fire [Tale 8d]

[*The story now shifts to incidents like those in Tale 1—creative acts.*]

They had no fire at all then. They had no way to make it.

The old medicine man said, "Fire way down in the water."

Everbody tried to get that fire by spearing. There were a thousand people there, every one of them tried, but not one could get that fire.

The old man said, "If I was you people, I'd be going to get that fire." He was awfully old, too.

All the young boys thought he couldn't do it, because they were younger and had more power, more strength. He said he could get it. They told him, "You cannot get it."

"Let me try it," he said.

He took a fish spear in his right hand first. He struck down but he missed. The rest of them said, "Get away! You can't do nothing."

Then he took his left hand. He went down with that spear.

He got that fire. Everybody got cold about that time, too. He got that fire out of the water.

There was a little island they stayed on, the whole bunch. He said, "Everybody look for wood." But nobody got wood.

That medicine man said, "If I was you, I'd be going to get wood."

They told him, "Go ahead and get wood."

Poor old man, he got blamed all the time.

He went out on the island. He brought a good cottonwood, a dry one, and packed it back. The boys cut it and made fire of that, nice and warm.

They were all talking. "How is it that old man get wood? Let's go out and follow him and see where he gets that wood," said the young boys to one another.

So they started to follow him where he got wood. Finally he found a wild rhubarb and broke it down. He made a cottonwood tree out of that. The rest of them couldn't do that. That old man, he could do everything better than those young boys could do.

The Crow Medicine Man
Doesn't Want to To Make Ground

Then the boys told him, "Let's make a ground [*i.e., land*]."

He said, "I don't want to do that. You people know better all the time. I'm an old man. If you want to do something, you go ahead and do it. Any time you stop, I'm always the man that can do it. Whenever you start anything I have to finish it. If I didn't, you people would do nothing. You people don't like me because I'm too old. If I wasn't with you people, you would be stuck already." The rest of them didn't like him.

So they talk about how to make more ground.

"Why don't you put me in as head boss?" he says.

But the rest of them said they don't want him. They said, "He's too crooked."

They left that old man. They started to make ground, but they couldn't do it. They called that old man again.

"You people don't like me. I don't see why I have to help you people," he said. "You young people know better, because I'm too old. I'm way on and can't do anything."

The Crow Medicine Man
Loses His Beak and Recovers It [Tale 8e]

[*The last segment reminds us of Tale 4.*]

So they were talking about him. Some of them want him. Rest of them don't want him because they think he was too crooked.

When he was asleep they took his beak off of him. They tried starving him that way, because he got nothing to eat with.

He went to the spruce tree. He went to the cones on top. He said to them, "Let's make a war on the village and destroy it."

He made the cones alive, just like people. All the cones, thousands of them, all wake up. He came home, that old man.

An old woman had his teeth (beak) in a sack. He knew the sack, but couldn't get it because too many were watching him. At night those Spruce Cone people were coming.

"Wake up!" he said. "War coming to this village. Run away! We got to run away. I'm going to carry this sack."

The old lady forgot all about his teeth in there. He told her, "I can carry this sack." The old lady told him to go ahead.

So he took his beak out of the sack. He left the sack right behind. He beat it to the other place. The old lady found out there was no war—nothing there, or anything. Well, she went back and looked for the sack. She looked inside and found the beak was gone. The man was gone, the teeth were gone. Now that old lady thought, "My goodness! That's how he did us, that time."

That man never went back to those people any more.

9 / The Man Who Went Through Everything on a Canoe

TOLD BY JOHN SILAS

Recorded by FdeL and NR

The Indians often said "on" a canoe instead of "in," and that was the title, as Silas gave it.

IN THE BEGINNING, ONE MAN MADE THE EARTH. ALL THE birds and animals were like men. All were talking.

He Leaves Home

Ch'eteetaalkane (Ch'etitalqani, "Noah") had two wives. Each had a son, both of them. The two boys were big enough to walk around. Their mothers told them to get snow to make water. They had a basket. They put stones in the fire. The boys brought snow in the basket. They took stones out of the fire and put them in the basket to melt the snow. It turned to hot water. They got dirty water.

One wife said, "Those kids brought dirty water."

"Noah" thought his wife must have told the boys to bring dirty water. He was lying down. He got up and said, "Give me that water. It's not dirty. I'll take it." He drank it right up, even though it was dirty. Then he went right out of his house altogether. [*He was angry.*]

It was winter time when he started. That was in this Alaska where he first started, they claim.

One wife went to follow him. She packed her baby, but the other wife got left. The one that followed her husband, loved him. She traveled all night, and toward morning she saw a fire. He was camping there.

She said, "Baby is pretty near frozen."

He was going to start, when his wife was coming. He had already started, but he came back to his camp when his wife called. It was early in the morning.

He said, "I will never stop. I will go through the country."

Well, finally, he got to a place, a village. He saw two wolves lying there behind a tree in front of the village. His wife got killed by the wolves, so he was all by himself now. He thought he would try to go through.

The Robin

Finally he got to one place, and he camped there. He didn't know where to go. Somebody talked, calling out from the hill someplace, "My toboggan! Toboggan! Toboggan!" He was sliding down the hill. It was night and the man couldn't see anything. He went to sleep and didn't pay any attention to it.

He got up in the morning and went to where he heard somebody talking last night. He found a Robin hanging from her toboggan. She had been caught on it and pulled down by her toboggan, and was choked to death.

He passed. He kept on going.

He Makes a Canoe

Spring was coming. He didn't know where to go. He found a river, Yukon River. He saw water going down the river.

"Well," he thought, "Well, how am I going to travel? If I could travel on the water it's so much better than walking."

He started to make a canoe and finally finished it. He went down the river on the canoe.

He Becomes a Fish to Steal Bear's Spear

He saw somebody fishing with a spear. He saw that man, so he left his canoe and went to cut off behind him. He went in the water just like a fish. He went upstream. The man saw the Fish coming up and he tried to spear it. *Ch'eteetaalkane* knew he would get speared, but he saw that spear point, and pulled it away. He went upriver with it, and went back to his canoe.

Then he went down on his canoe to that fisherman. It was a Black Bear.

So he said, "Well, how are you getting along?"

"It's all right," but the Bear thinks that man took his spear.

That man had hidden it under the bow of the canoe so the Bear wouldn't see it.

[*The bow part of the birchbark canoe used on the Tanana River and the Yukon was decked over for a short distance in the prow, and this is where "Noah" hid Bear's spear point. The Bear thought the spear point must be in the canoe and wanted to take it apart, but the man objected.*]

The Bear said, "I can fix your canoe over again."

"No," the man said. "You can't do anything with my canoe at all."

But Bear took the canoe apart and threw everything out of it, and tore it all up. But he forgot that one little place in the bow.

Then he put everything back.

Ch'eteetalakane started out again.

The Bear shouted, "Oh, partner, I forgot one place!"

But the man said, "I won't go back to you no more."

He Visits Frog and Mouse Woman

The man went down the river so far. He found a camp and landed there. There were two women there—no husband. One was on one side and one on the other side with a fire between them, like old days. They were lying down.

He went up to one woman. She was Frog but he didn't know it. She started to cook for him. She put nothing but grass on the plate for him. That's what frogs eat. She was nice to him, but he couldn't eat it.

Then he went to the other woman on the other side of the house. She was Mouse. She started to cook some Alaska "potatoes," called *troth*. They are good to eat. The top is like a bunch of grass; the root is long and narrow. [*It is a wild pea called* Hedysarum.] He ate that and then he left right away.

Rabbit

He found another camp. He was sleepy. He was going to sleep there, but he saw a head hanging down in that house, a dead person's head.

He thought, "I wonder what way the fellow that lives here kills people."

He saw that the man there had a sharp tail. *Ch'eteetaalkane* saw that when he walked around. So he lay down and pretended to sleep. He watched to see which way the man was going to do. He got a flat rock and put it on his chest, and he looked as if he was asleep.

The fellow jumped up on top of him with both legs. That's the way he killed men: he went right down on his chest with his tail. He struck that rock that *Ch'eteetaalkane* had inside his shirt. That was Rabbit.

So *Ch'eteetaalkane* saved himself. He went out and said, "You turn into Rabbit!"

That's why rabbits have brown feet. He was awfully sick. He broke his tail when he hit that rock.

Weasel and Otter

Ch'eteetaalkane went on a little more. He found another camp. He saw somebody lying in there, scraping a skin. It was a man's skin!

He landed there and the man took up his canoe. *Ch'eteetaal-kane* went into the man's place. He was scared because his canoe was taken. He stayed overnight with that man. His canoe was tied up to the ceiling, so he couldn't get away.

So he pretended to sleep because he wanted to get his canoe. When the other fellow was asleep, he took his knife and cut the moose thongs tying up his canoe. He threw the canoe right in the water, and beat it.

But that fellow was right behind him in no time.

Finally *Ch'eteetaalkane* got away from him. He thought, "I hope I never see that fellow again!" He thought he'd lost him altogether.

He stopped and made camp. He went to sleep. He woke up and found somebody was sleeping right close beside him. It was that same fellow. He waited to find out which way to kill him, then he got a club and killed him. Then he started to build a big fire and threw the body in it. He wanted to burn that body. He saw a Weasel come out of the fire. Weasel's tail was burned. That's why the tip of Weasel's tail is black.

That fellow that he killed got up and jumped in the water. He was an Otter. That's why he swimmed so fast that the man couldn't get away.

Wolverine's Trap

Ch'eteetaalkane went on then. He saw something opening and closing, down the river, two rocks coming together like a machine, to catch people. It was going to catch him.

"Well," he thought, "This is the time I'm going to get killed."

He took an arrow and shot it through the opening, and it got through all right, so he thought he could make it. He started down. He tried to paddle through, but he was caught. His canoe floated away from him. He got caught by his shirt. He lay there.

He heard somebody coming down the hill. That thing (the trap) belonged to him. He made that to catch people that travel on the river. *Ch'eteetaalkane* pretended to be dead. The fellow took him out of that trap and packed him all the way up the hill to his camp. *Ch'eteetaalkane's* canoe was lying just a little way down the river.

All the fellow's kids came running out. His daughter shouted, "Papa's got something to pack!" All the kids were glad because they had a man to eat. They took the man (in the pack) to their home.

The man looked for his knife. *Ch'eteetaalkane* thought, "I wish you lost your knife." So the fellow lost his knife. He looked for it but it was gone.

The man saw one of the kids climb up a tree and was watching him. She said, "Papa, that man can see!"

"No. He's so fat, that's why his eyes are open. He can't close them."

The fellow had no knife, so he brought his axe over, and left it by *Ch'eteetaalkane*. He turned to his wife, "Look at something running in my hair. Something tickles my head. You see what it is."

Then *Ch'eteetaalkane* grabbed the axe, and gave him one hit and killed him. Then he killed his wife, too. But the young kid that was up the tree was still there. Every time he shot an arrow at her, she would catch it in her hand. He had a hard time to kill her. When he tried to cut down the tree, she urinated on him. He tried to burn down the tree, she urinated on the fire and put it out. He tried to climb up, and she urinated on him, too, so he didn't like to go up. Finally he got mad and gave up. He started to walk away.

"I hope you will be crooked and steal all the time from one another. You're a dirty job!" (he said).

That was Wolverine. That's why they steal from your cache. He just got mad and said that. The Wolverine's trap was below Rampart on the Yukon River.

He went back to his canoe. He found it and went on his canoe down the river.

Noises in the Woods

At one place he stopped he heard a dog bark. He anchored his canoe with a stick through the loop in his canoe. (You can see the rock with the hole in it where he put in the stick. It's on the bank a ways below Rampart. His tracks are there, too.) He didn't know what was there. He looked for the dog but couldn't find it. Still he heard it, and hunted for it. Sometimes it sounded like it was up in a tree or in the air. He looked around, he thought something was strange, but he couldn't see anything.

He thought, "Maybe it's only in my ear. Still, it must be something."

He couldn't find anything, so he went back to his canoe. That's why now people hear things in the woods and don't find anything. If it wasn't for that, people wouldn't hear dogs barking or sticks cracking or whistles or any noise in the woods when nothing is there.

The Spruce Chicken Woman

He went on down the river and found a village. He talked with the people and stayed with them for a while. A woman went out and was gone for a while. He went out to see his canoe, and it was all torn up. He thought those fellows were going to kill him. That's why they destroyed his canoe.

He went back and said, "My canoe is broken." He knew that woman did it but he couldn't say anything. He took his canoe up and told that woman, "You fix it for me. Sew it up."

He worked with that woman so she wouldn't break it again. She didn't say that she did it. They both started to work.

He said he was going to leave.

She said, "No. You stay the night."

He stayed all night. He watched closely all night long and never did sleep. He took his canoe and left in the middle of the night. He didn't know what kind of an animal that was. She was Spruce Chicken [*Spruce Grouse*].

He Cheats Fox

He kept going down river and came to a little lake. He heard something holler out in the woods, ducks or water animals. So he went there. He saw a Fox running around on the shore of the lake. He went to the Fox, who said he had a camp at the other end of the lake. He said he had two ducks roasting in the ashes at his camp.

"We could eat them when we get there," Fox said. "You cut across the lake and I'll go around."

Ch'eteetaalkane went to the camp as fast as he could. He saw the duck feet sticking out of the ashes. He pulled them both out, and broke out the meat, and put the feet back in the ashes. He cached the meat so he could eat it later.

He saw Fox coming around, so he pretended to be just coming to the camp. Fox got into camp and the fellow came just behind. Fox pulled the ducks out—nothing but the feet!

"He said, "All my ducks got burned."

"Hellow, what are you going to do?"

"Well, I got something to eat yet, someplace."

He went out to his cache and brought in some rotten mice. He gave some to *Ch'eteetaalkane,* but the man didn't like them. He pretended to eat and put them in his shirt, so Fox wouldn't see.

He and Fox Chase Away the Giant

Fox told a story. He said, "There's a big man down below here, a Giant. He's got a good fishing place in the ice that he stole from me."

Ch'eteetaalkane went to the river with him and made a hole in the ice himself. But there were no fish there. He gave up and kept on going down the Yukon.

By that time it was just beginning the winter freeze up. He thought he would stay there until the freeze up. He didn't have much to eat, so he went back to visit Fox once in a while. He hadn't seen that Giant yet.

Ch'eteetaalkane said, "Are you going to get a nice fishing place?"

"No, he took the best place away from me."

"Well, the only thing to do is to fight to get that fishing place. Scare him away."

They went together to hunt for the Giant. The big fellow was awfully wild. He didn't like to see anybody.

Ch'eteetaalkane asked Fox, "What's he afraid of? Did you ever hear?"

"Yes, he's afraid of Chickadee."

"I'm going to make a noise like a chickadee, and you holler like a fox." He (the Giant) was scared of foxes, too.

Ch'eteetaalkane went in the woods and sounded like the way Chickadee sings. Fox on the other side hollered like a fox. That big fellow got up and listened. He looked around and got scared. Fox and Chickadee were getting closer all the time! Pretty soon he started to run home. They didn't see him at all.

So they started fishing on top the the ice there. They caught fish, and then they went back to Fox's camp and ate.

He Visits the Giant

Ch'eteetaalkane said to Fox, "Why don't we visit that fellow?"

"No, he's an awfully mean man. We will have a fight if we go."

"Well, I've come through lots of dangers. I might just as well see him, too."

Fox wouldn't go. He got scared of that big fellow. The Giant had stolen one boy from around here and kept him down the river for a long time. But he treated him just like a son.

Ch'eteetaalkane went to his camp alone. Giant heard somebody coming, so he went out. He went over to wrestle with the

man. Both of them were even, and they couldn't do anything to each other. He, *Ch'eteetaalkane,* called to his partner, Fox, to cut the cords of the Giant's heel. So Fox came up and did that. The Giant gave up then and sat down. *Ch'eteetaalkane* stood up. Giant called for that little boy he had stolen, and the boy ran up to him.

"Tell your mother to come out."

He ran back and told the Giant's wife to come out. She had awfully big breasts. She put them on *Ch'eteetaalkane's* neck, and it pushed him right to the ground. But he didn't do anything to her, she couldn't help it. That's why men don't fight with women now.

Well, that's all I remember.

10 / The Giant
and the Boy

TOLD BY JOHN SILAS

Recorded by NR?

These characters are those mentioned in the preceding story.

THE BOY DIDN'T KNOW ANYTHING AT FIRST. HE WAS OUT hunting and he found a porcupine hole under a rock. He couldn't move the rock so he thought he would go inside and get the porcupine. When he went in he could see the light from the hole, then pretty soon the entrance shut up. The poor boy thought something was wrong, and he started to cry. The big Giant had put his hand in the hole.

He told the boy, "It's me. I am grandfather to you. Don't be afraid of me."

The boy had never seen that kind of man before. He threw the porcupine out and crawled out himself. The Giant was afraid of that porcupine!

He said, "You go home with me."

The boy was scared of him and didn't want to go. But he (the Giant) said it was all right. He was a good man anyway.

He (the boy) saw a big animal running around in the Giant's hair. He was scared and started to cry.

"What's the matter?" (the Giant asked).

"There's something walking around in your hair."

"That's all right. It won't hurt you. That's my lice. You don't have to be afraid of anything around my body."

He put the boy in a pouch slung from his shoulder and packed him home.

He (the boy) was satisfied. He had plenty to eat. He called

135

the Giant "grandfather." He just ate a little bit but his grandfather ate a lot. He (the Giant) was awfully good to him. But the boy felt bad. He would like to go home.

They went up to the hills to hunt sheep, and the Giant got two of them.

"Grandfather, how are you going to pack them?"

"I can put them on my belt and walk."

They were just like rabbits to him. They went home and had a fine feed again.

It was winter time. The boy went out and hunted around the house. He found lots of beaver trails. He said, "How do you kill beavers?"

"Oh, it's easy to kill them."

"Grandfather, let's go out for beaver. I know where they are."

They went out together. Giant had big arrows. With one hit he broke open the beaver house. They went over there. Giant took off one of his mittens and put his hand in the hole. The whole lake rose. All the house was full of water and the beavers had to come out. They had no place to stay any more. They clubbed all the beavers when they came out.

The boy went with him all the time to see how he did (things). Everything was new to him.

The Magic Journey Home

Finally the boy felt very sad. He said, "I would like to go home."

"Yes. I'll let you go home."

The Giant started to build a sled, an awfully big sled. The boy thought, "I can't pull that sled."

"No, you can pull it easy." [*The Giant answered his unspoken thought.*]

They loaded the sled and piled it way up. The boy thought, "My goodness, I can't pull that sled. It's awfully high."

It was loaded with dried meat and fat and all kinds of grub. He was ready to go.

The Giant said, "You eat what I put right here on the front of the sled—that's all. Don't look at the back of the sled. Don't do that."

He pulled that sled like nothing. It went easy, fine. Every once in a while, when he got hungry, he ate and kept on traveling. Finally he thought, "I don't know why my grandfather said not to look at the back of the sled."

He was halfway home. He got on top of the sled and looked back. He saw his grandfather's rabbit fur hood hanging from the handles in back. He got down and put the thong across his chest again. He pulled, but nothing doing. He was stuck and couldn't move any more. He thought, "I'll go back to my grandfather."

So he went back again.

He said, "Grandfather, I did look back. That's why I'm stuck."

The Giant went back with him to the sled and told him to pull again. He said, "Don't do that any more until you get all the way home."

So he (the boy) never looked again. He knew where his family was. A little ways from there, he left the sled.

He walked to the camp. He packed some caribou grease on his back. The people knew that Giant had taken him. When they saw him the boys in the village hollered, "His grandfather's stolen boy came ba-a-a-ak!" They all came into his house to see him. They were all glad.

They said none of them had much to eat in that camp.

He said, "I have a sled down a little ways."

He passed that caribou fat to everyone, to the whole bunch in that house. He saw one little fellow behind the others. He looked like he was so hungry. He peeped out behind the others all the time. He (the boy) took his knife and broke that fat. He passed that dry meat to everybody.

He said, "Who's that, that sticks his head out every once in a while? He must be pretty hungry."

That grease was melting a little. He threw the grease at the

little boy and it splashed on his face. That was Marten. That's why they have white faces.

Everybody got a sled and went down to the big sled. All the women were pulling—they didn't have any dogs in those days, [*i.e., no dogs trained to pull sleds*]. They were surprised to see that awfully high sled loaded with grub. All winter they lived on it. When spring came, the ice melted and the sled sank in the river. It was so heavy they couldn't move it. Finally it turned into an island in the Tanana River down below (Manley) Hot Springs someplace. Right now if you hunt there you will find that the rabbits are awfully fat. Everything is good there.

In this story we have met the favorite and perhaps universal magical prohibition against looking around or looking behind when on a magic journey. Here the Giant's power seems to have been in his rabbit fur hood draped on the sled handles, and this power helped the boy to pull the loaded sled. In Tale 11, we meet again the admonition against looking around.

11 / The Girl Who Went to the Sky

TOLD BY JOHN SILAS

Recorded by NR?

She Chases a Butterfly into the Sky

THE FAMILY WAS STAYING AT A FISH CAMP. MOTHER AND father and two little girls were there. The mother was cutting fish and the father was busy. There was a little baby there, too—a boy. That baby was smart. He could see something. He saw a pretty butterfly.

One sister said, "Let's kill that and bring it to our brother. He will like that."

They ran and ran after that butterfly. One girl lost her sister and went home. She said, "We ran after a butterfly but couldn't catch it, and sister got lost."

They hunted for her but couldn't find her. She didn't come back all summer.

She ran and ran after that butterfly and didn't know where she was. She found an old woman in a camp. The old woman was glad to see that girl.

She said, "I've got lots of young boys. They're all hunting today, but they'll be back some time tonight. One of them is going to marry you."

The girl didn't like it, but couldn't get away. The old lady knew which was her best son and she wanted him to marry this girl.

She told the girl, "You get in this sack." It was that boy's sack. She put that sack under his pillow.

The boys came back. They said, "We smell somebody else in here."

"No," (said the old woman).

"If you cheat us, we are going to kill you."

"Yes. I put a girl in a sack. I don't know which one. Whoever owns that sack is going to marry her."

They all looked inside their sacks. The youngest had the girl. The others felt sorry; they wanted her for themselves. They told their mother, "What did you do that for? But it's all right, after all. We don't care."

They stayed there for a long while. They all treated her awfully well. She stayed with all the brothers. Finally she started to think about her home and family.

The Magic Return Home

That old lady had a flat rock in one corner of the house. She called that girl "daughter." Every time she went out, she said, "Daughter, don't move that rock." She (the girl) wondered why she said that.

When the woman went out (one day), the girl moved that rock. She saw through—there was a big hole there. She saw her fish camp way down there below. Her family was fishing down there. She started to cry. One day she cried all day long and the old lady found out then (what she'd done).

She said, "Did you move that rock?"

"Yes."

"If you go back, the boys will kill me" (the old woman said).

"I can't help it. I've got to get back some way."

"You make a long string, but don't work on it when the boys are here."

Whenever the boys were away, the girl worked on it all day long. Finally she had a big sack of string [*i.e., rope made of fine rawhide or sinew*].

One day the boys all went out again. The old lady tied her around the waist (with the string).

"When I let you down through that hole, keep your eyes closed all the way down!"

The old lady let her down. She wondered why the old lady told her to close her eyes. She started to look. As soon as she looked, she was on top of a cloud and couldn't get through. The old lady pulled her back again. She told (the girl) not to do that, and tried over again. Finally, she got down on the ground.

The old lady (had) said, "If they kill me, you will see black clouds come upstream and a little rain. Then you will know they killed me."

The girl sneaked behind her family's smokehouse. The baby had grown. He was shooting arrows. One arrow came close to his sister where she hid. She took the arrow and watched the boy.

She told him, "Come here. I'm your sister."

He had forgotten all about her. He ran back to his mother and said. "I saw my sister."

His mother ran back to her, too. It was she—the daughter!

The mother said, "Where have you been?"

She (the girl) said she didn't know where she was. She went after a butterfly, and walked and walked to a camp. She told the whole story to her family. She said, "If they kill my grandmother, you will see clouds some afternoon and it will rain."

She saw a cloud coming upriver and she started to cry again. She was sorry that her grandmother got killed. That rope was a spider web. Maybe Spiders were people then.

In stories from other tribes, the woman in Sky Land is indeed friendly Grandmother Spider, and it is she who spins the magic rope used to lower the girl. Perhaps it is implied, though not stated, that she taught the girl how to make the "string."

12 / The Caribou Husband

TOLD BY JOHN SILAS

Recorded by FdeL and NR

CARIBOU MAN WAS STUCK ON ONE WOMAN AROUND HERE. He didn't know anything about this Tanana River. He was stuck on a woman and married that woman. She wanted to come down here and see her family. So he came with her, but he didn't feel good down here because there was too much brush around.

He told his wife, "Don't sleep with me. Any time I sleep, don't look at me."

His wife thinks, "I don't know what's wrong with him."

After a while the woman's brother was coming. He was glad to see his sister and her husband.

She told her brother, "Don't look at your brother-in-law when he's asleep."

(The Caribou husband had his friends in the house. The woman's brother didn't know his brother-in-law was a caribou.)

Finally something came along at night, and the woman's brother thought he heard a caribou come in. That was his sister's husband coming back at night. He got up as fast as he could, even though he was awfully sleepy. He saw nothing but a caribou asleep there by his sister, where the husband and his friends had been. He thought a wild caribou had come in, he didn't know it was his sister's husband. He wanted to kill the caribou.

There were three or four rooms, all full of caribou asleep. He thought they were all wild caribou. He was awfully sleepy but he tried to kill them.

His sister woke up and grabbed her brother before he killed

one of them. They were all in bed, but they heard something and they all got up, just like caribou get up when they've been asleep.

That woman, she hollered, "Brother, those are my husbands!"

The caribou ran away as far as the river. The Caribou man heard his wife talking so he went back up a little ways. Even now, when you chase a caribou, he beats it, but then he stops and starts to come back again a little, to find out what's the matter. This story is the reason why they do it.

Afterwards, they all went off together to their home.

That's the end.

It was hard for Reynolds and myself to follow this story, and when one does not understand what is being said, it is difficult to write down what one hears. We were confused about the number of husbands the woman had, but on thinking over our texts and comparing them, I believe that the following is the correct explanation:

The reason why this woman called all the caribou her husbands was because she was married to a Caribou clan man, and the other men of his clan were potential husbands, if her first husband died. There was a Caribou clan among most of the interior Alaskan tribes. The story seems to pretend that all Caribou clan people are really caribou.

VI
TALES FROM
TANANA MISSION

At Tanana Mission we heard stories from four persons. The first was "Old Blind Joe," also known as "Kobuk Joe" and "Rampart Joe," who told Tales 13 and 14. He was reported to be eighty years old and the oldest inhabitant of the settlement. Although he had lived many years at Tanana, he had been born and grew up on the Koyukuk River and may have learned these stories there. Later he lived for a time in Eskimo country on the Kobuk River, which empties into Kotzebue Sound, and he also lived several years at Rampart on the Yukon above Tanana Mission, before he moved to the mission itself.

Mrs. Blind Joe, his second wife, who was nearly as old as her husband, told Tales 16 and 17. She had lived all her life in the vicinity of Tanana Mission.

These stories were translated as they were being told by Joe's nephew, Joe John, who added one of his own, Tale 15. This story, and Blind Joe's first, both dealing with the origin of the Sun and Moon, have for me a slightly Eskimo flavor, perhaps because Joe had learned them when he lived on the Kobuk and later taught them to his nephew. These tales were all recorded at one session, as we sat outdoors enjoying the sun.

Chief Luke, who told Tales 18, 19, and 20, was in bed. A "spit can" on the floor beside his bunk indicated that he suffered from tuberculosis. He interrupted the story of Crow and Hawk, Tale 19, to remark with a naughty leer: "Dirty work coming! You like dirty work?" and resumed the narration only after I had assured him that it didn't scare me. I suspect he was interested in seeing whether he could shock the young white woman. Respiratory trouble and the difficulty of speaking English probably explain why his three narratives are hardly more than outlines of the stories. Chief Luke also knew the story of Crow and the Goose woman, but he gave only the briefest of outlines which I have not included here.

151

13 / Crow and the Origin of the Sun and Moon

TOLD BY BLIND JOE

Translated by Joe John. Recorded by NR

THERE WAS A TIME WHEN THE WORLD WAS DIFFERENT than it is now. There was one big town and the chief there was the Crow. All those people were dying.

They asked the Crow, "What is the cause of these people dying?"

At the end of the world there was another chief.

"This chief at the other end of the world is the cause of my people dying," said the Crow chief.

He went to this fellow (the other chief). He went to this place to kill the chief. They fought and killed one another.

Crow said, "We liked each other and still we killed one another!"

"What are we going to do now that we are dead?"

"Well, the only thing to do now is for you to be the Sun and I'll be the Moon."

The End-of-the-World chief said, "As long as the world is standing up, I'll be shining down on the people. The world is going to turn around, according to me. I'll shine on the world as it turns." (So he became the Sun.)

Crow said, "I'm going to shine so the people can travel around any time. (So Crow became the Moon.)

14 / The Man Who Went Down the River

TOLD BY BLIND JOE

Translated by Joe John. Recorded by FdeL and NR

My spelling of the protagonist's name has been questioned, because the people of Tanana Mission now call him **Ch'etetaalkkaanee**. *I checked with my original field notes, in which I had recorded it as* **Ki**titalqani; *Reynolds heard the first consonant as* **G.** *Since Blind Joe (and perhaps his nephew, too) had traveled widely, we cannot assume that either of them in 1935 spoke the dialect later recorded at Tanana Mission. We did not hear* **Ch,** *or* **ch',** *so I believe the correct spelling of the name was probably* Kk'etetaalkkaanee *in the* ANLC *system of spelling, or* Q'etitalqani *in the system we used in 1935.*

He Leaves Home

KK'ETETAALKKAANEE [Q'ETITALQANI], "THE ONE WHO Traveled Among the Different Animals and People," had a father, a mother, and brothers and sisters. He said, "I'm going to leave you now. When my hair gets gray and as white as a rabbit skin (in winter), I'll come back to you people. When I come back, I'll be (a?) Coyote. My hair will be white." He was a young fellow then.

He started out from the end of the river, from the head of the Yukon, to come down the river. At that time all the animals and birds—the mice, rabbits, willow grouse, and chickens—were men.

He started out during the winter. It came spring and water started to run, and he started to make a canoe.

154

He Makes a Canoe

Where he started to make his canoe there was a den of Foxes.

He made the frame. He put birchbark and the roots to sew them by the frame and went to bed. Alongside where he went to bed were animal women: Mice, Weasel, Squirrel, Fox, and Crow women.

When he woke up, he looked up and saw all these women were sewing the canoe with roots. So he set the frame for the women and went back to bed again. When he woke up, the Fox and Weasel women were sitting on each side of the back end of the canoe.

He Gets a Wife But Can't Keep Her

He thought "I wish that Fox woman would lose her awl!"

And his wish came true. The Fox woman lost her awl and was looking for it. So *Kk'etetaalkkaanee,* that man, jumped and grabbed this Fox woman. But the Fox woman chewed up his hands on both sides, so he had to let her go.

He went to the door of this den, and a little Hawk peeked out and looked at him and said, "What about me? My sister said to ask, 'What about me?'"

But the man said, "No. You don't look like your sister. Your eyes are too big."

She went back in, and then the Weasel woman peeked out. He made a grab for her, and just got one of her braids, and pulled it off.

So he went inside and got a hold of the Fox woman.

He stayed there with her for a while. Then he put her in his canoe and started down the river. They were coming down, and the sun came up and it got warm. He heard something panting behind him. He looked around and saw it was a Fox behind him, panting with her tongue hanging out. She had turned back into a

Fox. So he landed and went ashore, and the Fox jumped off and ran away back up the hill where she had come from.

He Deceives the Brown Bear

So he started down river all by himself, and he landed a little below and went to sleep. Right below where he camped, around the bend, was a Brown Bear man. He had a home there. This Brown Bear's daughter was just a little below him on the bluff on the other side of the river, picking berries. The man, *Kk'etetaalkkaanee*, left his camp and went down to the Brown Bear's camp and wanted something to eat.

The Brown Bear wanted to fool him. He said, "We don't have any fish. I got a place on the bluff below here, where I hunt brown bears." He wanted his daughter to kill the man, and he said this to fool him.

So they left this camp and went over to the bluff. They saw this Brown Bear walking around on the bluff. They landed there. The man put his paddle in the canoe and shoved it out and told it, "Land below here a little way."

So they climbed the bluff up to the Brown Bear (daughter).

The Brown Bear (father) told him, "Friend, use arrows without any heads. Shoot over the bear, and as soon as it comes to jump, I'll take my knife and stab it."

So while the Brown Bear wasn't looking, the man stuck the point of his arrow behind his neck, under his collar. Then when they got close, and the Brown Bear girl was jumping, he put the point on his arrow. He shot the Bear in the chest and killed her.

Then he turned back, and as soon as the Brown Bear dropped, he turned and ran away from the Bear father. The Brown Bear (father) chased him, but he, *Kk'etetaalkkaanee*, turned into an Otter and slid down the hill right into a lake.

He Escapes from the Brown Bear

The Otter came up with his head under the lily pads on the lake. The father of the Brown Bear circled around the lake, crying. He was pulling back the green scum floating on the lake, trying to see where that man had gone. He walked around the lake, looking for that Otter.

On the shore there was a Frog woman. Bear said, "Drink up this lake. Drain it. There is a man in here that killed my daughter. I want to get him!"

So she was drinking, draining the lake. And when the water got low, the Otter saw a Snipe walking along.

The Otter said, "Brother, go over to that Frog woman, and bust her stomach so all the water will come out."

The Brown Bear heard him and shouted, "Hey! What are you talking about?"

The Snipe answered, "No, I'm just looking for little worms for my family."

So the Snipe looked over at the Frog woman. She was swelling up with water, as big as a mountain. He flew over there and began to pick up worms right alongside her stomach with his bill. All of a sudden he pricked her stomach with his bill, and all the water was coming out, filling the lake up again.

As soon as the Frog woman began to drain, Brown Bear set a fish trap at the outlet of the lake. Then the Otter picked some moss off the bottom of the lake and made a moss man out of it. He sent his moss man down to the trap. The Brown Bear caught it and began to fight with it. While he was fighting, the Otter sneaked down, slipped under the trap, and went down the creek.

When he got out to the river, he saw his canoe just below the creek. So he got into his canoe and went away.

There was a great deal more to this story, but Blind Joe did not tell it. Joe John, his nephew, said that Wolverine's trap was on the Yukon between the Rapids and Rampart. Eliza Jones consulted Effie Kokrines of

Tanana about its location, and reported that it was on the north bank of the Yukon, right below Garnet Creek, some eighteen miles below Rampart. It is called Nełtseeł Hutseeł Totaalyets Denh *(literally, "The Place Where The Water Current Wrecked Wolverine's Weir"). There are boulders and rocks in a line stretching out into the Yukon that are supposed to be the remains of this structure.*

15 / The Sun, Moon, and Stars

TOLD BY JOE JOHN

Recorded by FdeL

THE SUN, MOON, AND STARS WERE ALL BROTHERS. THEY had one sister. They didn't know any other people. They had never seen any other people. The girl was of age to be married.

She thought to herself, "When we get old, who is going to take care of us?"

So she went out to hunt for a husband. She walked, and walked. Then the others followed her, singly [*in a single line*], following each other.

Finally she got to the end of the world. She started to climb up (to the sky). So they all climbed up.

Finally they gave up. She lay down and died there, smiling. She was the Moon. The others done the same thing. The oldest brother is the Sun and the others are the Stars.

The sky is evidently a dome that comes down to meet the earth at the horizon. When the girl had walked to the end of the world she had been everywhere, and could go no farther on earth.

16 / Crow Recovers
the Arm of Marten Girl

TOLD BY MRS. BLIND JOE

Translated by Joe John. Recorded by FdeL and NR

Bears Take Marten Girl's Arm for a Rattle

THERE WAS A TOWN. THERE WAS A MARTEN GIRL AT THAT
town. There were three men came there: Brown Bear, Black Bear,
and Wolf. They were in human shape. So they got to the village
and grabbed this girl. They grabbed her arm and tore it off. They
took this arm with them, and took it to their home.

In this Brown Bear's house they scratched this arm all up,
clear down to the Marten claws. They had a bunch of claws of all
different kind of animals, strung into a round rattle. They put the
Marten claws in with the others.

Crow Sets Out to Get the Arm

And this old Crow went there in a canoe. So before he got there, he
got this little Tree Owl [*possibly the Boreal Owl*] and put him in the
canoe with him. So he landed at the Brown Bear's house, and he
told the little Tree Owl to hold his canoe to the bank with a paddle.

And this little Owl went to sleep while he was holding the
canoe, and it tipped over.

Crow Makes Himself Pitiable, with More Deceits

Crow had to walk over a portage, and he kind of starved himself. He came to this village, all weak. He was barely walking. The

163

people saw him coming, a poor starved fellow, coming to the village. So they took him in and cooked for him. He ate that.

They asked him, "Where do you come from?"

And he said, "I come from the south."

And after they asked him all these questions, he said, "Now, I'm going to dance for you, and give you entertainment."

He started to dance, and he danced all day and all night until the sun came up, and everybody went to sleep watching him.

He said, "Put me in the room where the Marten woman's arm is."

In front of the house were two old Bears, one sitting on each side of the door. The fire was outdoors. Crow kept going out all the time, and every time he go in, he take his knife and cut the string from one of those claws on the rattle. He kept doing that, and each time he said, "Oh, I got stomach ache!" as he went in and out.

Finally, by doing that, he cut all the strings off, and started to run away with it, and said, "Did you fellows give that arm away?" He stepped right in the ashes, and as he ran through the ashes, he kicked them and scattered them, and they kind of burned the old Brown Bears' backs. [*That is why their backs look burned.*]

Crow started to run back over the portage that he'd come on. When he got to the canoe, his canoe was upside down, and his nephew, that little Owl, was sleeping there, under the canoe on the beach. Just as he ran out of the portage, he kicked that canoe, and it landed right side up. And he grabbed his nephew by the head and threw him in the canoe. His nephew's eyes were wide open with astonishment. That's why Tree Owls have such big eyes.

Crow's Return

All those people were coming behind him all the time. Just as he shoved the canoe off, they grabbed for it, but couldn't reach it. So these people grabbed trees and pulled them up by the roots. They said, "I wish I could do this to that old Crow!" But they couldn't reach him.

While they were doing this, Crow was paddling, and he was saying, "I wish I could do this to those people," and he would jab his paddle in. And every time he paddled, he paddled so hard that an island came up behind him.

So he left that village and went downstream. He had that arm he took away, and he had that dried Marten's arm in the water to soak it. It had been dried.

So he was coming to his own village when he came down. Everyone came and said, "Take him out on the shore."

So he told them to keep the flesh part of that arm moist where it had been torn off. So he got ahold of this arm, and he hit the girl that had lost her arm. And he said to the arm, "Land back a little way!"

So that is why martens' arms are one-sided, with one of their front legs a little behind the other.

So the girl jumped around happy, "I've got an arm! I've got an arm!"

Crow's energetic paddling has here made islands, but in one of Jetté's stories, (1908–9:309–15), Raven ("Crow"), as a young man, threw a harpoon with such force that the wave he hit with it formed a mountain in the Khotol Range, "The-One-Whose-Top-Was-Hit-by-Raven," and on the rebound created "Dinale," "The-High-One," (literally: "That [Mountain] Which is Tall"), Mount McKinley, now more frequently called "Denali" in Alaska. Attempts to change the official name from McKinley to Denali have failed, according to Richard Nelson, and Miranda Wright reports that she has often heard the mountain referred to as "that shiny place in the sky where all the spirits go to."

17 / Crow and Willow Grouse Woman

TOLD BY MRS. BLIND JOE

Translated by Joe John. Recorded by NR

Crow Courts the Girl Who Won't Marry

THERE WAS A VILLAGE. ONE GIRL DIDN'T WANT TO GET married. All the boys were after her. There was another village above there. The boys came down and wanted to marry this girl, but she didn't want to marry anybody.

Crow said to his grandmother, "I'm going to go down and try." His grandmother said, "Oh, you couldn't do anything. You wouldn't get that girl."

In False Finery

Crow went out in his canoe and picked some grass and pitch and got some dog excrement. He hit himself on the chest and blew on the dog excrement and it became dentalium shell beads. He chewed the pitch and mixed it with the grass, and then he shaped it into clothes and a knife and sheath. He went down to the other village and everybody said, "The chief is coming! The chief is coming!"

The girl's brother was down there and he ran up and shouted, "Mama, I found a brother-in-law!"

Crow was holding his canoe against the shore with his paddle. He said, "I never step on the ground."

The girl's mother took all the sleeping skins and placed them in a row down to the river. Crow got out of the canoe then and

walked over the sleeping skins up to the girl and sat down be-side her.

When this Willow Grouse girl sat down, her dress was pegged to the ground. [*This perhaps indicated that she did not want to marry Crow.*] He (Crow) stayed there for a couple of days. He was worrying all the time that his pitch dress would melt. The girl fell in love with him, and went back to his village with him in the canoe.

His Fine Clothes Turn to Trash, and His Wife Leaves Him

They traveled all day. Crow had his wife's sewing bag in front of him.

Crow said, "Dear, look at me."

She turned around, and he was an ugly thing, an awful thing! All the pitch had melted off. She was broken-hearted. She got hold of Crow's clothes behind him and twisted them.

She said, "Dear, I want to get off for a little while." She had a pretty shawl of marten skins. She said, "You can tie a string on me so you won't lose me." She got off and went up on the bank.

He pulled the string and said, "That's far enough."

She went behind a bush and tied the string to a bush. He pulled the string and pulled on it. Finally he pulled it hard, and instead of pulling in the girl, he pulled in a little spruce tree.

He started to jump up, but his clothes were sewed to the thwart, and when he jumped up, all his clothes pulled off. He got off without his clothes. He went up in the brush and hunted all through the grass clumps, and everywhere, but the girl was gone.

While he was looking around, the girl sneaked around and jumped into the canoe. Crow saw her getting in and ran down to the shore. He reached for the canoe but just grabbed the stern piece, and his hand slipped off.

Crow's Ignominious Return

He started to walk up the beach without any clothes. The girl went down the river in the canoe. He got in among the thorns. His legs were all bleeding. He came back to his grandmother. The old grandmother just gave him a good bawling out. He was all tired out and couldn't do anything from traveling so far. His grandmother started to doctor him and tried to cure his wounds.

The Girls' Ball Game

There were lots of people in that village. The men were all out fishing with dip nets and all the young girls were playing ball.

Crow said, "Grandmother, take me out."

She said, "Oh, you poor thing! You'd better quit." But she took him out anyway, and leaned him against the house.

The girls were playing ball. He thought, "I wish the ball would roll to me."

His wish came true. The ball rolled alongside him. All the girls jumped on him to get the ball away. They kicked his sores open, and he started to bleed again.

Crow's Revenge

The fall came, and they started to have a potlatch. Everybody gathered for a big potlatch. The Willow Grouse girl was among the people that came. They had a feast, and all the young girls went down to pack water. The Willow Grouse girl was among them. Crow went down to the girls and he had a spear with him. The girls couldn't do anything against a man with a spear. He speared and killed the girl that had left him last summer. A Willow Grouse jumped out of the dead girl's body.

Crow's wish to have the ball come his way was probably made to attract a girl, but he was overwhelmed by the success of his wish and was left worse off than before. I suspect that his stabbing of Willow Grouse girl was used in a fuller version of the tale to explain why the grouse breast meat is white.

18 / Crow and the Seesaw

TOLD BY CHIEF LUKE

Recorded by FdeL

CROW USED TO BE LIKE A BIG MEDICINE MAN. CROW FIXED a seesaw over a rock, put a young boy on one end and a woman on the other end. Crow wanted a fat pregnant woman. He put her on the seesaw.

"I don't like a thin woman."

Crow sat in the middle and covered himself with a blanket. They asked him what he was doing.

"I am watching to see if the log will break."

But all the time he was pecking at it with his sharp beak. Soon the log broke in two. People fell down the bluff and all were killed. Crow ate them all.

Attla (1983:243–56) told a longer story which began with the episode of the seesaw. Mink is so angry at his uncle for killing the people that he throws him down a cliff. He later becomes lonely and regrets his act, as Raven had foretold, so he puts his uncle's body back together again, and restores him to life.

175

19 / Crow and Hawk

TOLD BY CHIEF LUKE

Recorded by FdeL

CROW CALLED HAWK, HIS NEPHEW. CROW SAID, "I'M going to hunt with you."

So they go hunt on an island.

Crow fool him.

"I wait here and get something."

Crow stole Hawk's canoe so he can't go. Hawk was looking for him. Then he saw Crow and called to him to come back. He don't come back.

Crow stole Hawk's wife.

Next spring he look for Hawk. Then Crow (went) back (to the island). Nobody there. No sign at all. (Crow thought that) Hawk had starved to death.

He had to watch his canoe, but he was alone, with nobody to watch it. So he made dirt [*excrement*], and made a man out of that.

He said, "Can you talk?"

Dirt said, "Yes."

"When somebody comes down by my canoe, you holler."

So Dirt watched it.

So Crow said, "I wish I find that Hawk." He was singing.

Then Dirt began to holler. Hawk was in the canoe and all the way up.

Old Crow cry, "Nephew, come on! Come on! No more I fool you!"

But Hawk didn't pay any attention to him. He was paddling away.

"How you kill animal that you eat?" (Crow called after him).

"Only mice. And any animal I see that swims across. I hit it with a rock. By and by all the bones are smashed," Hawk said. "Then I eat it." Hawk was fooling him. Hawk went away.

By and by a little mouse came and Crow killed it. Crow smashed it with a stone and ate all the broken bones. The old man Crow choked on the bone.

Then Hawk saw his wife. She was a nice fat woman. She had a big fat belly. [*Crow had made her pregnant.*] Hawk kicked her belly, and all young crows came out and hollered. Lots of them.

After that, he took his wife and cleaned her, and married her again.

Crow died. Hawk went to look for Crow. He walked around and by and by he find his feathers and bones. He knew he had gotten choked by the bone.

20 / Crow and Seal

TOLD BY CHIEF LUKE

Recorded by FdeL

CROW HAD A MALE SEAL FOR A PARTNER. THEY WENT IN A canoe on a lake to hunt ducks.

"One place there is shallow water. But you can't walk because you sink," Crow said. "When we get there, you see me (watch me)."

Then he paddled, and he slipped across, and didn't get stuck. Seal was afraid.

Crow said, "Come on! I make it for you. I fix it so you could cross."

Seal paddle hard to cross, but in the middle he is stuck.

Crow said, "I'll come in close."

Seal said, "That's why you did this, to fool me."

Crow made help. He got out of his canoe. He could walk. He said, "You get out of your canoe. See, I can walk. I don't sink."

Seal got out and sink down. Crow fool him. Crow (pretended to) try to help him. Seal tried to get out (of the mud).

Seal said, "Don't fool around my back!"

But Crow pull his guts from behind, through his anus, and ate all the guts, ate all of Seal.

Then he came back to camp.

Somebody said, "Where's your friend?"

Crow said, "My friend got a headache. I tell him to go back."

Crow had a wife. He sit down. He got something in his canoe. He took out his own stomach (intestines). He put his own guts on the canoe. He cut himself open with his knife.

He said, "I got only caribou guts. I kill a caribou but he fell

180

down a crack [*crevice in the rocks*]. I couldn't get him. All I could do was hook up his guts."

By and by he eat fish eggs. (They were boiled and made into soup.) He drank them. Crow's child, Crow's little boy, lost one of his mitts. He looked for it. He thought his father was sitting on it. He pulled the mitt out. Crow had corked himself with it, and when it was pulled out, all the rotten fish-eggs soup went all over.

Crow flew up a tree, and sat down there. All the young boys got an arrow and tried to kill him. Finally one boy killed him with an arrow.

Crow, he was (always) stealing things. He was thinking all the time to eat people.

If you tell stories it makes the winter short. When you finish, say "*kk'udaa* (Q'uda)—That's enough. Water dripping from the door already (because spring has come)."

As Eliza Jones knew the story (from Koyukuk Station), Crow gave his own guts to his mother-in-law, who commented to her daughter on its nasty smell. When Crow's wife reported to her husband what her mother had said, Crow told her to tell her mother that was because the guts got sour. But the mother-in-law did not put the guts into the fish-egg soup that Crow drank, as in our Tale 36a from Nulato. The version recorded here does not specify what became of Crow's guts.

VII
TALES FROM
RUBY

Mrs. Altona Brown was a remarkable woman from a remarkable family, as her autobiography indicates. Her grandmother, for example, made her own underground house when she left her husband. She also made a caribou fence and snares and successfully took caribou, which she dispatched with a spear and butchered with a slate knife.

Altona was like her. After an arranged marriage that was anything but satisfactory, Altona broke with tradition and selected her own husband. She and "Dago Kid" Brown, a white man, were happily married when we met them in 1935. She was apparently very skillful and energetic in cutting fish for drying, and with her husband running the wheel, the couple had done very well in supplying dog feed to the prospectors and miners who "stampeded" into the area in 1910, when Ruby was founded. The Browns also bred sled dogs for sale at that time. In 1935 they were boarding dogs not needed by their owners during the summer, and had between fifty and a hundred animals staked out near their fish wheel. Later, Altona had her own snowmobile with which she visited her own trapline and showed that she could do all the work traditionally handled by men. Her English was distinctly better than that of most of our informants, owing to her English-speaking husband and to her many white friends at Ruby.

21 / Crow and Whale

TOLD BY MRS. ALTONA BROWN

Recorded by FdeL

CROW LIVED IN A BIG VILLAGE. THERE WAS A WHALE. There was a girl that everyone wanted to marry. She was Willow Grouse.

Crow wanted someone to go hunting with him. But the old folks didn't want their children to go hunting with him because he would eat them. They asked him who he wanted to go hunting with him.

Crow said he wanted the Whale, because he was so big and strong and husky. Whale was a young fellow. He went with him. They went up the river. There was a lake where they could kill lots of hell-divers [*red-necked grebes*]. The Whale didn't want to get off the canoe. He was afraid of Crow.

Crow said, "Sh! Listen to those ducks. I'm going to get out of the canoe to see them."

He went into the woods, and then he killed the boy (Whale).

He tore the kid's stomach [*intestines*] out. He ran with it into the woods and put it under the trees. That's what made the roots. [*Crow presumably ate the rest of Whale.*] Then he went all the way to the portage.

Then he didn't know what to say to get away with it. Finally, he pulled out his own guts and put that in a basket. That's why crows have no gizzard.

He took his guts home.

He was singing [*a eulogy for Whale*] and crying.

The people said, "It's a wonder you never come home with people that come hunting with you."

He (Crow) was married. He told his mother-in-law and his two wives to go to the canoe and get the guts. They went down and said it smelled awful, and so they came back.

He (Crow) said, "Oh, the animal was all crushed up. That's what made it smell. Bring it up and fix it up. There is nothing wrong with it."

So they fetched it up. They cooked up some salmon eggs in a big pot, and other things. They had a potlatch. They started to ask what happened to the boy that went with Crow.

He said they were going up the canyon. They saw caribou on the rocks. He told the boy it was too far to kill them. But the boy killed it, and it fell down. So the boy went to get it with a hook, but he fell off the cliff and was killed. So then Crow claimed he hooked up the caribou guts, and that's what he brought home.

All the people were in the feast house. Crow's boy had a (pair of) rabbit skin mitts. Crow was the big eater. He gobbled up everything they got. On purpose, they gave him lots of soup. So Crow stuffed himself with the mitt [*in his anus to hold in the food*]. Crow was plumb full and couldn't move. The people told the boy to get wood. So he went to go out, but couldn't find his other mitt. Then all the people began to look for the mitt. So finally he saw it, and pulled it out.

"Here's my mitten!"

Then everything in Crow ran out, and the place was flooded. The people had a terrible time to get out. Crow turned into a bird and flew up through the smokehole. The boy jumped into a [*wooden or bark*] pail and floated up through the smokehole. The people all turned into different animals to get away.

Crow's body was dead, floating around, and he was thinking, wishing himself sitting on the tree, watching all the people trying to get away.

Then he was wishing he would like to see pretty Willow Grouse cry for some of his feathers to put in her hair.

Afterwards she began to cry. Everybody asked what she was crying for, but she couldn't say. Her mother asked her, but she finally told her small sister that she wanted some of the feathers of the old dead Crow. So the little girl told her mother that her sister wanted Crow feathers. So the mother went to her daughter and asked her "What for?" And the girl said she wanted them to make her hair pretty.

Then her father got disgusted. And still she was crying. So they went and got a few feathers, and she put them in her hair. So that's why willow grouse has black feathers on each side of her neck.

[*Were Crow's guts in the soup he ate?*]

Crow ran away with a girl in his canoe. Whenever he got tired, he would dip his paddle in deep and would pull up a little ground. They would spend the night there. That's why there are some islands in the sea that go down and come up.

22 / The Man Who Went Through Everything

TOLD BY MRS. ALTONA BROWN

Recorded by FdeL

He Becomes a Fish to Steal the Fisherman's Gear

IT WAS EARLY IN THE MORNING AND THE MAN WAS COMING down the Yukon River. He saw that somebody had his fishhooks out. So he came ashore and hid his canoe in the woods. Then he made himself into a Fish and went to the hook and was caught on it.

The old fellow who had put out the hooks was glad to get this Fish, and put him in his packsack and started to pack him home. But the Fish made his muscles tight, and so the old fellow couldn't carry him. Then the old fellow would put down the pack and pound the Fish. "Now you will die," he said. But the Fish made his muscles soft, so he wouldn't get hurt. He did this every time, every step the man took.

Finally, they came to the big house. The old man left his packsack outside the door and went in. He was getting ready to cook the Fish. He got some wood, and then the man got out of the sack. He stole the old fellow's hook and line and went back to his canoe. He went on down the river.

[*The above episode belongs* after *the man had made his canoe, and lost his wife.*]

He Makes a Canoe

At first, the man walked the land. That was when he did lots of stunts. When he camped he didn't know how to make a canoe, or how to start.

He started to walk the land. He came to a place where the river makes a circle and there is a short portage between the bends. He took a piece of spruce bark, threw it in the water, and walked the portage. He waited for the piece of bark, and waited, and waited. It didn't float down. It must have sunk.

So he sat down and thought. Then he took cottonwood bark. He threw it in the water and walked the portage. He waited for it. He didn't get that, either. It didn't float.

He done that to lots of trees that got long bark. Finally he came to the birch tree. He barked that. He threw that in the river and walked the portage. Then it floated down. So he thought, "That's the kind of material to make a canoe."

So he got some bark long enough to make his canoe. He got some spruce roots. But he didn't know how to make the front turn up. So he killed a hawk and took off the lower jaw and measured that. But it didn't fit. He did the same with an owl. So finally he got a spruce hen and took off the lower jaw, and then made a pattern from it that fitted.

Then he got everything ready, but he was too lazy and went to bed. He was wishing he had a girl to sew it for him.

Then all of a sudden he woke up. He heard something working on his canoe. He didn't know what it was. So he stuck his head out of the blanket and saw a bunch of girls, sitting on each side of his canoe, sewing it. Then he started to move and they all ran away. He didn't reach one of them, and he didn't know where they went. Then he worked some more on it (the canoe). He went to bed again.

He Gets a Wife but Loses Her

Then he woke up and they were all working on it, and they were almost finished. He wanted to pick out the girl for himself. There was only one he wanted. She was a big girl and he got stuck on her. She was pretty. So he made a big jump for this girl and missed her. So he put his canoe in the water and tried it out.

But he couldn't go. He was stuck on this girl and had to have her with him.

He saw they (the girls) went in a hole. He blow and blow in the hole, but not a sound. Finally a Mouse came out.

"What do you want?"

He said he wanted that girl. The Mouse went in and came out again and wanted to know if she would do.

But he said, "No. One side of your eyes is smaller than the other."

[*Since the Dena never criticized anyone to his or her face, the Traveler was very rude.*]

Then she started to cry and went back in.

So all small animals like Squirrels and Weasels came out and asked if they would do, but he didn't want them. And the girl he wanted didn't come out.

Finally somebody talked to him from inside and said that if he wanted to come in he had better make the hole bigger so he could walk in.

He did. He walked in. There were all different-looking girls sitting around the house. The one he wanted was sitting near the old man, their father. He asked the man if he could have the girl.

So the man said yes, but he would have to take good care of her. He would have to put something over her so the sun wouldn't hurt her. He would have to keep away from the water because she couldn't swim.

So the man promised, "Yes."

Then the old fellow gave him the girl. Then he took her on his canoe with him and went downriver.

When the sun was coming up, she started to cry. He got mad and threw her in the river. She started to sink, so he took her on the canoe again and put her ashore. She ran home. She was a Fox. She was singing.

Mrs. Brown stopped here, though it was not the end of the story, and told a bare outline of Porcupine and Beaver (not included here).

193

VIII
TALES FROM
KOYUKUK STATION

We again obtained eleven stories from the same community, largely through the assistance of Ella Vernetti, the young wife of Dominic Vernetti, a white storekeeper at Koyukuk Station. Good-looking, vivacious, educated, and very intelligent, she impressed all of us with her abilities and good nature. Her mother was the daughter of a shaman from Dulbi ("Dolby") River, an eastern tributary of the Koyukuk, and her father was a white man. She acted as interpreter for her uncle, Andrew Pilot (Tales 23 and 24), and had herself already recorded and translated three stories (Tales 31, 32, 33). We know nothing about the narrators, except that the first was an old woman. The wording of these tales is, therefore, Mrs. Vernetti's. She did more "editing" of these last three stories than of the two that she translated as Andrew Pilot was telling them. Ella also tried her hand at writing romantic fiction, based on the true story of how a young Native killed two white men who tried to rape his wife. It contains all the clichés expected in that genre.

23 / Crow Gets the Sun and the Moon

TOLD BY ANDREW PILOT

Translated by Ella Vernetti

Andrew Pilot, over sixty years old, was reputed to be a medicine man and the son of a wealthy Native trader at "Dolby" at the mouth of the Dulbi River. (Eliza Jones has identified the father as "Red Shirt," whom Allen [1887:105, pl. 28] believed was a medicine man implicated in the Nulato massacre of 1851.) Andrew Pilot's third wife, Sally, was a young woman from "Cut-Off" on the lower Koyukuk. We visited them at their fish camp, only a short distance from our camp.

Crow's False Finery

CROW WAS WALKING ALONG, FEELING SAD BECAUSE HE had nothing. He took grass and beat it against his knees, and it turned into wolf skin leggings. Then he got spruce cones and alder cones and beat them against his breast, and they turned into a wolverine skin mantle. He took wild rhubarb and the green berries and slung them from his right shoulder across his chest, and they turned into dentalium shell beads. He didn't think that was enough, so he thought for a while. He started to chew spruce gum and chewed quite an amount. He put it around a stick and formed a dagger with a double handle [*a handle with double spirals at the end*] and hung it on his wolverine dress. Then he was prepared to fight if he had to.

Crow Goes to Get the Sun and Moon

All the land was in darkness, and the Sun and Moon were on the other side. He wanted to bring them to his country. He was all dressed up. He passed through all the villages. He came to the last village, and no one there was fit to have him as a guest. They didn't know who could have him, for none had anything to compare [*with his obvious wealth*]. They decided that the man who had the Sun and Moon should have him. So he entered that house.

This man had a beautiful daughter who wanted to marry the handsome stranger. Crow stayed there for a while and finally consented to marry this girl. He married the girl and lived with her, and a little child was born.

The baby kept crying, and they didn't know what to do for it. Crow said that he wanted the Sun and Moon as playthings, and the grandfather brought them over and hung them above the baby, and it stopped crying immediately.

Crow's Return

For several months before, Crow had been having trouble with his clothes, to keep them from changing back to their original form. He thought he couldn't keep up his pretense any longer, so he flew away with the Sun and Moon and Stars, at night when everybody slept. And as he flew, he lit up this country here. The wind took them up and placed them around.

Before the people had light they made long strings of rocks and set them out to their fish traps and wherever they wanted to go, so they could find their way back.

24 / How the Three Clans Got Their Names

TOLD BY ANDREW PILOT

Translated by Ella Vernetti

THERE WERE WARRING TRIBES. THEY ALL CAME TOGETHER one time, and the three headmen from the three groups of people met. They wanted to decide what to call one another, and to make a peace.

They asked the first man, a Black Bear, "What do you want to be called?"

He said, "I did not come from on top of the ground. I came from underground, and in coming through the ground I passed copper and all kinds of different minerals. So I want to be called 'Copper. *Noltseene* (Copper people).'"

"Well, you have to prove that you came from underground. What have you to prove it?"

So he brought a sack with a piece of copper in it to prove it.

They asked the second, the one that came sunwise, what he wanted to be called. He was a Marten man.

He said, "Well, I have come over a long stretch of water. I swam part of the way and I came by boat part of the way. So I want to be called 'From-Out-of-the-Water people.'"

"Well, give us proof that you have covered a great body of water."

He brought out a string of dentalium shells. So his people were called '*Toneedze gheltseełne*' (Tonidza ʁeltsiłna).

The third said he came from the caribou country, far away. So they called his people "From-Among-the-Caribou people, *Bedzeyh Te Hut'aane* (Bedzex Te Xot'ane)." He was a Caribou man.

199

25 / Crow Gets the Sun and Moon

TOLD BY LARSON CHARLEY

Recorded by FdeL

Staying at Andrew Pilot's camp was Larson Charley, a Native about forty years old, born at Old Louden on the Yukon. He had previously been married to a woman from "Cut-Off," on the lower Koyukuk, and had lived there with her for several years. He and his partner, an Irish man named George Storres, were apparently planning to fish at Pilot's camp that season. One evening they came upriver to visit us, and Charley told us this story.

Crow Made the Sun

CROW WAS THE CHIEF OF THE COUNTRY AROUND HERE and he had the Sun. It was a little thing then. He made the Sun and it was up there, but it didn't work. It moved around but gave no light. Finally, he discovered the right stuff to make it light. The Sun got bigger and bigger all the time, and finally got broad daylight.

A Chief from Away Tries to Get the Sun

A chief from another country wanted to get the Sun.

He said to Crow, "I've got another kind of sun up there in my country. Let's you and I trade."

The Crow didn't believe that. He had one sun for night (the Moon), and one for day, so he knew the other fellow was lying.

The other chief said, "You haven't seen that sun that I'm talking about around here?"

"No, I've never seen that sun and moon anyplace."

"You know that I'm a medicine man."

Crow said, "I'm a medicine man myself, and I've never seen anybody that could beat me with medicine."

The Sun was coming up in the morning, and the fellow that had come to Crow was watching it to see how to get it. He watched it all day, and that night he saw another one come up.

He asked, "Is that the same one coming back again?"

"No, that's another one I have. Now that you've seen all of my Sun and all of my Moon, I want you to tell me what kind of sun you have."

After the Contest, the Other Gets the Sun and Moon

The fellow was stuck then. He tried to figure out what to do. He made medicine and the wind started to blow. He told Crow, "You stop the wind blowing now!"

Crow started to make medicine. They were both making medicine at the same time. Crow was working to stop the wind, and the other fellow told Crow he was helping him, but he was really trying to get the Sun. He got the Sun, but Crow didn't know it. He got the Moon too. It was at night time. Then he went away without Crow knowing. He found out afterwards that that fellow had taken the Sun and Moon, and had gone.

That chief got back to his camp and held the Sun and Moon for three days. It was dark here then. Then he threw up the Moon and made medicine, and it stuck on the bottom of that other earth above us. It started to move around and do work. After the Moon set, he took the Sun and threw it up, too. And the Sun started to go to work like the Moon. So they had daylight up there, and we had darkness here. That chief knew he had the Crow beat with medicine then.

Crow Goes to Get Back the Sun and Moon

Crow didn't know what direction to go, but he finally found that chief's track and he followed it. It was a hard job, too. Finally, he

came to daylight and he knew he was getting closer. He had Mink with him because he couldn't kill any animals himself. Whenever Mink killed anything, Crow ate it.

When he got close to that place, he told Mink, "You stay here until I come back."

He came to a big village. He went back a little way and made medicine to get fancy moccasins and parka.

People saw him coming a long way off, and shouted, "He! he! he! he! The biggest chief in Alaska is coming!"

Crow Marries the Chief's Daughter

He came closer and saw a girl packing water.

He thought, "I wish that girl would get thirsty and drink water."

She went down to drink, and he took a spruce needle and threw it in the water. She saw it in the water and threw it away. Crow threw another one in the water, and she threw it away again. The same thing happened a third time. Then the fourth time, she got mad and drank the water right down and the needle with it. She was the chief's daughter.

Crow went right up to the chief's house. He thought Crow was a big chief from another town. He stayed there three or four days, and then the chief told him, "I'm going to take you for my son (-in-law)."

"All right."

So he stayed there and married the daughter. Right away they started to have a baby. The spruce needle turned into that baby. Half a year he stayed there and they didn't find out he was Crow. The baby was born and started to grow faster and faster and became a little boy. The chief was fond of his grandson and used to carry him around.

The Boy Cries for the Sun and Moon Pictures

The chief had pictures of the Sun and Moon hanging up in his house. When he took the Sun, he had taken pieces of birchbark and made medicine. Then he held them up, and they turned into pictures of the Sun and Moon.

The baby sat up and cried.

His grandfather said, "Oh, no wonder he is crying. He wants to play with those pictures."

So they took them down and tied them together with a string. The boy played with them and rattled them together.

Crow Makes off with the Sun and Moon

Crow started to make medicine again. Still nobody knew he was Crow. He made medicine to have a dog steal a king salmon from a cache.

At once somebody said, "A dog got away with a king salmon!"

Crow went first and the chief behind him, trying to catch the dog. Crow turned around and went back to the house, and took the Sun and Moon away from the baby. He kicked the baby, and it turned into a spruce bough. Then Crow left.

The chief came back with the king salmon, and the Crow was gone, the baby was gone, the Sun and the Moon were gone!

He was sad and said, "Now, that Sun and Moon are going to disappear from here."

After Crow got a little way off, he held up the pictures, and the Moon came right to the picture, and the Sun did the same thing. Then he left, and that country was dark, and there was no moon.

Crow got back to his home. He made medicine and sent the Moon up first. He told it, "After you get up there, you go to work!" The Moon stuck up there and went to work. Then he did the same thing with the Sun.

The chief of that other town asked his daughter, "When you went down for water that time, did you drink anything?"

"When I got down there I was thirsty, and I drank water."

"What did you drink in that water?"

"I saw a spruce needle, and threw it away. Then I started to drink again, and another spruce needle was in the water. The fourth time I drank it."

"Oh, that's how he got away with that Sun," the chief said.

Crow Guards the Sun and Moon

Crow said to his people, "Any time when I'm out hunting, and anybody comes, don't let them in my house until I get back."

Three or four years after that, Crow said, "I don't think he's going to come now, but watch anyway." He had a guard there all the time.

One fellow came while the Crow was out hunting. It was the other chief's son this time. His father came halfway with him, and stayed there. His son came to the village while the Crow was out, and wanted to go in the house, but they wouldn't let him.

"If you came in while the chief is out hunting, he'll kill all of us!"

"All right." So he stayed in another house until Crow came back.

They told Crow when he came back.

"Well, bring him over and let him eat with me."

Crow had never seen him before, and he started to ask him questions. "Where did you come from?"

He said he was from a different town from the one where the chief used to have the Sun and Moon, but Crow didn't believe him.

He stayed there a whole year, but wouldn't do anything. Crow found out he came from that chief.

He said, "I found out you came from that chief."

"No, I'm from a different town."

They took him out and sent him home.

He went to his father and said, "I couldn't make it. He found out and sent me away."

Four or five years after he got the Sun and Moon, Crow went to make Stars. He found what kind of medicine to use, and his hand was just full of it—some shiny dust. He talked to those things, "After you get up there, go to different directions and stay there."

They got stuck up there on the bottom of that other earth [*Sky Land*], and at night they started to shine.

Athabaskans commonly have one word for both Sun and Moon. They may distinguish between them by saying "day Moon" and "night Moon"; or "day Sun" (Dzaanh Zo'), and "night Sun" (Tledaał Zo'). The vault of our sky is just the bottom of Sky Land, another earth similar to ours, but above us.

According to the Ingalik, who live on the Yukon below Koyukuk Station and Nulato, there are actually four levels of the universe. The first is the familiar one where we live now. A level below is where Raven lives in a house beside the river that most of the souls (yeg) of the Dead must cross to reach their final abode. Osgood (1959:104–5) tells the story of Raven and his mother-in-law which explains this arrangement. The third level, "on top of the sky," is the afterworld of the souls (yeg) of those who met tragic deaths: who froze, or were killed in war or murdered, or died in childbirth, or were suicides. Their bodies were cremated. The lowest level is the afterworld of those who have drowned, where their yeg live in a village near those of the different kinds of Fish. But no specific mention is made of where the Sun and Moon are in relation to the world "on top of the sky." Presumably they are on the under side of Sky Land, and Osgood (1959:103) reports that they are believed to travel horizontally around the edges of the earth, appearing and disappearing behind the hills.

26 / Crow Gets the
Sun and Moon

TOLD BY JOHN DAYTON

Recorded by FdeL and NR

John Dayton, usually called "Johnny," was born in 1892. His mother had come from Kateel on the lower Koyukuk River, and his father from a village twenty miles farther up the river. The stories he told (Tales 26 to 30) he had presumably learned from them. He also told us many interesting bits of ethnographic information. When we were leaving Koyukuk Station, we briefly visited Johnny and his family at their fish camp a short distance below the town. We were impressed by its tidiness and air of prosperity. Madeline, Johnny's second wife, was born in 1905 up the Kateel River, the daughter of an Irish man, Harry Lawrence, who apparently did not support his children. Her mother, being single, gave her, and later her younger brother and sister, to Mrs. Cecelia William of Nulato, who also raised Altona Brown. That is why Madeline calls Altona "sister." After Johnny's death in 1942, Madeline married Herbert Solomon (1914–1980). (See Solomon 1981)

Persuading Crow to Get the Sun

ONCE IT USED TO BE DARK. THERE WAS A TOWN AND ALL the people there were starving. This Old Man Crow was living there and he was starving, too. It was so dark that the people had ropes strung all along their trap lines. At every trap there was a cross string so they would know that a trap was there.

One evening they gathered and started to talk about the Sun. They asked one another who could get it. They said they knew of only one fellow who could get it. They asked one another who that was. They said, "Old Man Crow."

They sent somebody after him. This fellow told him that the

people wanted to see him. Old Man Crow asked what they wanted to see him about. The messenger said they wanted to talk to him about the Sun and Moon. He said he wouldn't go unless they offered him big pay.

The messenger went back to the meeting hall. He told the people that the old man wouldn't go unless he was offered big pay. The people thought this first messenger wasn't smart enough to talk to Old Man Crow, so they decided to send another messenger.

They told this messenger not to tell Crow that they wanted him. They said to tell him that somebody was going to get the Sun. They said to ask him to come over just for his pleasure to see somebody get it. They were going to fool him that time.

As soon as he came to the hall, the people started to talk to him about the Sun and asked if he could get it. They were asking him what he wanted to get it. He said he was hungry all winter and he said he wanted nothing but food—enough for the rest of the winter.

He asked the people, "Who owns the Sun up there?"

They told him that there was a wealthy man with wife and children that owned it. They said that lots of different people had gone up there and asked for it, but the owner wouldn't accept anything for it. Then Old Man Crow asked the people if this man had daughters, and they told him yes, he had two grown-up daughters.

He told them he would let them know in the morning. He wanted to think about it.

Next morning when he woke up he went back to those people again. He told them he was going to try his best and for them to keep their promise to him. He told the people to have food ready for his trip, so they did.

Crow Marries the Sun Owner's Daughter

He left in the morning, and when he was about two weeks out, he started to get into a country where there was a little daylight. It took him another two weeks to get to that town they called *Kkaa-*

yeh (Qayex), "Big City." Just before he got to this big city he put on his best clothes, the best of everything he had, and he looked younger.

There was big excitement outside. Everybody was playing outdoors. The people saw him coming and they said to one another, "There is a fine-looking rich man coming. Where shall that man stay? We've got to give him the best place we've got." The only place they could think of was the house of the owner of the Sun, a wealthy man. This wealthy man told the old man to stay in his house.

After a little while he got pretty well acquainted with those people. Pretty soon he got acquainted with the oldest daughter, and they got married together right away.

Crow's Son Cries for the Sun, and Crow Fools the People

This wealthy man had the Sun in his house where nobody could get at it.

After a year they had one child already. When the child was able to sit up, he started to cry. They tried to stop him, but no, he just kept on crying, crying. His grandfather then asked the young couple what the kid wanted, anyway.

Crow said, "I think he wants to play with the Sun for a while."

Old Man Crow started to figure out how to get away with the Sun while his kid was playing with it. One night he made up his mind to fool these people, and he had everything prepared before he fooled them.

One morning while the people were playing outdoors, he went out and told them that there was a dog stealing a king salmon out of a cache. The whole crowd got excited and ran up to that cache. It was about a quarter of a mile away from town. The owner had guards over the Sun, but they left, too, for the excitement. There was not a soul left in the whole city.

Old Man Crow went into the house and got hold of this Sun

and went out immediately. He started flying in the air with it toward home. The people could notice that. They said it was getting dark. They got excited.

"What's wrong with the Sun? Somebody is getting away with it!"

Nearly every one of them got lost. They couldn't find their houses. It was too dark already.

Crow's Return

Old Man Crow flew home with it (the Sun), and the people were overjoyed to see him bring home the Sun. They rewarded him with all kinds of supplies of food. He didn't want clothes or anything else. Just food was all he wanted.

The people started telling (asking) him about what they were going to do for light in the night. Old Man Crow told them he was going to cut a little piece out of the Sun and make a Moon for the night (out of it). And so he did.

Ever since then we have had the Sun and Moon for light.

27 / Crow and a Whale Story

TOLD BY JOHN DAYTON

Recorded by FdeL

ONCE CROW AND WHALE WERE GREAT CHUMS, LIVING together in one town. This Whale had lots of grub of all kinds, and the Crow didn't have much. He was kind of half-hungry all the time.

It was during summer time. One evening, old Crow decided to go out hunting for ducks, young ducks that can't fly, and his nephew the Canada Jay offered to go with him.

[*John Dayton called this bird the "blue jay," but Eliza Jones identified it as the gray Canada jay.*]

But Crow told him that he was too light, he was not the kind of fellow to go with him. He said he would rather see his friend Whale go with him. This Whale was an awfully fat man.

They started to paddle up the river, the two of them in different canoes. There was a lake that used to be full of ducks that can't fly in the summer, and Crow knew about it before, but Whale didn't.

Crow told him, "This is the lake where people before us used to hunt only in the night when it's dark."

While Whale was preparing some lunch, Crow went into the lake. He walked along the beach to find a place with soft mud, so his friend would sink into that. When he went back to his friend he brought back a lot of feathers that he had pulled from his own wings. He colored the feathers with all different kinds of colors to make his friend believe that they were duck and goose feathers.

"That's where I found these feathers. So you would be sure, I brought them home to you."

After they had lunch, it was pretty dark, but Crow told his friend that they ought to start right out anyway. The Whale said to him that he didn't think he could get any ducks during the dark.

"Well," said Crow, "if you can't, I'll show you how to do it." His friend didn't believe that he could hunt in the dark, but he went out with him against his will.

Whale asked his friend who should take the lead, who should go to the lake first.

Crow said, "I'll go first in my canoe."

Crow was heading for that muddy beach all the time. And when they got to that place, his friend started to sink. He said it was too soft for him.

Crow told him, "Oh, just run. Run part way, then run again. Then you'll get over it."

But instead of getting over that muddy place, he sank, and his friend told him that he would help him. He said the Whale had lots of fat, so to help him, he was going to get some of it from his back. Whale started to yell for help, and the more he yelled, the more his friend ate him, faster and faster. He (Crow) wanted to finish him, so he stuck his spear right across his head, and towards morning there was only a skeleton left of the Whale. During the night, Crow had eaten the whole thing up!

He went home towards morning and went to bed at the camp. He was figuring out what to tell the people about his friend. Next morning when he woke up, he pulled some more feathers out of himself and colored them so they looked like duck and goose feathers. He went back to that lake where he had eaten his friend up, and there was no sign of him. While he was standing around there he heard somebody talking out in the lake. This fellow that was talking told him what a mean fellow he was, how he had killed and eaten him, and now he had to stay in the water all the rest of his life. And he wouldn't stay in that country any more, but was going into the ocean where he would never see Crow any more.

So Crow went back to his camp, filled his canoe with his own feathers, and started down the river. He sang a kind of love song for his friend. [*Probably the kind of eulogy that was commonly composed for the dead.*]

The Canada Jay said, "Ah, you are just trying to fool us."

Crow told him, "Oh, has this friend of mine, this Whale, come home early? Is that why you talk to me that way?"

He started to tell his story about their hunting trip. He said that his friend didn't know how to hunt during the night time while it was dark, so he told him, "Well, I'm going out into the lake. You can stay and sleep all night if you like." When he got enough ducks, he came back to the camp where his friend was sleeping. He could hear his friend snoring away, and he left the ducks under his canoe and went to sleep. When he woke up, there was nobody around, and there was nothing left of the ducks but a few feathers, and he thought his friend had taken them and gone during the night.

The people could hardly believe him. Canada Jay told his uncle that he believed that he had killed his friend. Crow said if they didn't believe him, he was going to stay in the air all the time.

And they told him, "Show us how you can stay in the air all the time." They asked what he had done with all his feathers. They noticed he had no feathers left on his wings.

He told them, "While I was cooking lunch the first evening I burned my feathers off."

There was one medicine man living in that town, and he asked some of the young fellows to bring him one of the feathers that Crow had brought home. He told them that if this feather didn't burn, it belonged to the Crow and that he had killed his friend, but if it burned it was a duck feather.

He put one of the longest feathers in the fire, but it wouldn't burn, so he sent for all the feathers that Crow had brought home. He put all the feathers in the fire, but they wouldn't burn. They tried all sorts of different ways, but the feathers just turned black. So the medicine man told the people that Crow had killed his friend and eaten the whole thing up.

They all liked this Whale, and they said they were going to

take revenge for their best friend, and that they were going to kill the Crow. Meanwhile, somebody told the Crow that they were going to kill him. So he thought he better try to fly, and he borrowed some short feathers from Canada Jay. That's why Canada jays, even now, don't have enough feathers on their wings.

Just when Crow was flying up, people saw him. They started to shoot at him with arrows, and he lit on a high tree, and he told the tree to grow up with him. Immediately the tree started to grow, and the people had a hard time to reach him with their arrows. At last, when the tree was so high that they couldn't do anything to him, he yelled down to the people and confessed what he had done. He said that he had killed his friend and eaten the whole thing up.

Ever since that time he has always been living in the air. And that's the end.

Another version of this story from Koyukuk is Attla's (1989:149–69) "Great Raven Killed a Whale."

28 / Porcupine and Beaver Story

TOLD BY JOHN DAYTON

Recorded by FdeL and NR

THERE WAS A SMALL-SIZE TOWN AND PORCUPINE WAS living there, but he wanted to go out of town. In those days Porcupine did not know how to swim, so he could not get across (the river), and everyone refused to take him. He went down to the beach and was standing on the edge of the water. He started to cry.

He said to himself, "I wish somebody would come along with a canoe to take me over."

Pretty soon he saw a Muskrat coming along. Muskrats were bigger in those days. And the Muskrat asked, "What are you crying about?"

Porcupine told him, "I wanted to cross over to where there are all kinds of willows and spruce trees for me to eat." He was getting hungry while he was staying in town.

Muskrat said, "All right. Get ready and I'll take you over."

And Porcupine asked him, "How are you going to take me over?"

The Muskrat said, "Just get on my tail."

Porcupine didn't believe that he could ride on the tail, and he didn't want to take the chance. He said his tail was too narrow. Muskrat got angry because he said he had a little narrow tail, so he told the Porcupine to go to China [!], and left him there.

So Porcupine began to cry again and wished for somebody to come along. After a little while there was Mink coming.

He asked, "What are you crying about?"

So Porcupine told him the same thing he told Muskrat. The Mink said he would take him over.

And Porcupine asked him, "How are you going to take me over?"

The Mink told him to ride on his tail.

Porcupine said, "Your tail is too short and bushy. There's no place for me to cook while we travel."

"Well then, you stay right here where you are!" and Mink started off.

Porcupine started to cry again, and he wished for another one to come along. After a while Beaver came.

Beaver said, "What do you cry about?"

And Porcupine told him the same thing as before.

Beaver told him to get ready. Porcupine said he was awfully glad to get ready, and he got on the Beaver's tail. He said, "Your tail is wide enough to carry six people," and he asked him if he could take enough load with him.

They started out, and Porcupine asked if he could start to cook. He told him he had taken a little wood along.

And Beaver said, "Get your things ready that you have to cook. Get them ready before you start a fire."

When they started across, Porcupine asked Beaver if he could cut out little chunks from his tail.

Beaver told him, "Well, not too much," so he took out little chunks from different places. That's why beavers have hollow places in their tails.

Beaver told him that he couldn't stand fire on his tail longer than to get to the middle of the river, and they were nearly there already.

Porcupine said, "I'll have the meal done pretty soon, before we get to the middle of the river." And then he thought to himself, "I wonder why he can't stand it. I'm going to keep my fire a little longer and see what Beaver does."

When they passed the middle of the river, Beaver said, "Ouch! My tail is burning!" and he shook his tail, and Porcupine drowned. Beavers have no hair on their tails because of Porcupine's fire.

Porcupine started to walk toward the shore right on the bot-

tom of the river. When he got out of the river and on the beach, he tried to run, but he was so stiff that he couldn't. That's why porcupines can't run fast—he got stiff under the water. He was one kind of man when he drowned, but when he came out of the river he saw himself that he was different again. He was a (real) porcupine now.

He thought to himself, "I can't run fast, and all the other animals are faster than I. They are liable to kill me." He thought to himself, "I'm going to learn how to climb trees."

When he got to about the middle of the tree, there was Mr. Bear coming along, and the Bear told him, "My, you smell fine. You are made to be eaten."

Porcupine told him, "Well, you are just a little too late. If you had caught me on the beach, you might have eaten me alive, but now I'm in the tree."

The Bear said, "Well, I can climb, too." And he started up the tree.

When he got to this Porcupine, he (Porcupine) hit the Bear with his tail, and Bear got sharp quills in his nose, and he tumbled right down. He said he would not forgive Porcupine for that.

That's the end.

This is the only version I know in which Porcupine is not a woman. Since Athabaskan verb forms do not distinguish between "he," "she," and "it," we can understand how such switches in gender are possible when translating into English.

29 / Uncle and Nephew Story
[The Jealous Uncle and His Nephew]

TOLD BY JOHN DAYTON

Recorded by FdeL and NR?

The Nephew in a Hollow Log

THERE WAS A MAN WITH TWO WIVES. HE HAD HIS NEPHEW (*boze,* sister's son) with him, a big boy. Once the uncle went out hunting and this boy stayed home with the two women. The man told him to keep away from the women and not to make love to them. He was awfully jealous of his wives.

When he came home late in the evening he found out that someone had made shavings in the house. He asked his wives who had done that, and they wouldn't tell him because they knew he was going to get mad. He said if they didn't tell him, he would lick them both. So they told him that his nephew was over to visit them. The nephew hadn't really been fooling with his aunts. He just went in the house to cut shavings.

Next morning, the man wanted his nephew to go out with him. It was summer time. When they got to a patch of timber, he cut down a big spruce tree, and cut off a log about ten feet long. He split that right down the middle and hewed it out big enough for a man to lie down inside. He told his nephew to try and get in there. He tried, but it was not quite big enough.

Then he fixed it so his nephew could lie down fine inside, and he put it back together. He left a little food inside with him, and he tied the log around with roots. He threw that log into the river, and it floated down the river and out into the ocean.

It is always stormy out on the ocean, and the wind blew him across the ocean. It took him a month to be floated across. Then

he felt that he was hitting against the rocks, and he knew he was across. But he couldn't get out. There he was working there, pretty near two weeks, stuck.

He was just about to starve inside, when something started to feel that log. He heard a noise of something chewing on that log. And all of a sudden the log went to pieces and opened up. He saw a porcupine beside him. That was the one that had chewed the roots off. So he got a club and killed that porcupine. That was the first animal he had killed since he landed. Then he started to live on that porcupine.

Adopted by a Giant

One morning he saw somebody coming along the beach, an awfully big man, a Giant. He was afraid of this Giant so he went into a cave that was near. The Giant came to the cave and wanted the boy to come out, but the boy wouldn't, he was so scared. The Giant told him that if he didn't come out, he was going to put a big stone at the door of the cave, and then the boy wouldn't get out alive. This way, he made him come out.

He said he was going to adopt him, and he took him home to his wife. He told his wife to make clothes for this boy, and they brought him up. He became a fine man, a handy man. He called the Giant "grandfather."

When the Giant got old, he started to work for him and feed him. After about twenty years had passed, the Giant asked him where he came from, and he told him that his uncle had done cruelty to him. He started to feel lonesome for his mother. He asked his grandfather if he could go home across the ice.

The Magic Return Home

The Giant said, well, it was all right with him. He had caribou for dogs. He told the young man to take two "dogs."

One evening the Giant told him he was going to dream about

the boy's uncle, to see if he was still living. He dreamed that the boy's uncle was living yet. [*This dream proves that the Giant was a shaman.*]

The boy asked his grandfather which direction to go. The grandfather had a cane, and he told his grandchild to come down on the ice with him. He stuck the cane up on the clear ice and told his grandchild to go in whatever direction the cane fell.

One morning the Giant told him to get ready, fill the sled with supplies, with food. So he did. He took all kinds of grub with him, enough to last two months. He and his grandfather hitched up those two caribou "dogs." Then they went down on the ice again and stuck up that cane. He told his grandchild to keep inside the sled cover all the time. He mustn't look out. He told him that when the "dogs" stopped going, that was the time he had to get out of the sled.

It took him ten days. Then all at once, the "dogs" stopped. When he got out of the sled, he was across the ocean. He turned the sled around and let the "dogs" go home by themselves. Then he started to look for signs of people.

It was winter. One morning he found some signs of people, and he got that cane and used it the same way as before. He found a trail where somebody had been out hunting, and he followed that trail. After he camped for two nights on the trail, he caught up with some people. There were about three families. There was an old lady pulling her own sled, and he caught up with her first. She was behind the others. All at once the people saw him coming behind, and they all stopped.

He told her that twenty years ago his uncle had done cruelty to him, told her what he had done. The old lady was surprised, and fell down and started to cry. That was his mother! She just took the boy in her lap, she was overjoyed to see him. He asked his mother who those people were, and she told him that one family was his uncle's, the one who had been cruel to him. He had married a second time. He had lost his first two wives and had married two young girls. The boy introduced himself to those people and told who he was.

The Nephew's Revenge

He had been there about a month when the old uncle started to get jealous of him again over his two wives. One morning he told his nephew to go out hunting with him. This time the boy was ready. They got to a patch of timber, and he asked his nephew to give him a lift with a log. When he was stooping down to lift that log, his uncle struck him on the back with a stone axe, but he didn't hit him hard.

He pretended not to be mad, and told his uncle he would cut down a tree for him. He cut down a giant tree, and told his uncle to lift one end, but he couldn't move it at all. Suddenly he grabbed his uncle by the throat. He held him with one hand, and lifted the log with the other. He put his uncle crossways under that log and let it fall on him.

He told the old man, "You tried to kill me once, but I came back alive."

The uncle begged him to take him out from under the log, and offered all kinds of pay, but he wouldn't listen. He told his uncle what a cruel man he was and that he tried to kill him once. "Now it's my turn to kill you."

Well, he just left him there to die easy [*i.e., slowly*]. He went home and he married those two aunts of his, and while he was living with those aunts, his mother died.

That's the end.

See Attla (1983:139–70) "The One Whose Uncle Put Him in the Water in a Log," for another Koyukuk River version of this story.

Jetté reported (1908–9:314–15) that the Koyukon applied the word "dog" to signify any tame animal, since the dog was the only tame animal they originally knew. Thus "brown bear dogs" would mean tame bears, and "caribou dogs" would mean tame caribou (reindeer), without necessarily implying that the bears or reindeer were being used as dogs. In this case, however, the caribou do pull the sled, and this suggests that the boy had drifted across the ocean to Siberia, where reindeer are used like sled dogs.

30 / Two Little Boys Story

TOLD BY JOHN DAYTON

Recorded by FdeL

THERE WERE TWO LITTLE BOYS PLAYING WITH BOWS
and arrows. They were shooting up in the air, and they lost their
arrow in the woods. While they were looking for it, they found a
house in the woods.

They said to one another, "Let's go in."

There was nobody inside, but there was a lot of grub in there,
and among this grub they found a box full of "ice cream"—caribou fat mixed with fish oil and fresh blueberries.

They said to one another, "Shall we eat some of it?"

One of them said, "No, that's stealing if we do."

The other one said, "Well, let's have a taste of it anyway."

They just ate a little of it. Then they waited a little while, and
they said to each other, "Well, we might as well eat half of it."

After a while they were tempted to finish it all, and they said,
"There's nobody to tell on us, anyway."

When they went out, they heard a noise. There was somebody
coming through the brush. They ran into the house again, and
they saw an old man coming through the woods. One of them hid
under the bedding and the other hid under a (hollow) log stool.
Soon they saw the old man come in, and he started to prepare his
supper.

The old man had a kind of Mouse in the house for his companion. The Mouse could talk to him, but the boys didn't know
anything about him. After a while the man found out his "ice
cream" was gone. He called out to this Mouse and asked him who
had done that, if he had done it, or if somebody had come in.

The Mouse said he didn't do it, and he told the old man, "While you were out two little boys came in and they ate it."

The old man asked him, "Where are they?"

The Mouse told him, "One of them is hiding in your bedding and the other one is hiding under your stool."

Fortunately the man had his door locked, so the boys didn't have a chance to run out when he started to look for them.

He lifted the bedding up and found one of the boys and ate him alive! And he found the other one and did the same thing to him.

While they were in the man's stomach, they started to talk to each other. One asked his friend if he had a stone knife with him. The boy said, "Yes," and he asked if he had a whetstone.

They started to sharpen that knife, and when they got it done, they asked each other, "Shall we cut him open?" And they started to cut him. They felt the old man running around with them. Then they cut him open and both of them jumped out. The old man fell dead.

One boy asked what his face looked like, and the other told him that his upper eyelid was red.

So he said, "Well then, I must be Ptarmigan."

The other asked, "What do I look like?"

And his friend told him, "You look like Mink, because your nose is red."

"Well, I must be Mink."

All of a sudden he became Mink and ran down the beach. And the other became Ptarmigan and flew away. That was how the first ptarmigan and the first mink started.

Despite the typically Athabaskan ending of this story, the plot and situation suggest to me a European folktale: children (or a child) find a house in the woods, enter, and are tempted to eat some treat. Its depletion is marked as "Top Off," "Half-Gone," etc. Then they are discovered and must escape—Hansel and Gretel, Goldilocks and the Three Bears, and similar tales come to mind. What is the origin of the log stool?

233

The emphasis on eating and being eaten, while encountered in some of the Grimms' stories, is typically Athabaskan, however. This tale may have mixed antecedents, although I cannot prove it. Eliza Jones knows it under the title of "Wooden Dish, Who Ate out of You?"

31 / The Man Who Traveled among All the Animals and People

TOLD BY AN OLD KOYUKUK WOMAN

Recorded by Ella Vernetti

K'etetaalkkaanee, the Bungler

ONCE THERE LIVED AN OLD WOMAN WITH MANY WORTH-less children. She got tired of slaving to get them food and to keep the house warm, so one day she told her oldest son that if they wanted anything to eat thereafter, he would have to get it. She told him to build a fish trap and to put it in the lake. He made one and went out to a lake and chopped a hole in the ice and put the fish trap in wrong end up. Time went by and she finally told her son to go out and look at the fish trap. She accompanied him and found the mistake he had made and told him how to put it in. A few days later he went to look at it and he brought home several baskets full of "devilfish" [*blackfish*], which lasted for quite a while.

One day there was nothing more to eat in the house, so she told him to go out and put up some snares to catch snowshoe rabbits. She made him a bunch of snares and he took them and went out. He threw a snare on a willow every now and then, until he had used them all up and went home. She went with him to bring home what he had caught and found he did not set the snares at all. She again showed him how to fix all the snares, and they returned home. Next day she sent him out and he brought home a big load of rabbits.

When these were all gone, and again they were on the verge of starvation, she sent him out and told him to bring home something to eat from the trees. [*She could not name the game directly, for there was a taboo against it. So she called it* "something bent, or

235

crooked," *which any Dena should know refers to the hunched back of the porcupine.*]

He didn't know exactly what he was sent for, but he went anyway and came home with his parka full of bent twigs, saying that was all he saw on the trees. When his younger brothers and sister heard him coming, they were delighted and helped him to lift the sack down from the smokehole of the dugout where they lived. The sack landed on the floor with a crackling, and when they looked and they saw nothing but bent twigs, they all sat down and wept. She (his mother) explained the method of killing a porcupine when up in a tree, and again he went out and late that evening came in loaded with porcupines. There was great joy, and a big feast followed.

She told him that the wood supply was almost depleted and for him to go out and chop down some trees. He set out with an axe and cut into a great tree. The sap oozed out and he cried, "I can't bear to chop it down, for it is bleeding!" He cut into several trees with the same results, so he threw away his axe.

As his mother said that he could not enter the house again until he had proved himself, he set out from home.

Visiting Animal People

He walked a great distance and soon came to a country of Animal people. He spent the night in many of their homes but they never served him anything to eat, because as soon as they rose in the morning they set out for their feeding grounds. The Ptarmigan went to feed on the trees and so did the Willow Grouse, and the Bear people went to the berry fields or down to the streams for fish. They weren't very sociable either, as they all seemed intent on foraging and taking care of their homes. He tired of them and went on all over the country, and nobody paid much attention to him.

He Makes a Canoe

Soon spring came, and he needed a canoe to travel on. So he took the bark of the spruce and threw it in the river. He watched it float out, but it sank before going very far. He took the bark of a cottonwood tree and put that in, but it sank also. So he tried the bark of a birch, and that floated as far as he could see it. He got a lot of it together, and lay down to rest, thinking he would start making the canoe in the morning.

The sun was high when he woke, and he thought he heard a hum, so he raised his head. And he was surprised at what he saw. There was the framework of his canoe already made, and all the different Animal women in human form were seated around the canoe, sewing on the birchbark. They were all so busy that not a one saw him, and he lay there and watched them working.

He Gets and Loses a Wife

Among them was a beautiful girl whom he desired very much, and he was figuring a way to get her. They were almost finished, so he hid her little awl that she used to puncture the birchbark before putting the root through. They were all finished now and were leaving, and she searched all over for her awl. She begged the others to wait for her, but they were soon gone, and she was still looking for her awl. He (the young man) rose up behind her and caught her, and she struggled in vain to get away. He finally made her understand that he loved her and desired her for his wife. They stayed there a while longer and then started down stream.

The sun came up and shone brightly all day. He had his wife behind him in the canoe, and he thought he heard an animal panting. So he turned around. He found that the sun had thawed his beautiful wife back into the animal she was, and so, instead of the beautiful girl he had captured, there sat a Fox, panting with the heat. He paddled ashore and threw her out and went on his way.

The Giant and His Wife

He paddled on down the river and soon came to a divide in the river and the water was very swift. An immense Giant was there and gobbled up anyone coming down that way. It so happened that the Giant was taking a little nap when the man arrived there, so he quietly steered his canoe through the rushing water between the Giant's legs. He steered and nosed it out between rocks and trees and finally made it into quieter waters.

He went around a big bend and saw a big house high on the mountainside. He landed and went up to the house and entered. He saw the Giant's wife sitting at her spinning wheel.

When she saw him, she cried, "How did you get by my husband at the rapids?"

He told her and she gave him something to eat. He thanked her and went on.

No sooner had he gone than the Giant came home.

"I smell somebody," he roared. "Where is he?"

"He has gone away," said the Giantess.

He dashed down to the river and started slapping the water and thus created great waves.

"May his canoe sink!" he roared.

The man's canoe broke in two, but he changed himself into an Insect and floated ashore on a leaf. His canoe drifted in and he fixed it up and got into it. And he continued on his way around the world.

This is only a small part of the whole story that the old woman knew, but Ella Vernetti grew tired of writing it down. Her excellent control of English is shown in this translation of what the old woman had told, and the introduction of the spinning wheel indicates some knowledge of English folklore, probably as children's stories she read at school.

32 / Crow and
Foggy Man

Recorded by Ella Vernetti

There is no information about the storyteller from whom Ella Vernetti recorded this version.

Crow Meets and Kills Foggy Man

THIS IS THE STORY OF THE CROW.

It was midsummer and all went out hunting, but none returned. The Crow asked the rest of the camp to give him all the food they had on hand and he would go and find the hunters. He paddled his canoe down the stream and soon came to a landing. He got ashore and pulled his canoe up on the bank and started thinking.

He started to chew gum during his meditation. He chewed so much gum that he made a canoe out of it, also a dish, a knife, a spear, and several other useful articles. He finally started to portage his canoe across country, and soon he came to a place where there were many canoes, half wrecked.

He was frightened, so he kept repeating aloud, "Alligator, swallow me!" while he paddled along.

All of a sudden, the lake began to get hollow, or the water began to get dish-shaped with him [*a vortex*], and a canoe with someone in it came up out of the water.

Frightened Mr. Crow began saying, "My dear friend! My dear friend! Don't you remember me? You are my partner. I saw you long ago." He had never seen him before.

The someone in the canoe didn't do or say anything, so Mr. Crow asked the stranger's name.

The reply was, "They call me Grandmother's Needle, *Netsoo Tl'aaghadakkone* (Netsu Tɬ'aʀedeqone)."

"How strange. They call me that also," said Mr. Crow, "so that makes us friends."

They talked together for quite a while, and so they were to go on their way, but the Crow said, "You know, in the old days, friends used to give each other everything they had."

So the stranger and Crow exchanged everything. In fact, one stepped out of his canoe and into the other. As the stranger was making his departure by starting to disappear under the water, the Crow jabbed him in the back with his spear. And the stranger retaliated by sticking his spear into Crow, but it (the spear) was made of gum so it broke in pieces. He then disappeared under the water and the Crow landed ashore.

Crow Kills Foggy Man's Mother

He started walking ashore and up a little trail when he came to a little house with smoke curling out of the chimney. He entered and found two old women. One was taking a nap and the other was seated at the stove, warming her back. He killed the old woman that was napping, and then the other, and he dressed in one of the old women's clothes.

He started out on the trail, but the old woman's pants began to hamper him as he tried to walk. He walked like a decrepit old woman, and coughed until you thought surely it was an old woman.

When he entered [*another house?*] he found that it was her child that he had stabbed in the lake, and he was now dying from the spear that he (Crow) shoved into him. The Crow saw what he had done, so he rushed out of the house to go home. And all in the house started to chase him. As he was running along, he was greatly hampered by the old woman's clothes, and the others were catching up to him. So he got out his knife and ripped himself out of the clothes. He just made his canoe, and jumped in, and paddled out into the lake in the nick of time. The followers started scolding him, and he came back with repartee.

He crossed the lake and came to the portage and took his canoe across. He went up the stream, and when the people at the camp saw him, they shouted for joy and cooked a big feed for him. He told them of his adventures and how he had killed the ogre and they gave him lots more food and they all lived happily ever after.

Note the elements of Euro-American folklore introduced into this story and others written down by Ella Vernetti. These include not only beautiful girls, ogres, spinning wheels, stoves and chimneys, but "Once there was. . . . And they all lived happily ever after."

Attla's version of this story (1989:133–47), "Great Raven Who Killed a Water Monster," resembles ours by including the episode of killing the mother of the water monster and escaping in the old woman's clothes. It also explains why Raven made a dish out of gum. In Attla's story, this dish is filled with birch shelf-fungus, looking like human ears, which makes Foggy Man believe that Raven is a man-eater like himself, since he carries a similar dish. The "Alligator, swallow me!" as translated by Ella Vernetti becomes "Swallow me, enveloping water thing!" (Attla 1989:137). Was this taunting the monster in order to attract him? It is not explained.

33 / Porcupine
and Beaver

Recorded by Ella Vernetti

Again, there is no information about the narrator.

"MY, BUT I WOULD LIKE TO BE ON THE OTHER SIDE OF the river, right where the birches and alders grow so thick," said Porcupine to herself. "It's so nice, and the evening sun shines so warmly there just before it goes down behind the mountain."

"I'll take you across," said the Muskrat, swimming up to where the Porcupine was sitting.

"I should say not! Your tail is like a towline," replied old Porcupine.

"Who would want to carry you anyhow, you old Bit Nose!" cried the Muskrat as he swam away, very much insulted.

"I'll take you across," said the Otter as he was going by.

"I should say not! Your tail is like a stove poker," again replied the Porcupine.

"Who would want to carry you, you old thing with wide nostrils!" said the Otter as he swam away, very much insulted.

"I'll take you across," said the Beaver, coming up to the Porcupine.

"Oh, thank you! Just come in a little closer and I'll load my things on your back, and I shall sit on your tail," cried the Porcupine, so happy.

As soon as they started across, the Porcupine thought she would like a cup of tea and immediately built a fire on the Beaver's broad flat tail and put the kettle on. No sooner did the kettle start to boil when the Beaver felt his tail get hot. And he dived.

Well, old Porcupine just sank right to the bottom of the river and she walked on the river bottom until she got out on the other side where she had wanted to be.

She climbed the bank and was drying herself when she heard someone say behind her, "Get out of my way or I shall stomp on your gall bladder!"

She turned around, and bless me! if it wasn't a big Brown Bear.

"You can't step on my gall bladder, for I haven't any," replied the Porcupine.

"Then I shall stomp on your liver," the Bear growled, but she said she didn't have that either.

Whereupon the Brown Bear charged the poor old Porcupine, but she quickly prepared herself for the attack, and flicked her tail at the right instant. The Bear rolled on his back and roared with pain [*as her quills went into his nose and mouth*].

"Take them out or I shall eat you alive!" he cried, but old Porcupine was no fool. She didn't budge one bit and the Brown Bear couldn't stand the pain any longer, but said, "Wet them and take them out, and I shall never bother you again, and we shall be friends forever."

So the Porcupine took them out, and to this day the Brown Bear gives a wide berth to the Porcupine whenever he meets her.

The Koyukuk River title is "She's Crying on the Beach" (see Attla 1983:65–76). This version is very similar to Vernetti's except that Attla introduced a Baby Beaver whose offer was also rejected.

IX
TALES FROM
NULATO

Francis McGinty, from whom we recorded the following stories, had been recommended to us as a guide by the Catholic Fathers at the Nulato Mission when we discussed our plans with them about visiting the Khotol River–Kaiyuh Slough area in the floodplain east of the Yukon. It was a happy choice, for he could not only direct us to the sites along the tributary waterways and name for us the various creeks and other landmarks we passed, but he enlivened our boat trip and evenings in camp with stories and bits of ethnographic information. When we rejoined the Yukon again, and left him as requested at Kaltag, we parted from each other with regret on both sides and the wish that we might meet again.

Because of his upbringing, Francis McGinty was better educated in English than were most of the other Native storytellers, but he had probably forgotten more narrative incidents than they.

But we will let him introduce himself.

The Autobiography of
Francis McGinty, Nulato

Recorded by NR

THEY TELL ME THAT WHEN I WAS LITTLE, MY OLDER
brother was going to get married. He had saved up lots of money
and stuff, and he had trapped all winter and saved all his skins.

He was out traveling with a sled, gee-poling ahead [*i.e., steer-
ing the sled with a pole*], and another fellow was behind, pushing. — It was that old fellow, the first one that came up to our camp
the other day at Kaltag. — The fellow reached up on the sled to
push the gun back; it had started to slip. The trigger caught on the
sled crosspiece. My brother got shot in the back, and died. The
other fellow loaded him on the sled right away and brought him
into town to my folks and told them what happened.

They got mad, and I think my mother started to get crazy.
They gave away all my brother's stuff, all his skins and money and
everything, gave it away to different medicine men so they would
make medicine against that fellow. But it didn't work. That fellow
is still going strong—you saw him the other day. They say maybe
he gave the medicine man more money than my folks. But I don't
believe in that business.

Then one of my sisters died, and then my other brother. I
guess my mother went clear crazy again and kicked me out, didn't
want me any more. I had an adopted sister, a girl from Old Louden
that my mother had adopted. She had got married, and they took
me in.

They treated me fine, she and her husband. Later they had
two small kids, two little boys. One spring we were all traveling together up the Kaiyuh to our camp, traveling on dog sleds.

That was the time I told you about when they found a white man starved to death. My sister got sick, but she wasn't very bad, so we kept going. Then one day she got real sick and that night she died. Pneumonia, I guess it was. We brought her back to town and buried her.

I stayed with my brother-in-law for quite a while after that. I stayed home and took care of the kids while he was out hunting and trapping. Anything I wanted I could have. But after a couple of years he married a widow woman, a woman way older than himself with several kids of her own. He gave away his two kids to his mother, but they kept me.

Right away she began to nag me and boss me and make me do all the work. I didn't like it. I was only twelve or thirteen and I wanted to be out playing with the other kids. Then, of course, my brother-in-law sided with her.

That summer we were at a fish camp on an island below Nulato, on the other side of the Yukon. My brother-in-law came to me and said, "If you don't do what I tell you, I'm going to shoot you!"

Of course I got scared. I ran away into the woods as fast as I could. I stayed back in the woods and walked up the island and came out on the beach on the upper end. A party of Natives came in a rowboat going to Nulato. I hailed them and they took me with them.

I went right to the Mission at Nulato and told the priest, "I just can't get along with my brother-in-law at all. He treats me awful mean. I would like to go to school at Holy Cross."

Father said, "All right, Francis. Our gas boat is going down to Holy Cross in two or three days, and I'll let you know."

So I said, "All right," and went and hid in the woods back of town because I knew my brother-in-law would grab me if he came in. I watched them load the boat. And when they were all ready to go I ran down and jumped aboard.

So I went to Holy Cross and stayed in school there for three years. I didn't learn much—I was too old, I guess—just enough to get along. I had no chance to go to school before, taking care of these kids all the time. I sure wish I had some more education. But I picked up quite a bit just by reading. I read some detective stories and some magazines. My wife and some of the Native fellows are all the time asking me to tell them stories about Outside and what's happening in the world.

Well, I left Holy Cross and went over to the coast to Unalakleet to herd reindeer for some of those Lapps. Paul Esmailka went with me, that fellow that had the fish camp just below you at Nulato. Pretty near all the people at Unalakleet were Lapps. The younger people were half-breeds. I think the Lapps only brought three women with them, and most of the men married Eskimo women. [*The Lapps had been brought, along with their reindeer, by the United States government in an attempt to introduce reindeer breeding among the Alaskan Natives.*]

The Lapps are fine people, all the time good-natured and laughing. They used to wrestle, for fun, or if they get into a little argument. Paul was always wrestling with them. One time two of them started to wrestle with me, and Paul just stood there and watched. I got one of them down and the other one was on my back. I reached around with one hand and managed to get the other one under me, too. The Lapps laughed about that for a long time afterward.

But those Lapps were funny—they wouldn't eat seal meat, wouldn't trust it at all. Once I shot a seal in the summer when it was fat, and Paul roasted it in front of the fire. He is pretty handy that way. Then we gave some to the Lapps but didn't tell them what it was. After that, they were just crazy for seal meat and couldn't get enough of it.

Sometimes we had to work pretty hard herding, in the fall when the deer were rutting. There were four of us with a big herd along the river, and we had to keep them from mixing with another herd on the other side. Those Lapps wouldn't trust each other, and if the herds got mixed they might butcher some of the other fellow's deer. We worked two at a time, going around the

251

herd to keep them together. About three in the morning the deer started to move, and we had to get up and work until about eleven at night. Then the deer quieted down a little.

That time of year they used to fight a lot. Sometimes they broke each other's legs; then we had to shoot them and butcher them. Sometimes they got their horns locked together. Once we found two females with their horns locked. They had fallen into a little trench about a foot wide and they couldn't get out. One was drowned and the other died before we could get her loose.

The Lapps used to make good money then, driving their deer to Ruby. They got big money for the meat—it was the time of the Ruby stampede [1907–1910]. It doesn't pay any more. The prices are low and the deer get pretty poor from traveling. They still ship some meat up the river in the fall and winter. Some of the deer broke away and there was a pretty good-sized herd running wild on the Kaiyuh for several years. I guess the Natives have killed them all off now. The white men took a big herd up in back of Kokrines, but they couldn't keep track of them in the brush and they all got away and mixed with the caribou.

They sure have some smart dogs, those Lapps. They brought them from Lapland. They look something like a shepherd dog—pointed ears, small feet, long head, and curly tail. Some of them are mixed with other dogs now. If they are a long ways off, maybe a half-mile or a mile, you just have to whistle to them and point with a stick which way you want them to go, or motion with the stick for them to go ahead or come back. I had a little old dog, must have been ten years old. His legs were too short. He would run along and fall down between the grass clumps, and then he would get mad and leave me. Some of the reindeer got smart. They used to chase my dog and he couldn't run fast enough to keep ahead. They would catch him and trample him, and then he got mad and went home.

It sure is a good life, herding reindeer; plenty of meat any time you want it. One old Eskimo woman at St. Michael owns lots of reindeer. Every time before she eats, she says, "*Quyaana,*

Jesus, government me him to eat!" [*Thank you, Jesus, that the government gave me them to eat.*]

No, I never saw the Lapps use reindeer milk.

Once when I was walking through town, through Unalakleet, an Eskimo girl came up to me. Her family was away and she had the key to the cabin. She said, "Come on, won't you marry me?"

I said, "Better ask your mama."

She said, "No, you ask her."

I said I wouldn't do it and I walked away.

Next time I came to town she was married to some fellow.

That was the best time of my life, that herding reindeer. Why didn't I stay? Well, I came back to Nulato just for a visit. I had been talking nothing but English at Holy Cross and Unalakleet. And lots of fellows come to me to be an interpreter, but I couldn't do it. I had hard time to understand my own language. That winter the influenza came and they quarantined the portage from Kaltag to Unalakleet. Then I got engaged to the one I'm married to now, and I had no chance to go back.

Four or five fellows in town were after that girl, but they wouldn't ask her. I just went up to her and said, "Will you marry me?" And she said, "Yes, I'll marry you."

Then I worked all year to get enough money. I worked on the boat that went down to St. Michael and clear up to Fairbanks. I just got into town once in a while. But I knew I had a girl then.

Other Natives say, "Francis McGinty got eight kids, but he never been stuck [*broke, penniless*] yet."

34 / Toheege (Foggy Man) and Crow Meet Each Other

TOLD BY FRANCIS MCGINTY

Recorded by NR

This is the translation of the title given by the narrator.

CROW WAS LIVING AT A VILLAGE HALFWAY BETWEEN NULATO and the Kaiyuh Slough. The people kept going up the slough and they never came back. Finally some of the people came to Crow. He was a big medicine man. They told him to find out what was the matter.

He went alone in his canoe up the Kaiyuh Slough. Just before he got to the Forks he saw pieces of a canoe on the beach. Then he went ashore and stopped. He went where there were lots of old rotten birch. He broke off and took out the old rotten centers. He put the shells [*of birchbark*] on his legs. He closed his eyes, then he looked at his feet—it was brand-new boots he had on! Then he put birchbark around himself. He closed his eyes again. When he looked at himself, there he was with a nice, brand-new parka! He went around to look for a spruce tree and found some nice gum. He chewed at that and made it into the shape of a bow and arrow and a spear. He closed his eyes. He looked again and there was a brand-new bow and arrow and spear! Then he stood up and looked at himself—just perfect!

He got in his canoe and started out. Just after he passed the Forks, the water started to go up and down on both sides, and he thought, "Something is going to happen now."

All at once a young man came out of the water. Crow asked him, "What is your name?"

"Oh, my name is Grandma's Needle—*Netsoo Tl'aaghada-kkone* (Netsu Tł'aʀedeqone)."

"Oh, that's the same as my name. They called me that because when I was little I used to crawl around on the floor and play with my grandma's needle. You and I have the same name. And we have the same kind of clothes, the same kind of bow and arrow, the same kind of spear. We are matched alike. Let's go shoot."

His partner [*namesake?*] shot first, and Crow shot after. He shot a little farther. Then Crow told him to throw his spear, and Crow threw after him—a little farther. They went to get their arrows and spears.

Crow said, "Let's trade."

So they traded everything except the canoes.

Then Crow said, "Let's go back. You go first."

As the partner went ahead, Crow shot him in the back. When he (Toheege) felt the arrow, he turned around to shoot, but the bow and arrow (he had traded from Crow) turned back into spruce gum. The man (Toheege) went to the beach and died as he climbed halfway out of the water.

Crow went back to the village. As he paddled, he sang, "Ask, 'Did I and Toheege meet in a canoe?' (*Toheege yeł nełts'edaałe-kkaanh hee' duhnee?*)."

Then they knew that Crow had killed Toheege. The place where he died is called "Where Toheege Slipped up the Bank (*To-heege Todlegok Denh*)."

Although the Minto Flats might be a logical locale for the Nenana version of this story (Tale 2), the locale of the Koyukuk Station and Nulato stories (Tales 32 and 34) is definitely the Kaiyuh region. That is a wide stretch of the Yukon floodplain lying between the present course of the river along the western rocky shore, and the bedrock hills of the Khotol Range to the east. It is a low-lying area of swamps and lakes, traversed by the Khotol River that rises in the east and enters the Yukon below Kaltag. In former days there were many settlements here. When coming from the Yukon, one may enter this region from upstream via the Kaiyuh

Slough which breaks away from the Yukon below Nulato to join the Kho-
tol River at the "Forks." The Kaiyuh (Qayex, village), so called because of
the many settlements formerly in that area, is (or was) alive with ducks
and other water fowl in summer. There are few obvious landmarks, and
one could easily lose one's way in the maze of marshes and ponds.

35 / Crow Eats Seal

TOLD BY FRANCIS MCGINTY

Recorded by NR

CROW WAS LIVING IN A BIG TOWN ON KAIYUH SLOUGH. He told one man to come duck hunting with him. That was Seal. They came to a portage. Seal didn't know much about the country, but Crow did.

Crow said, "Here is the place where old grandpa and the old people used to stop and get some ducks."

They stopped and walked back to the lake and saw lots of ducks. Then they came back, and Crow said, "Let's stay overnight and tomorrow we'll pack our canoes over and get some ducks. Let's make a camp."

When they got the fire going, Crow said, "When the old people used to stop here overnight, they cooked their own feet."

Seal stopped and looked. He never heard such a story. Pretty soon Crow got a knife and cut off his own feet. Seal didn't want to do that, but he had to follow Crow's advice, and besides, they had nothing to eat.

Finally he shut his eyes and cut off his feet. It hurt him pretty bad, too. Then Crow put his feet on a stick and put them in the fire. Seal felt pretty sick. He put his feet on a stick and turned his back. Then Crow got a birchbark basket under Seal's feet to catch the dripping oil. Crow's feet were pretty poor—no oil in them at all.

Crow said, "Gee, your feet are pretty lean. There's no oil in them. Let's trade."

So Seal said, "All right," and they traded.

They ate their supper. Crow was satisfied with those fat feet, but it was just like chewing on dry sticks for the other fellow. They went to sleep pretty late.

Early in the morning Crow got up and called his partner. That fellow didn't move at all, so Crow went over and shook him, but he was stiff and dead. Then Crow started to eat him. It took him the whole day to eat him all.

He went back and started to sing as he neared the village, "*Sughudaa'e!* (Suʀuda'e!) *Sughudaa'e!* My partner! My partner!"

The people heard him and went to the bank. They hollered, "What's the matter?" He was half crying. They crowded around to see what was wrong.

He told them, "My partner and I were going up the river and we saw a tree leaning over the water. There was a seagull's nest in the top of the tree. My partner started to climb up to get the eggs. Before he got to the top, one of the limbs broke and he fell in the water. I rushed over there and grabbed him, but he was already full of worms while he was falling."

They didn't believe him at all. They knew him—always full of lies.

All at once he became Crow and flew up through the smokehole. "*Sughudaa'e ghegedaatl* (Suʀuda'e ʀegedatɬ)—I ate my partner [*cousin*]."

They got mad and shot at him with bows and arrows. He was in a tree. No matter how they shot, he would see and duck the arrows.

A poor boy there, an orphan, was living with his grandmother. He said, "Grandmother, I'm going to shoot him."

The old woman was a medicine woman. She got the arrow and pulled it between her legs and gave it to the boy. He went out and shot at the Crow. Crow didn't see (the arrow) at all and didn't duck. It went right in his eye and Crow fell from the tree. The people went and got him and plucked him. They put all his feathers on themselves because he was a big medicine man. That's why all the birds have black feathers somewhere. They are all

259

Crow's feathers. Ptarmigan have black feathers in their tails, and willow grouse have some around their necks.

Because a man's partner, who often was also his cross-cousin and brother-in-law, was the closest friend a man could have, Raven's brutal treachery to Seal is truly awful. The notion of eating one's own feet is also a nice horrible idea, matched only by that of eating one's own intestines (see the story below).

Since no woman should handle or step over a man's hunting weapons in real life, lest he lose his hunting luck, it is evident that the old woman possessed great magical power which she imparted to the arrow when she pulled it between her legs.

36 / Crow Brings
His Own Guts

TOLD BY FRANCIS MCGINTY

Recorded by NR

This was the Native title to the story, according to the narrator. The plot falls into two parts, a and b.

Crow Brings Home His Own Intestines [Tale 36a]

CROW WAS THE HEADMAN IN A VILLAGE ON KAIYUH SLOUGH. He had two sons, and a wife, and a mother-in-law. He started out alone up the river, hunting. He couldn't see anything, and he was a poor hunter, anyway.

He thought, "Gee, I've got to get something!"

So he reached up his anus and pulled out some of his guts. Then he went home.

His two sons came down to the beach to meet him. He told them to pack up the meat.

Then all the people gathered, and he told them, "I was going up the river and I saw a bear away up on the hillside. I shot at it and killed it, but it rolled down and caught on the rocks. I couldn't get it, but I got a hook and pulled the guts out. That's all I could get."

The mother-in-law got busy cooking the guts with salmon eggs. Some of the fellows said, "Gee, it smells like somebody defecated."

While they waited, some of the men were wrestling. Mink was the strongest and he kept throwing Crow down. Every time he got thrown, he rattled like an empty barrel.

He said, "I've been traveling all day and I've got nothing inside me."

They all gathered for a big feed. It was soup—just like water. Some of the fellows couldn't eat it.

The mother-in-law said, "What happened to my mittens, anyway?"

The two boys started looking for them and saw them under the Crow. He was sitting on them. He had stuffed them up himself in place of his guts. They pulled them out, and Crow burst open, and the whole place started to flood with the soup he had eaten.

One of the boys jumped in a wooden bowl in the corner. The water was rising in the house. All the other people turned back into animals then. The boy floated up through the smokehole.

The Boy Escapes from the Fire Woman [Tale 36b]

He was floating for a long time. There was no land—the whole country was flooded. Pretty soon he found ground and landed.

He left his bowl there, and walked until he came to an old house. There was an old woman there. He stayed with her and they became friends. She told him to go out seal hunting. It was on the coast. He got lots of seals and the old woman took them and butchered them.

One day the woman said, "Don't kill any female seals today. Just kill males."

He went out, and he could tell the difference all right, but just for meanness he killed the females, too. Before he came back, he butchered one seal and piled up all the fat in front of him in the boat. He got back and the old woman started to feel all the seals to see if there were any females. As soon as she found one, she got awful mad and started to holler.

The boy pushed off and paddled away as fast as he could. He looked back and saw something following him that looked just like a flame of fire. It was coming closer, even though he paddled as hard as he could. He grabbed a piece of fat and threw it in the water. Then the thing quieted down for a minute. He kept throw-

263

ing fat back every time the thing got close. Finally he was nearly out of fat.

He saw a cabin a long way off. Then he speeded up some more. When he got near, he saw a crane on the top of the cabin, and it started to holler. A little girl ran out of the cabin and took the crane back in. He saw them take the crane in.

He landed there. When he ran into the porch [*the entryway*] the thing was getting close to the beach. When he went in, there was a big wolf tied on each side of the porch with a short chain. After he got in, the man there went out and made the chains longer. They closed the door. They could hear that noise coming into the porch, then they heard the wolves growl. They opened the door, and there were just the wolves licking their lips.

That's all.

37 / Crow Pretends to Die

TOLD BY FRANCIS MCGINTY

Recorded by FdeL?

THERE WAS A BIG VILLAGE WHERE CROW WAS LIVING among the people. He got sick and everybody was worrying. Pretty soon he pretended that he died. Closed his eyes and held his breath. He wanted to see what the people would do. Everybody gathered in the house and started to cry.

The small loon, *Tokotsegh* (TokotseR), the red-throated Loon, made a song about him as he lay there. "Poor fellow! Everybody scolded him. Then he died."

The other loon, *Tokkaa'a* (Toqa'a), the red-necked Grebe, said, "That fellow is not dead. I can see his toe moving!"

Crow said to himself, "They ought to do something to that fellow when he talks that way. They ought to grab ahold of him."

They grabbed him and held his throat to the fire. That's why *Tokkaa'a* has a yellow streak on his throat.

Then Crow thought, "That other fellow, *Tokotsegh*, made that mean song about me. They ought to grab him and put their fists in his eyes!"

They scraped down his eye. That's why *Tokotsegh* has red streaks around his eyes.

Crow thought, "The women ought to cry and cut themselves."

One cut herself up the breast and let the blood out. That's why willow grouse has white meat.

38 / He Went Around the World

TOLD BY FRANCIS MCGINTY

Recorded by FdeL and NR?

This was the Native title as given by Francis McGinty in English. Eliza Jones gave the Koyukon River title as Yo Maagh Nodaaldledenh (Yo Maʀ Nodaldleden), "One Who Traveled Around the Edge of the Sky," when she corrected our transcription.

The Bungler Acquires Medicine Powers

HE WAS A LITTLE BOY LIVING WITH HIS PARENTS. HIS father was raising him. He became a big boy, but never did anything—he was stupid. They told him to work but he didn't know anything. They told him to go out and cut a tree for wood. He went out with an axe and took one cut at a tree. The tree said, "*Emaa!*—Ouch!" So he went home. They told him, "Go out and put some snares in the willows." He went out but just threw the snares in the trees and came back. He was so stupid he could do nothing.

He got sick. They laid him in a big wooden bowl in a corner of the house. He was laying there, half dead, and his spirit went out and started to travel. His parents didn't know he had gone.

Visits the Wolverines and Wolves

He was traveling in the winter, he didn't know where. When it got dark he saw a house in front of him with a fire in it. He went in, and there was a young girl on one side and an old woman and man behind, and some boys were on the other side.

268

The old man said, "You must be cold. You had better stay with us."

They took him to the girl, and he stayed with her.

The old woman said, "Did you see our trail where we were working at a beaver house? We left an axe there."

"No, I found a wolverine trail there."

The old man got mad. "Wolverine trail? Where did you get that?"

He reached back on the wall and got his bow and arrow. The bow was unstrung. He got the string and started to string the bow.

The boy said, "Oh, I found an axe all right. It's in my bag there."

The old man said, "You should have said that in the first place. Sit down." He told his wife, "Give him something to eat. He must be hungry."

She reached back and took out nice "ice cream" and other things to eat. He was satisfied.

They all went to bed. The boy had no bedding and slept with the girl. When he woke up he felt cold. He raised his head and he was lying on the snow—no house, nothing. He looked and saw some wolverines on the hills far away. He saw one sit down and look back and howl. That was the girl.

He got up and started again. He went and went. About evening he came to a wolf trail. He saw where the wolves had been working at some beaver houses. He found their quiver there and put it in his sack and followed the trail. As it got dark he saw a house with a fire in it. He went inside and it was the same way—girl and old lady and old man on one side and nice-looking young boys on the other.

They said, "Gee, where did that fellow come from? He must be cold. Sit down beside that girl."

The old man said, "Did you see our quiver today where we were working at a beaver house?"

"Quiver?" he said. "I found only a wolf trail."

The old man got mad and started to fix his bow. He put up his arrow and was all ready to shoot.

The boy said, "Oh, I found the quiver."

The old man said, "You should have said that in the first place. Give him something to eat. He must have traveled all day."

The old lady gave him the best she had.

They went to bed and he slept with the young girl. Early in the morning he woke up and was cold. He got up and saw the wolves climbing on the hills far away. He saw one hanging back and howling. That was the young girl.

He did that every night to all the animals that live.

[*The Wolverine man and the Wolf man were angry because the Traveler had used their real animal names, instead of the respectful circumlocutions that are normally used for such important and powerful game animals. In addition, the common word for wolverine,* neɫtseeɫ, *sounds like* nedetseeɫ, *"he has continuous diarrhea" (Attla 1990: 52, n. 2). Miranda Wright believes that the animals were angry because they had laid a trap for the Traveler, but he had outwitted them.*]

He Meets a Helpful Giant

One time he was walking all day. Suddenly he felt something on his head and he fell down senseless. Soon he came to and got up. There was a big arrow beside him, and it had come from way up ahead somewhere. He picked it up and shot it back the way it had come. He listened and heard a big noise.

He walked and walked for quite a while. There was a big Giant lying on the snow with his scalp knocked off. The arrow was lying there. He put the scalp on (the Giant), and the Giant got up and started to talk.

He told the Giant, "Will you kill some caribou for me? I need them to live on until spring."

"All right."

They went to a place where there were lots of caribou. They

271

killed as many as they could. The Giant left him and he stayed there until spring.

He Builds a Canoe

As the spring came near, he started to think, "I've got to do something. I need a canoe."

He got birchbark and sticks for it and fitted them together, ready for sewing. He made a little house and lay down for a nap. He slept for quite a while. When he was waking up he heard noises—girls laughing and having fun. He sneaked to the door. All kinds of girls were around his canoe sewing it up, and there was one good-looking girl there.

He thought, "I wish I could have that girl."

Suddenly he jumped out and all the girls disappeared—nothing there. He looked at the canoe—all sewed, ready to pitch. He went back to bed again and slept. When he awoke he heard some girls again. He sneaked to the door, and there were the same girls pitching the canoe.

The Fox Girl

He tried to get the same girl again—the Fox girl. The other girls were different kinds of animals.

[Francis McGinty forgot what followed, but we know that he did get the Fox girl, but that she could not stand the hot sun in his canoe as they were traveling. She began to pant like a fox, and to smell like one, then turned into a real fox, jumped ashore, and ran away.]

Seagull and Crow

When he was coming down the river in his canoe, he ran out of grub. He landed on a sandbar and pulled his canoe back in the brush. Then he took off his clothes and pretty nearly covered himself with sand. Soon Seagull and Crow flew up and lit right beside him.

Seagull said, "We're going to have a feed now. I'll take the eye."

"All right. I'll take the hip. But we better take a defecation first."

So they flew a little ways off, but they left their knives behind. The man jumped up and grabbed their knives.

They flew back screaming and hollering. "Give us back our knives! Give us back our knives!"

"All right, I'll give your knives back, but you have got to get me something to eat first."

"We'll get you something to eat. We'll get you a caribou."

"Get several caribou. Then I'll kill one for you and have one for myself."

Crow and Seagull flew away across the hills. Pretty soon a bunch of caribou came running over the hill and down into the river. Crow and Seagull were flying behind, hollering and screaming. The man killed two caribou. He left one on the beach with the two knives in it. He butchered the other one and put it in his canoe and went on.

This was all Francis McGinty seemed to know of the story. He did not add what we were expecting to hear: That this episode explains why seagulls and crows (ravens) keep alert for a hunter butchering his kill, waiting for the meal that the conscientious hunter will leave for them. Or, that this tale explains why a hunter can appeal to these birds for luck.

Sullivan (1942:80–82) reports that when the Ten'a are hunting caribou they sing songs which they believe are pleasing to the spirits (yega) of the caribou. Another magic song appeals to the spirit of the Canada jay, that "is always around when they kill a caribou," that it may assist them in the hunt. This custom is based on an attitude and belief very similar to that expressed in the last episode of this story.

39 / Mosquito's Grandmother

TOLD BY FRANCIS MCGINTY

Recorded by NR?

This is the Native title.

MOSQUITO WAS LIVING WITH HIS GRANDMOTHER. THEY were living near a lake in the wintertime. The little fellow did all kinds of work, packing wood and getting water. He was bringing in a big load of wood, and he got very thirsty. He went down to the water hole in the ice and drank so much that his little belly was dragging on the ground. When he stooped over to go in the doorway, a blade of grass pricked his belly and he burst open. The water poured into the house. His grandmother put his skin on a frame and began to work it. Then she saw two men coming over the hill, so she hid his skin and put up (on the frame) the skin of a salmon instead.

The two men came up. They were nice-looking fellows. They said, "Grandma, we will snare some snowshoe rabbits for you, and you get us something to eat."

So they went on and she went into the house. She pulled the skin of her face tight to take out the wrinkles, and then put little pointed sticks through to hold it.

Soon the two fellows came back with some rabbits. She put them in a pot to boil, but the men were afraid to stay when they saw how she looked. One of them slipped out the door and went over the hill. She grabbed the other one and told him. "You stay here with me," she said. "I'll cook for you and treat you nice."

Finally he said, "I have to go outside for a minute."

She made a little harness and put it around him and tied a rope to it. She kept hold of the rope.

In a few minutes she pulled. "All through yet?" she asked.

"No, not yet."

In a few minutes she yelled, "All through yet?"

"No, not yet."

Then he got out of the harness and tied it to a stump. He ran over the hill after his partner and found him waiting. They went on together.

Soon the old lady asked, "All through yet?" No answer.

Then she pulled on the rope. She pulled again and again, and finally pulled so hard that she tore up the stump and dragged it into the house. She got mad and kicked the pot in which the rabbits were cooking. She didn't have any shoes on, and it hurt her feet. So she got real mad, and kicked harder. The hot water splashed all over her and killed her.

The next year the two fellows were traveling that way again.

One said, "Let's go down and see how Grandma is getting along."

So they went down and looked in through the smokehole. They saw her lying there, dead. They caved the house in and set fire to it. Then they went away.

40 / The Loon

TOLD BY FRANCIS MCGINTY

Recorded by ?

THE LOON HAD A CABIN ON A LAKE. HE HAD A WIFE AND three boys. One day, during the winter, they were out of fish, so the Loon went down to his fish camp to get some dried fish from the cache. He took his sled with him. He was getting fish from the cache when it fell down on top of him. He couldn't get out because it was on top of his back.

Finally, after many days, he got out, but his back was all rotted off. He could barely walk. He managed to drag himself back to his house. One of his boys ran out to meet him. The boy was glad to see him.

The father asked him, "What will we do if someone comes to this lake?"

But instead of answering, the boy was looking at his father, and asked, "Where is Daddy's tail?"

The Loon asked him again, "What will we do if someone comes to this lake?"

But the boy only said, "Where is Daddy's tail?"

Finally the father got mad and killed him with his knife.

Then the second son ran out of the house. The Loon asked him, "What will we do if someone comes to this lake in a canoe?"

The boy only said, "Where is Daddy's tail?"

So the father killed him, too.

The mother was listening inside the house. She told the last son, "When he asks you, 'What will we do if some one comes to this lake?' you say, 'We'll dive down and hide under the grass.'"

So the boy went out.

The father asked him, "What will we do if some one comes to this lake?"

And the boy answered him, "Dive down and hide under the grass."

Then a hunter did come to the lake in a canoe. So they turned into loons and dove down under the water and came up in the grass, and hid under the grass.

That is why loons are heavy and can't walk, and why they have no tails. That is why they dive under the water and come up and hide under the edge of the grass. That is why they kill all their eggs but one.

41 / Owl on the Portage Was Sitting

TOLD BY FRANCIS MCGINTY

Recorded by FdeL

This was given as the literal translation of the Native title.

THE OWL WAS SITTING ON THE BRANCH OF A TREE BESIDE the portage. He looked down and saw a little mouse walking over the portage. The Owl wanted to get that mouse, so he shut his eyes and dived down after him. He struck the place where the mouse was, and grabbed up a handful of stuff. Then he came back to his tree, and sat down on the branch.

When he opened his hands, there was nothing in them but old dried leaves.

Then he looked down, and there was that little mouse, still going over the portage.

So the Owl went after the mouse again. He closed his eyes, and dived down on that mouse. He grabbed up handfuls of stuff again. Then he flew back up to his tree and sat down on the branch.

When he opened his hands, he found a lot of leaves. And finally he found the tiny mouse. He (killed it) and put it on the branch beside him.

"This is too much food for me to eat all by myself," he thought. "I'll get somebody else and we can have a big feed."

So he shut his eyes and flew off. He flew and he flew. He flew for a long time, until he got so tired that his wings were hitting the ground. So he flew up into a tree and sat down.

He opened his eyes, and looked all around to see where he was. And there he saw that little mouse on the branch beside him!

So he set out again to find some people.

"Well," he said, "Might as well fly straight this time."

So he shut his eyes and flew off. He flew for a long, long time. At last he was so tired (that his wings and tail were dragging on the ground) and he had to sit down on a tree.

When he opened his eyes and looked all around, there was that little dead mouse on the tree beside him. The little mouse was all dried up.

"No use to look for other people," he said. The Owl had been flying for many days.

My memory is that Francis acted out the Owl diving with closed eyes, coming back and opening them again, and that he showed the Owl opening first one set of claws, then the other. Since this is the way I tell the story, I cannot trust my memory, especially since the Koyu-kon were supposed to tell such stories in the dark!

"Water is dripping from the roof."

Commentary

MYTHS AND
CHARACTERS

DENA ORAL LITERATURE

"STORY-TELLING, AMONG THE TEN'A, IS CONSIDERED QUITE an accomplishment. With what success they cultivate the art—if art it may be termed—I shall leave the reader to judge for himself after he has perused these pages. I shall endeavour to present a selection of Ten'a tales, sufficient to give a fair idea of their folk-lore."

So begins Jetté's introduction to the twelve stories he analyzed and published (1908-9:298). To the tales in Dena oral literature, we should also add their riddles (Jetté 1913), the amusement of the days past the winter solstice, as the stories amused and enlightened them in the dark nights before the solstice. Both storytelling and riddling, in their own ways, hastened the coming of spring, riddles being associated particularly with the lengthening days, and tabooed during the six months of shortening days. Riddles, like proverbs and wise sayings, belong to the Old World (Eurasia and Africa) rather than the New (the Americas), yet seem to have spread to some Indian groups of northwestern North America. Thus, the Ingalik, Koyukon, and Ahtna tell riddles and also have a few pithy sayings derived from their myths, as do the Tlingit. An example might be: "Finally, a little chunk of something (fish egg, or pellet) floated into my mouth," referring to the weak fish-egg soup served to K'etetaalkkaanee, the Traveler, which now might be used to comment on a stingy helping; or "Just like 'Grandpa, I have come to you,'" characterizing the stubborn person who, like the man in the tale, never listens (Attla 1990:7 n.; C. Thompson 1990:5-7, 62-63).

Jetté's Classification of the Tales

Jetté (1908-9:299-300) stated that Koyukon stories might be "divided into three classes. First, the inane stories, that are perfectly insignificant and meaningless." These are used by lazy storytellers who can't refuse outright when asked for a story, or by others who have been asked for more when they have just told a very interesting one, or who have found that the audience isn't sufficiently appreciative. The example given by Jetté is an apparently pointless tale about a grandmother and a grandson (1908-9:300-2).

But is it as pointless to the Native narrator and the Native audience as it is to whites? Is it, perhaps, a story of such hoary antiquity that the meaning has been largely drained out of it through repeated tellings over the years? Or, is the meaning so obvious to the Native that it does not need to be mentioned explicitly? But even if the meaning is gone, there must be some "point" to the skeletonized story for it to have been told at all. In our collection, perhaps Tale 41 about the stupid Owl and the mouse he caught is an "inane story" only to someone who lacks the Dena sense of humor. Perhaps our Tale 40 about the Loon is another, and also Tale 28 about Porcupine and Beaver.

Chapman (1914:5-6) also noted such stories as falling into a special class that included "the nursery legends and tales evidently invented for the entertainment of children. For pure vapidity, some of these are not unworthy to rank with the classic story of Old Mother Dory." Although he does not identify them, I would place in that category his Tale 16, "The Knocked-down Mouse"; Tale 25, about a mother Hawk who fed her children with mice; Tale 26, "How the Fox Became Red" with anger when he failed to catch some goslings; Tale 27, about an old woman who fell down and drowned while looking up at the geese whose gizzards she'd like to eat; Tale 28, about three little girls and a Mink; and Tale 33, about the "Adventures of a Mouse." With these should we not class Jetté's tale of "The Mouse" (1908-9:483-87) which has a delightful "crazy" character? Do all stories without transformations belong here?

Jetté's second class of tales are "myths, or stories connected with facts acknowledged as having really happened," and he assigns his second, third, and fourth tales to this class. They are: about how Raven fetched the Sun; about how the earth was repeopled after a flood; and about a woman from Kateel on the Koyukuk who became a *Nenele'in* (transformed woman) during a famine. The first two of these are certainly myths of Distant Time; the last, however, is not (see below).

Jetté's third class are "stories analogous to our works of fiction, having no relation to historical events or personages, and often [are] modified by the narrator." His fifth tale he calls a transition from stories of the second to the third type. This is a story about a woman's adventures when she fled from an unfaithful husband. First, she eluded a cannibal (?) who followed her until she made him freeze to death; then she was taken by a Gull man who would feed her only mucus; but finally she was rescued by a handsome young Eagle man (Jetté 1908-9:320-37). The rest of the stories in Jetté's collection are "decidedly fiction."

Chapman's Classification

Chapman also recognizes three classes of Ingalik stories, although they do not correspond exactly to Jetté's categories. Chapman's first class are apparently myths about the Creation, about "moral good and evil, and the life of the future" (1914:4). Examples are three stories about the Creation (three versions of Tale 1), which Chapman believed were truly aboriginal, not influenced by Christian doctrine, although this is debatable. Other examples are Tale 2, "Origin of the Feast for the Dead," about a woman who was taken to the Land of the Dead but who managed with the help of a ghost woman to escape; Tale 3, about a brutal revenge taken by one man for the murder of his brothers upon the daughter of the murderer; and Tale 4, about the "Origin of the Sun and the Moon" from the incestuous brother and sister, a tale particularly well known among the Eskimo from Alaska to Greenland. These stories would correspond roughly to those in Jetté's second class.

Chapman distinguishes clearly between the Creator and Raven, citing the words of an old Indian: "The Creator made all things good, but the Raven introduced confusion" (1914:4). The "second class of legends is taken up with tales of the Raven," although his true name is never mentioned in them and he is known as "Your Grandfather."

I do not think that we can really separate Raven the Creator of land and of men and women, from Raven the Marplot, and Raven the Glutton. The Raven Cycle stories Jetté classed in his second category (of myths).

Curiously enough, Chapman puts in his class of vapid fictional tales the saga of the Traveler, described as "the personal adventures of some fictitious character, frequently a wanderer like Ulysses, and with no better morals than he had, and without his ambition" (1914:6). I believe this indicates a lack of appreciation of the seriousness of these stories as indirect conveyors of knowledge about the natural (and supernatural) world, of man's place in it, and of how he should behave. Here also Chapman includes tales about the stock character of the "One-who-does-not-want-to-marry," for her fastidiousness gets her into trouble, while the same trait in a man makes him ridiculous, yet seems to rouse the narrator's secret sympathy. Chapman thinks that these stories may have been originated by someone who liked to fancy himself (or herself) as the hero (heroine) to whom the beautiful reluctant girl (or handsome youth) finally succumbs. Incidentally, Dena stories lack heroes and heroines, in our sense, although many plots deal with the struggles of a protagonist against evil beings, especially cannibals and man-eating animals.

History and Myth

Chapman (1914:3) makes the point that the Dena of Anvik really "have no history, in the proper sense of the term." They do not hand down the names of famous men, or tell tales of their ancestors' deeds.

The small-pox epidemic of 1839, and the appearance of the first steamboat on the Yukon, in 1869, furnish dates by which the ages of the older generation can be ascertained. . . . The arrival of the Russians, and subsequently of the Americans, the traditions of one or two famines, and the account of an Eskimo raid or two, comprise nearly all the historical events with which they are acquainted. As to their former condition and manner of life, they always represent themselves as far more numerous in ancient times than at present, and they point to the vestiges of their old villages as evidence of this fact; but this does not signify much, for they are always moving around, and especially when their places are visited by sickness. It seems probable, however, that their numbers have been somewhat diminished since the great epidemic of 1839. (Chapman 1914:3)

They also told of the abundance of game in former times before the introduction of firearms, and of their life when they depended on the bow and arrow, snares, stone implements, and fire-drills (Chapman 1914:3–4). The Dena are not alone among Indians in viewing the aboriginal past as a golden age.

Similar observations about the shallow time-depth of Native "history" could be made about the Ahtna, for whom the passage of Lieutenant Allen through their country in 1885 and the Gold Rush of 1898 served in 1954 to fix the ages of their most venerable elders. However, Ahtna traditions of earlier events, about Russian expeditions and "Aleut" (Chugach) raids, both types of invasion ending in victory for the Ahtna, the historian can assign to the first half of the nineteenth century, although the Ahtna do not place them in any specific time period. Tlingit memories go back farther, perhaps, and the Eskimo are noted for the accurate details in their historical accounts.

Perhaps closest to history are the Koyukon stories referring to clans. (The Ingalik, of course, lack clans and therefore have no stories about them.) Our Koyukuk Tale 24, "How the Three Clans Got Their Names," ascribes the origin of the names to the claims of the three men who were representing their respective clans. Attla (1989:317–37, "Deeneegidzee") tells about a war between the *Nolseena* or Black Bear clan and the *Bidziyh Ta Hʉt'aana* (Bedzix Ta Xot'ane) or Caribou clan. Our Tale 24 renders the first name as *Noltseene* or Copper people, claimed by a Black Bear man who came from underground with a piece of copper. Attla (1989:319n) translates the Native name as meaning "made while descending," adding that "This clan is called the Sky Clan in other areas." This fits the Ahtna story that this clan originated from the union of a woman with a Star husband and that the clan came down from the sky to the lower Copper River. The clan may well have originated there and diffused through intermarriage from the east to the west and northwest, perhaps along with traded copper.

The representative of the second clan was a Marten man, according to our story, who claimed to have come across a great body of water, bringing a string of dentalia as proof. We heard the name of the clan as "Tonidze ʀaltsiɬne [plural]," but Attla (1989:319n) gives the name as *Toneedza ghaltseela* (Tonidze ʀaltsile [singular]), meaning "one being made continuously in midstream," and calls them the Fish or Dentalia clan.

The Caribou clan is rendered by Attla as *Bidziyh Ta Hʉt'aana* (Bidzix Ta Xot'ane), meaning "People Among the Caribou," as in our story. It was suggested that the Caribou husband in our Tale 12 may have been both a Caribou man and a member of the Caribou clan. Tale 24 may reflect actual clan migrations, and Attla's an actual feud.

Native Classification

No one classification of Dena stories is completely satisfactory, unless we can accept the distinctions made by the people themselves, if we can discover them. Thus, stories about the Distant Time are called by the Koyukon *kādōn-tsedeni,* meaning "In old times, it is said," (Jetté 1908–9: 399, like the "Once upon a time" with which we begin tales of a similar long ago), or *kk'adonts'idnee* (q'adonts'edni) (Nelson in Attla 1983:1–2). We would call them myths, not to denigrate them, but to indicate that, like the ancient sacred stories of other peoples, their truths are not those of the present day, but of time long past, Myth Time. Some of these stories may be funny, others horrifying, and still others sad. Above all, however, these stories instruct, not only describing the characteristics of animals and birds of which the Dena should take note, but teaching the difference between right and wrong conduct in dealing both with other people and with "other-than-human persons," the sentient beings that share our common world. And telling such stories brings good fortune to both teller and listeners, especially if the stories have a happy ending.

Telling a story was like praying, praying to the spirits for a good life and for the spring to come soon. "Long ago, when times were hard, people would appeal for mercy by telling stories. It was their way of praying" (Attla 1989:27). But some stories, like Attla's about the feud between the Fish and Caribou clans, were not told often because they possessed "so much killing medicine power. Catherine says that before telling this story, people long ago would burn bones in the fire to appease the bad spirits" (Eliza Jones in Attla 1989:337n).

We note that Attla did not classify any of her stories as anything other than myths, for they are all set in Distant Time. So, for that matter, are the "inane" tales of Jetté, Chapman, and some of our informants. Yet the Dena do have some stories that might seem to fall into more recent time. In addition to those mentioned above, we can cite Jetté's (1908–9:315–20) story of the wild woman from Kateel on the Koyukuk who finally married down near Holy Cross, so that the inhabitants of Kateel and Koserefsky now feel that they are related. We also heard something of this story (see *Travels Among the Dena*). Eliza Jones reassures me that the Dena themselves would class it as "historical," *yoogh dona* (yuʀ done), in the same sense as accounts of the Nulato massacre, which we also heard, one told by a man who had heard it firsthand from a survivor.

Catherine Attla's first book of stories, *As My Grandfather Told It* (1983), does not pretend to arrange the tales into categories; rather, the book includes episodes from the Raven Cycle, stories of cannibals, of Willow Grouse woman, and of Porcupine and Beaver. In her second book, *Stories We Live By* (1989), the tales are arranged in five categories: (1) Power and Compassion; (2) Raven; (3) Love and Jealousy; (4) Death; and (5) War. While war stories might belong either to Distant Time, or to historical "times long ago," *yoogh dona* (yuʀ done), and, although the world then was already as it is now, all the tales in this volume she classes as *kk'adonts'idnee,* or myths (1989:276). Her last book, *K'etetaalkkaanee: The One Who Paddled Among the People and Animals* (1990), is devoted to a single version of the Traveler Saga. Thus, so far, the published Dena stories include very few narratives that the Dena themselves might classify as historical but long ago. Athabaskan languages allow, or rather necessitate, that the narrators indicate how they learned what they are telling: for example, there is a form that indicates that the statement is based on personal experience; another form if it was deduced, as one would deduce the movement of an animal from its tracks; and lastly, "they say" or "it is said," indicating that one is repeating hearsay, which is particularly appropriate to the myths of Distant Time. These distinctions suggest one way in which narrations might be classified.

CHARACTERS

Animals

The forty-one stories we recorded in 1935 belong chiefly to the Raven Cycle and the Traveler Saga. And there are additionally thirteen miscellaneous tales. Almost all are myths. In such stories of Distant Time, the characters, with few exceptions, are animals, but animals or animal spirits in their original human guise, when "everything was man" and animals could talk. The ability to speak seems to be what most clearly distinguishes people from animals; for the animal's outward form was like a garment or pelt that might be donned or removed. It is interesting that these human-animal characters never really die, but when "killed" assume the forms and habits by which we know the animals and birds of today. This is also true of Raven ("Crow"), and of Whale, even after Raven had eaten him. The cast of characters is large, with some animals appearing in different guises in different tales. For example, the "Spruce Chicken" (Spruce Grouse) girls kindly sew up the Traveler's canoe, but the Spruce Chicken woman he meets later he suspects is a cannibal. The Wolverines are nasty man-eaters in most versions of the Traveler Saga, but in the Nulato version (Tale 38) they are friendly to the protagonist, to the extent that their animal natures permit.

Among the birds, besides Raven, we have Seagull, Goose, Canada Jay, Hawk, Great Horned Owl, and the smaller Boreal Owl and/ or Tree Owl, Red-Throated Loon, Red-Necked Grebe, Snipe, Robin, Ptarmigan, Willow (or Ruffled) Grouse, and Spruce Grouse. Birds smaller than Raven may appear as his sororal nephews: These are a small Hawk, the Tree Owl, and the Canada Jay. (There are no crows in the interior.)

The list of animals is also impressive: Brown Bear, Black Bear, Wolf, Wolverine, Caribou, Seal, Whale, Beaver, Porcupine, Muskrat, Mink, Otter, Marten, Fox, Mouse, Squirrel, Rabbit, Weasel, and Frog. To these we may add Gnats and perhaps Mosquitoes. (The Lynx and a few other animals are represented in the Dena myths collected by Attla and Jetté, although not in ours.)

It is noteworthy that among all the animal characters, Dog never appears. This is not because dogs were absent in the distant past of Myth Time, since there were dogs for Raven to eat, and smelly dog skins to make his robe. Yet there are no stories in which the Dog acts on his own or speaks. (The dog in the story of "The Woodpecker Who Starved His Wife" (Attla 1989: esp. 191–211) is the only exception I know. The dog brings food to its starving mistress, as a dog might do, but at the very end of the story is provoked into speech.) It was once explained to me by a Native of another Alaskan group that the Dog is the animal without a soul, a "thing" in the service of man, hated by the animals on which the Natives depended for survival, because he betrays the animals by aiding man in the hunt. Yet this was not the attitude of the Dena.

R. K. Nelson (1983:189–94) has clearly explained that the Dena believe the Dog to have a powerful spirit, since it seems to have a remarkable "sixth sense" that enables it to know when evil spirits are around or when someone is going to die. Although dogs act as protectors, pull sleds, and formerly carried packs, they are far more than work animals, for the Koyukuk River Indians regard them with affection, almost like members of the family. They are given personal names, and are called the "grandchildren" of their owner, who is known as their "grandfather" or "grandmother" (a form of teknonymy, like that of the Ahtna and Tlingit, in which the owner is know as the "father" or "mother" of his/her favorite dog or pet). Their dogs' behavior is a constant source of interest. The word "dog" in Koyukon was used as we would use "tame" (Jetté 1908–9:314–15), so that in a few stories we have "dog caribou" (reindeer) hitched to a sled, "dog bears" and "dog wolves" like watch dogs on either side of the house entrance. In Koyukon, the plural of dogs is formed in the same way as that for human beings, not as in other categories of nouns. Because dogs are so close to people, it would be unthinkable to eat their flesh, or to wear a garment of dog skin; this would be something like cannibalism or the revolting practices of Raven.

Nevertheless, there are, or were, feelings of ambivalence.

Nelson reports the tradition that in Distant Time dogs could speak; but Raven took away their ability to do so, knowing that people would otherwise become too fond of them, so that to lose a dog would be like losing a relative. There was also a taboo against people speaking to their dogs. It was taboo as well against letting them into their houses, because this might make the children act like dogs (i.e., eat dirty, unclean things, and behave in a rough, animal way). And because dogs are unclean, they had to be kept away from the carcasses of the important animals, and never allowed to eat their flesh or gnaw their bones (R. K. Nelson 1983:193–94). I suspect that, like the Hare Indians (Stavishinsky 1975:488), the Ahtna and the Tlingit, the Koyukon also could not kill their own dogs when the latter were of no further use because of age or injury, but formerly abandoned them, as the aged and sick members of the family had to be abandoned when the family moved in starvation time. Just as killing a dog, for so many tribes, has meant that a family member would die, so some of the Koyukuk River Indians are uneasy about shooting a dog when someone in the village is dying, for fear of similar consequences (R. K. Nelson 1983:193). Finally, the bodies of dogs were cremated, not cast aside for other animals to eat.

Many of these old rules were no longer observed in the 1970s, when Nelson was doing most of his fieldwork among the Koyukuk River Indians. People could then talk to or yell at their dogs. Also, pets of many breeds (but not those used as sled dogs) lived in the house. Some persons were no longer careful to keep dogs from the remains of important animals, and useless dogs were shot.

Important animals like the Bear, Wolf, Wolverine, and Lynx, were offended by and inimical to women, especially when freshly killed and their *yega* were still with their flesh and skins. This necessitated precautions and taboos in handling their pelts and their meat. No use at all was made of a bear skin by the Upper Koyukuk Indians, but they hung it near where they had killed the bear for the chickadees to peck. It was too dangerous to bring into the village (C. Thompson 1990:21). The Yukon Dena, however, were not afraid to make use of the pelt, though they treated it with caution.

One of Jetté's stories, "The Bear-Skin" (1908–9:337–46), in fact, tells about a wife whose husband pretends to die and has himself and all his hunting equipment placed on an open rack. Soon a little bird informs his wife that he is really living with two other wives in another place. The aggrieved woman, wearing a bear skin (and form) in which to travel, finds the two wives. In her human form she kills them by pushing their heads into a boiling pot. One dies with a smile on her face, the other with a frown. The husband finds them in this condition. The "bear" on the hillside reveals the face of his first wife, and then, as a raging bear, kills her husband and all the people in the town. On the way home, she is careful to keep pushing the bear skin from her face, until, distracted by a raven, she forgets. When she finally tries to push it back, it is stuck, and she becomes a bear for good. Jetté commented (1908-9:343):

> In this story, for instance, the bear is the avenger of a woman's wrongs, and works its vengeance directly and specially against two women. In several other stories the bear appears as peculiarly hostile to women. The peculiar fear which the Ten'a women have of the bear is traceable to no other source than these legends, in which the bear is always represented as the woman's deadly foe. Now, as this fear exists, and is universal among the Ten'a women, it is fair to conclude that, even though they profess to disbelieve the stories, there is still some vague and unconscious admission in their minds that the stories have been or might have been true. The same may be said, I believe, of ghost-stories among . . . [other] races.

I do not believe that this story is the source of women's fear of the bear. This fear is partly justified by the actual danger of the bear's attack if surprised or if it is a sow responding to an apparent threat to her cub. But the fear is more deep-seated than this, and the story is only one of several ways in which this fear is communicated. I suspect that if we could dig deeper here we would find that danger from the bear is inherent in its "breath" or "spirit," and that this lingers about the remains of the bear even when dead, when it could make sick those with weaker spiritual powers: children and women—sometimes even scaring away their souls. That is why they may not come near the fresh carcass, or eat the flesh (especially that of the head—the seat of power), or make use of the fur for clothing or blankets, and certainly not utter the bear's true name at night! At least this is the explanation for such a fear among the Ahtna, and I suspect that it holds true for the Dena as well. The story only serves to express the Athabaskan's fear of the spiritual power of the bear, a power which is possessed to lesser degrees by other carnivores.

Chapman (1914:42–49) recorded what was essentially the same story, one common also among the Eskimo of the Yukon River and the Chugach of Prince William Sound. A similar story was published by Sullivan (1942:97–99) from the Koyukon of Nulato; in his version, however, the husband is killed only when he follows his first wife home to kill her for murdering his two new wives, and they all turn into lynxes. In the story by Attla (1983:77–86), only the guilty husband becomes a lynx at the end. All these stories agree on two important details: the wronged wife is informed by a bird that her husband is living with two new wives; and when she has killed them by pushing their heads into a boiling pot, their faces retain their expressions, one smiling, the other frowning. It was only by accident, I believe, that we failed to hear this story in 1935.

It is interesting to note that in other stores, the Bear, though the largest and most dangerous of all the animals that the Dena meet, is treated as just a little stupid, and not too hard to outwit. He is no match for the wiles of Raven, or of the Traveler; and he is ignominiously routed by Porcupine, who is generally a female character. Because Porcupines are food that is easily obtained in times of hardship, they may not be called by their true name when one is going to snare them, but are referred to as "that which is crooked," referring to their crooked or arched spine (Eliza Jones).

Most tales of the Traveler present the Wolverine as a man-eating monster that later becomes the robber and defiler of caches. In actual practise, however, the Dena treat a dead Wolverine like a chief (*doyonh*), as they do the Wolf, and welcome him to the hunter's cabin, put fine clothes on him, and spread a banquet before him. The essence of these things he will take with him, and characteristically, while the Dena men enjoy the food, women are carefully excluded (Sullivan 1942:101–3; R. K. Nelson 1983:148–53). Jetté (1907:157–58) published the myth explaining why the Wolf and Wolverine should be treated in this fashion:

There were once two rich, influential men who went on a long hunt, persisting against the advice of a poor but wiser companion, even when there was no game. They starved and eventually turned into Wolverine and Wolf. The third man, on his long journey home, survived a number of perils, including a forest of dancing trees and snapping cliffs on the river, and so became the first medicine man of the Dena.

In Attla's eleventh episode of the Traveler Saga (1990:49-54, "Wolverine") and in our Tale 38, the Wolverine and the Wolf are presented in not unfavorable light, amiable hosts but dangerous when insulted and when the Traveler shows that he has guessed their trick. In Tale 16 the Wolves who have stolen the Marten girl's arm, and their Bear guards, are outwitted by Raven.

One popular story about animals is that of the Porcupine who is crying on the beach because she cannot get across the river to a better stand of the trees on which she feeds. The trading of insults with the unsuitable animals, Muskrat, Mink, and Otter, who offer to ferry her on their tails, must have been greatly relished by the audience, as well as her discomfiture when Beaver dumps her in midriver. But note that she gets ashore anyway, walking on the bottom. Since porcupines can and do swim, is her crying for assistance in crossing part of the joke? On her arrival at the farther bank, she insults with impunity the Bear who threatens her, in some versions actually killing him with the quills on her tail (Tales 28 and 33; Jetté 1908-9:354-59; and Attla 1983:65-76). This story is one especially enjoyed by Dena children. Miranda Wright explained for me the moral inherent in the tale: Because Porcupine has grossly insulted those who offered her help, her insolence and rudeness result in her being dumped in the river by Beaver. While this moral lesson is an important one for children to learn, it is best conveyed in a story, which will hold their attention without appearing to lecture them.

The characters of the other creatures are not so clearly drawn. Mouse woman is neat and serves the Traveler edible food, although the portion is rather small. Mouse man, however, is more of a comic character with big pretensions (Jetté 1908-9:483-87). The old man in Tale 30 has a talking Mouse as companion who reveals to him the hiding places of the little boys who have stolen his food. Mouse, Squirrel, Weasel, and Fox, when specific animals are identified, are the girls who sew up the Traveler's canoe. The Fox girl is apparently the prettiest, but cannot stand the heat of the sun. (Hawk and Crow women are also mentioned in this incident in Tale 14.) Fox is a man with whom the Traveler makes a temporary alliance against a Giant, but he is also cheated by the Traveler out of his roast ducks. Mink appears in Tale 25 as Raven's companion on his journey to bring back the Sun, and hunts for them both. Raven's hunting partners, Seal and Whale, seem to be amiable, fat, but overly trusting young fellows. Rabbit is a man-eating monster with a sharp, knifelike tail with which he stabs his victims, but the Traveler makes him the harmless creature he is today. Otter, once a man-eater, was also subdued by the Traveler. Otter women are depicted as overly eager for sex, and may also be man-eaters, but they are "tamed" when the Traveler kills one with a club. In another version, the Traveler himself assumes the form of an Otter in order to escape the Bear, whose daughter he has killed. Then follows an episode often associated with the theme of the False Plea, in which the Bear gets a Frog woman to drink dry the lake in which the Traveler-Otter is hiding, but the latter gets "Brother Snipe" to prick her belly and let out all the water, and so escapes in the flood, while the Bear is fighting with a dummy made of moss. Marten is the hungry little boy whose face gets splashed with grease, and Marten girl is the pretty one whose arm was stolen by the Bears and Wolves.

Birds

A Raven and a Seagull collaborate to drive caribou to the Traveler, who leaves one carcass for them. The Owl may be stingy and mean (Tale 7; Jetté 1908–9:467–75), or else a bumbling figure of fun. Raven's nephew, Hawk, is the only one of his hunting companions who is able to defeat him. Robin is a poor woman who apparently gets strangled by the rope on her toboggan. Willow Grouse woman is the desirable woman that Raven fails to win, although she cries at his death. Geese appear only as the woman that Raven marries and her relatives who are forced to abandon him when he tires on their migration flight across the ocean. The Loon and Grebe seem to be rather stupid.

Human Beings

Although there are a few stories in the collections of Jetté, Chapman, Attla, and our own in which human characters appear, this is exceptional. The Traveler and his family come first to mind, but we must remember that in Attla's version (the only one I know that has an "end"), this final episode seems to fade out with the protagonist becoming a Pine Grosbeak. There had been nothing about him to suggest a bird, except that the name of this species is "traveler," *kk'ogholdaale* (q'oʀoldale) (Attla 1990:149n), and this transformation comes as a curious anticlimax to us. Does it seem thus to the Dena listener?

These tales, with their emphasis on animals, are in striking contrast to those of the Eskimo, where the emphasis is upon human beings, even though the Alaskan Eskimo also have many Raven tales. But, as we shall presently see, the behavior of some of the animal characters does reflect the way human beings feel and act.

Shamans

The characters who are most detached from bonds of kin and place are those who are shamans, or who are becoming medicine persons. Their powers are gained or augmented by overcoming the obstacles thrown in their way as they travel on their medicine journeys. In the tales, as in real life, they seem to be persons driven by the strong internalized forces of their calling. Despite their role as protectors of the community from the evil spirits, and as directors of ceremonials (especially among the Ingalik), shamans are seen as touchy and irascible, anti-social and self-centered, jealous of their power, and at war with rival practitioners as well as with themselves. The prototype of medicine journeys is that of the Traveler (see below). Shamans can "dream" of persons far away and, on awaking, report on their condition (Tale 29).

The Raven medicine man in Tale 8c–d illustrates the stereotype of the old shaman. He is resented by the young because he is too old, and too crooked to be trusted. He knows how to get fire, for example, and they don't, so out of meanness they steal his beak (teeth). His journey under the water to rescue Raven, who has been taken by the Fish people, partially resembles the underwater exploits of the Koyukon shaman to ensure a heavy fish run. The man with power doesn't hesitate to show it, as is illustrated by Raven's boastings when he made land or secured fire.

299

Monsters

One last category of characters would include the various monsters that people the Dena world of the imagination. Prominent among them would be the transformed person, usually a woman who has become animallike during a period of starvation. Such was the woman from Kateel on the Koyukuk who became a "Goblin" or *Nenele'in* that slinks about and steals food (Jetté 1908–9:315–20). One who has been driven by famine to eat human flesh becomes such a creature, called "Woodsman" by R. K. Nelson (1983:194–99), who adds a number of details: the ability of these creatures to move swiftly without tracks and to disappear; spending the winter in dens; and stealing children to rear them as their own. Stories about such creatures are common among the Tanana and Ahtna, and usually deal with personal experiences.

The "Foggy Man" in Tale 2 is *Ok dena,* literally, "Man of Fog." "Foggy Men" are also mentioned that make it foggy when they rise from the lake. In Tales 32 and 34, and in Attla's (1989:133–47), the Foggy Man monster that had killed so many hunters until Raven got the better of him, is named Grandma's Needle, and Raven claims to be his namesake. Ella Vernetti (Tale 32) evidently envisioned him as a very large creature with huge jaws, for she called him an "Alligator," and Attla's description is of an "enveloping water thing" or whirlpool (1989:137). Foggy Man's other name, *Toheege* (Toxige), means "mirage," a distorted image on the horizon, a common phenomenon in Alaska, or else a large "eddy" or "whirlpool."

One characteristic of supernatural beings is that they can detect the presence of human beings by smelling them. This is true of the youths in Sky Land (Tale 11), and of the Giant (Tale 31). This was a supernatural ability often mentioned in Chugach stories.

XI

THE BUILDING
OF DENA MYTHS

LOCALIZATION OF MYTHS

WITH A FEW EXCEPTIONS, THE COUNTRY IMPLICIT IN THE tales of Distant Time is that familiar to the Dena themselves. It includes the great river, the swampy lowlands with their maze of lakes, sloughs, and winding streams, and the mountains that rim the river basin. The headwaters of the river are in the east, where the Sun begins its daily journey and near where the Traveler began his; the several Lands of the Dead are also there. The river leads down to the ocean, across which the Geese make their annual migration flights. The youth whose uncle put him in a hollow log was carried down the river and across the ocean to the farther shore (Siberia?), where lived the Giant who hitched "caribou dogs" to his sled when the ocean was frozen. It took the youth ten days' travel with the Giant's sled for the trip back to Alaska (Tale 29).

Below the surface of the water were the homes of the Fish people. These might be visited by powerful shamans, either to rescue a captive who had blundered into the Fish's domain (Tale 8c), or to persuade the Fish to make the generous runs on which humans rely for the greater part of their subsistence. The home of at least one group of Fish people was like a hill in the middle of the ocean. In the lowland floodplain waters lived the Foggy Men, man-eating monsters whose emergence was marked by swirling eddies and the fogs and mists rising from the marshes. Raven, who lived in a village halfway between Nulato and the mouth of the Kaiyuh Slough, met Foggy Man and killed him just beyond the Forks where the Kaiyuh Slough meets the Khotol River; and that place is known to this day as "Where To-heege Slipped up the Bank."

301

Above this earth was a similar world: Sky Land. The sky itself was evidently conceived of as a dome that comes down to meet the earth at the horizon. The sun, moon, and stars were stuck onto its lower surface. The girl who went to the sky simply wandered up there by mistake while chasing a butterfly. The girl who searched for a husband walked all the way around the horizon in vain, and then climbed the vault to become the Moon; her brothers became the Sun and the Stars (Tale 15). Raven formerly lived in a great big town, but the chief at the other end of the world was somehow the reason why the people in Raven's town were dying. After a fight in which Raven and the chief killed each other, Raven became the Moon, and the End-of-the-World chief became the Sun (Tale 13). The Ingalik conceptualized the world as having four levels (see comment at Tale 25). There is no apparent consistency in the way the cosmology is pictured in the different stories.

If we were to make a close examination of place names in Dena country, I suspect we would find many that had been derived from myths. Jetté's unpublished dictionary, (which we examined briefly in Nulato), as well as his published stories, give evidence to the localization of many mythic episodes, as well as historical reasons for place names. One of the mountains in the Khotol Range is known as "The-One-Whose-Top-Was-Hit-by-Raven," because it was formed when Raven hit a wave with his harpoon. On the harpoon's rebound, Denali the High One was created (Jetté 1908–9:309–15). Another mountain in the Khotol is the body of a Giant who died there of exhaustion; Bishop Rock just north of the Yukon is his pack. And Kateel on the Koyukuk River is where a woman became transformed in a time of famine, yet the Kateel River is "the luckiest river," according to our informant, suggesting that there is yet another tale.

Some places are associated with the Traveler's adventures. Thus, a hole in the rock somewhere below Rampart is where he anchored his canoe when searching for the noise in the woods; and his tracks are there, too. A line of boulders stretching out into the river from the north bank of the Yukon is the remaining wreckage of Wolverine's Weir or Trap Fence. The place is said to be right above Garnet Creek and about eighteen miles below Rampart. The trap itself, a pair of cliffs that come snapping together, is certainly suggested by the scarps along the Ramparts.

The most interesting landmark of this kind was the cliff with red paintings on its face, right where Moose Creek enters a slough of the Tanana River about eighteen miles above Fairbanks. These pictures marked the place where Raven is supposed to have made women from men (fig. 1). The pictures were found by U.S. Army engineers in 1941 when they cleared trees and bushes from the face of the bluff. Fortunately, archaeologist Louis Giddings saw these pictures and was able to sketch and photograph them before the engineers blasted the cliff to get material for a dam. Only a little piece of painted rock is preserved in the museum of the University of Alaska Fairbanks.

These pictures covered most of a rather smooth, underhung surface of rock, about twenty feet high and fifty feet long, with a smaller group of pictures farther up on a vertical rock face. Although the incurved shape of the cliff suggested a shallow rock shelter, Gidding's trenching failed to uncover any sign of an old camp site, for the soil there was recent river silt. Some of the pictures had been defaced by weathering or hidden by moss. The pictures are of human or humanoid figures in various attitudes, ranging in size from five-and-a-half to twenty-five inches in height. We reproduce here the sketches made by Giddings and published in *American Antiquity* (1941), but unfortunately the three photographs in the article did not reproduce well.

The largest figure, I suggest, is Raven, standing erect like a person, his skinny wings like outstretched arms. Other pictures are of persons in groups. In one group, the people apparently are all marching in the same direction. In another, three persons are enclosed in a circle, with three others outside; this may represent three people looking down through the smokehole into a house with three occupants. Of particular interest are the two representations of people in boats: five (women?) in one boat, with four tally marks above, and five men in another, with eight tally marks above. What is surprising about the boats is that they seem to be dugouts with raised prow and stern.

Pictures in very much the same style are known from Cook Inlet and Prince William Sound (de Laguna 1934, 1975a). Cook Inlet is at present within the territory of the Tanaina Athabaskans, but in

Fig. 1. Moose Creek pictographs, on a slough of the Tanana River, about eighteen miles above Fairbanks, Alaska. From Giddings 1941, pl. 9. Not to scale: (a) Raven (?), 25 inches tall; (b) Marching figures, 5.5 inches tall; (c) Marching figures, 5.5 inches wide; (d) Three figures on houseroof, looking through smokehole at three in house (?), 17 inches wide; (e) Five figures in a boat, four talley marks above, 11 inches wide; (f) Six men in a boat, eight talley marks above, 31 inches wide.

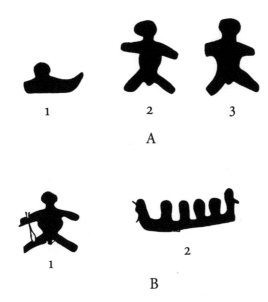

Fig. 2. Red pictographs, Tuxedni Bay, Cook Inlet. From de Laguna 1934 and 1975a, pl. 63. Group A: (1) Man in kayak; (2) and (3) Anthropomorphic figures (men or bears). Group B: (1) Man or bear; (2) Six persons in a canoe or umiak; or four persons in a canoe with a high prow and stern. Scale: Boat is 7½ inches. All pictures to same scale, traced from the original and reduced 1:3. Broken lines indicate indistinct outlines; hatched lines mark cracks or breaks in the rock.

former times, like Prince William Sound, it was the home of Pacific Eskimo—Chugach or their relatives. Could the Moose Creek pictures possibly be mementoes of an Eskimo raid? Or are they Athabaskan records left by travelers to inform others, serving the same function as the pictures sometimes scratched on trees or stumps by their modern descendents? Certainly such rock paintings are rare if not nonexistent in the interior, but they are not uncommon among the Northwest Coast Tlingit and Tsimshian.

MOTIFS AND THEMES

Traveling

A number of themes seem to run through several tales and to characterize the collection as a whole. The first is traveling. As a coastal Tlingit woman said of the interior Athabaskans: "All they have to do is walk around."

Like the sun's daily journey from east to west, life itself is a journey. Life's journey, driven by the food quest, does not end at death because the spirits of the dead, it is believed, return upstream to the far-distant headwaters of the Yukon, reversing the journey of life. The spirits of the dead will eventually leave this distant place when they are reborn to life as babies (see Chapman 1914:12–19). In myth, also, journeys are usually downriver and are but briefly interrupted by visits to settlements and camps. In many stories, as well as in the Traveler Saga, the characters seem always to be on the move from place to place, giving us the feeling that social ties, and sometimes family ties, are not permanent or tightly binding. Yet this impression is partly false, for the wanderers may eventually think with longing of home or of their parents and, if given the chance, will eagerly return to find them. The happy reunion with an aged mother may end the tale. Although marriages were formerly arranged in actual life, the loss of a spouse is nonetheless a traumatic event. In the stories, such loss leads to bitter grief, or to savage revenge in cases of infidelity or abduction. There is less often displayed a longing for the particular place we would call "home," perhaps owing to the seasonal movements from camp to camp. In this respect, Dena stories contrast with Eskimo stories of wanderers. An exception is Jetté's tale about the

Eagle-Man (1908–9:320–33), in which his happily married wife finally cries from homesickness, and in our Tale 8a, when Raven is sitting, lost, after dropping out of the flock of migrating Geese: "He didn't know which way to start; he didn't know where his Alaska was. . . ."

Transposable Episodes

As the journey depicted in the tales is punctuated by overnight visits to the cabin or camp reached at day's end by the lonely Traveler, so the incidents of a cycle seem to be threaded like beads on a string and, like beads, may be shifted from one string to another. Thus, in "Raven and the Goose Woman," the episode of making a canoe (Tale 8b) seems to be lifted bodily from the story of the Traveler. As an example of a reverse shift, from the Raven Cycle to that of the Traveler, we can cite the episode, "He Cheats Fox" (Tale 9), in which the protagonist unexpectedly changes character and utilizes a trick that would be characteristic of Raven. The episodes in which he steals a fisherman's gear also suggest the well-known story of how Raven stole the fisherman's hook, although Raven lost his beak in the attempt, while the Traveler escaped scot-free.

Stories about stock characters, such as the rich man's daughter who refuses to marry, may be used in almost any story where it seems appropriate to place it. (See Chapman 1914, Tale 5a, "How Raven Brought Light;" Tale 5e, "How Raven Stole the Rich Man's Daughter;" and Tale 12, about the woman who married two Bears. See also our Tale 17, "Crow and Willow Grouse Woman.") In societies in which marriages are usually arranged—as were many in Alaska—the girl who refuses to marry even the most eligible suitor must be made to suffer for her obstinacy, as happens when she accepts the worst suitor of all, even though she eventually has to escape from him. This lesson for all young women appears often in American Indian stories: Don't be too choosy!

Magic Journeys

There are also magic journeys described in the stories, all of these apparently journeys home. The two stories of a youth who lives with a

Giant tell how the Giant started the young man for his trip home with a loaded sled, in the first case propelled by the magical powers of the Giant's rabbit-skin parka, and in the second pulled by two "caribou dogs" (reindeer). As is usual on such trips, the human beings are told not to look out, or back. When the first youth does so, the heavily loaded sled comes to a stop and he cannot budge it. When he returns to confess his fault to the Giant, the latter sends him off again on a second, successful journey. In the second tale, the man obeys this injunction and arrives safely across the sea, sending the "caribou dogs" home to their master. (Does this incident suggest a knowledge of Siberian reindeer sleds? Note that in Attla's version [1983:159] the team is made up of different big game animals.) In order to go in the correct direction, the Giant sets up his cane on the ice, and the way it falls is the way the man should go. The cane that points the correct way also figures in Attla's story of "Eagle Man Who Carried People Far Away" (1989:85–109) where it is used by the husband seeking his kidnapped wife. This cane also belongs to Ahtna folklore. These are all motifs that are familiar to us from our own "fairy tales," even though they seem quite at home here, and may be part of the universal (or nearly universal) stock from which mankind builds a vision of the wonderful.

A somewhat different magical journey is undertaken by the girl who followed a butterfly into Sky Land. Here, despite the warning of the old woman, she moves the rock cover of the hole through which she can see her own family down below on earth, and so is filled with longing to return. Finally the old woman lowers her to earth on a cord the girl had made. The return is interrupted on the first try because the girl disobeys and looks down, though she has been told to keep her eyes shut. The same incident is used in Attla's story of "The One Who Secured His Axe to the Sky" (1989:29–69). This man follows a woodpecker and also finds himself in the house of an old woman in Sky Land. He disobeys her by moving the rock and sees his mother down on earth. This time it is the old woman herself who braids the rope of sinew by which she lowers him to earth. The rule against looking down is not mentioned, but he does disobey her injunction not to cut the rope, an act which means that people now use rope to hang themselves. The notion that Sky Land is a world just above our visible sky, and that there is a hole in it, properly covered by a rock, is found in a number of Indian stories, often combined with the theme of the Star husband. The Wanderer is usually lowered safely on a long cord made by Grandma Spider, in Indian tales of the Plains and Southwest.

Magical Objects and Wishes

The Dena stories also contain objects of magical power, in addition to the Giant's rabbit-skin parka and the direction-pointing cane (Tale 29; and Attla's story of the Eagle-Man, 1989:85–109). The latter tale also includes an old woman's caribou skin pants that give superiority in wrestling, and a wolverine skin that facilitates escape. The grandmother in Tale 35, who was evidently a medicine person, pulls an arrow between her legs and her grandson uses it to shoot Raven. An ordinary woman doing this would ruin any man's luck, for it was taboo for a woman even to step over a hunter's weapons.

To a people who had to work hard to make an uncertain living, the notion of magical objects has always been attractive. But the Dena add an even more wonderful notion; namely, the potent wish. With a potent wish, the medicine person or a character like Raven has no need of magic implements or of elaborate rituals and spells. The wish itself, when thought, accomplishes the desired end. This point is more clearly revealed in Attla's stories than in our collection, perhaps because it was harder for our informants to express it.

Big and Little

As might be expected, there is some playing with the contrast between big and little. In the stories about Giants, examples include the incidents at the end of Tale 9, where the Traveler and Fox frighten the Giant away and finally defeat him; the final episodes of Tale 10; the whole last part of Tale 29; Tale 31, where the Traveler meets "The Giant and His Wife"; and Tale 38, where the Traveler meets a helpful Giant. In the last episode of Tale 5, the roles are reversed. The man becomes the Giant when he visits the tiny Gnats.

The last two episodes of Attla's version of the Traveler Cycle, "Little People," and "Giant Woman" (1990:139–45, 147–49) also contrast the small and the large. In the first, the Traveler wantonly and purposely kills some of the small people. The survivors then try in vain to kill the Traveler, but he kills them all to prevent their being here today. In the second episode, he himself dies when he tries to sleep with the Giant woman. In our Tale 5, the Traveler seems to be rather callous when the waves he creates drown a number of the Gnat people, although he does not kill them intentionally and is able to rescue most of them.

Giants seem to be fond of taking little boys in order to adopt them as "grandsons." They treat these boys well and are fairly amiable most of the time, with a few exceptions. In Tale 31, the Giant is a cannibal but his wife a kindly soul who shelters the Traveler. In Attla's version of the jealous uncle, the Giant's wife is "one who kills little people," and her husband must protect his adopted grandson from her (1983:149). Despite their size, Giants are afraid of certain small animals such as chickadees, porcupines, and foxes.

The playing with big-little contrasts is carried out in typical Alaskan style when the mouse swimming in the stream is a "moose" to the Gnat people, who use porcupine quills as barbed spears; and the mountain sheep that the Giant carries on his belt are just "rabbits" to him. And his hair lice are "big animals."

Ruses and Stratagems

A number of ruses are part of Raven's stock in trade. When his beak is stolen, he diverts the attention of the old woman who is guarding it by making armed warriors out of pine cones. He starts a pretend "war" on the village, during which he makes off with the sack containing his beak. Another ruse is pretending to be sick, so that a girl will get wood for his fire, thus giving him the chance to steal her clothing with which he will turn men into women. He pretends to die in order to hear what people think of him. He distracts people by crying out that a dog has stolen a king salmon from a cache, a serious enough theft to send everyone in pursuit. But in Tale 25, Raven, who has made the Sun and Moon, loses them to a rival chief, apparently while trying to stop the wind that the other has called up. One gathers that Raven himself is distracted by this contest of medicine powers.

A common stratagem for escape is to pretend that one has to go ashore, or into the bushes, to relieve oneself. The captive slips off the cord that has been tied around his/her waist and puts it around a stump. By the time the captor has discovered this, the former captive has made his or her escape (Willow Grouse girl in Tale 17; the young man caught by Mosquito's grandmother in Tale 39). A variation of this ruse is employed by Raven in Tale 16. He first makes himself pitiable so that the Bears and Wolves who have stolen Marten girl's arm will take him in; he dances all night to put them to sleep, so he can steal back the arm; and he works it loose from the rattle every time he goes outside again, feigning he is sick with diarrhea.

A delaying tactic employed by the Traveler is to wish that one will lose something, thereby enabling the Traveler to accomplish his aim. Thus, he makes Wolverine man lose his knife so that he will bring his axe, which the Traveler uses as a club to kill him. The Traveler characteristically uses a club. In Tale 14, he wishes that the Fox woman will lose her awl and grabs her when she is searching for it. In Tale 31, however, he just hides it himself. Another stratagem is to create a magical "man" or "men" out of inanimate matter to serve some particular purpose. We have seen how Raven (Tale 8) raises an army of spruce cone men. He also makes a man out of his own excrement to act as a watchman to prevent the theft of his canoe (Tale 19). On the coast, he more often makes a man out of an old stump for such a purpose.

Rich Clothing

In the stories there is great emphasis on clothing, especially on fine boots and parkas trimmed with wolf and wolverine fur, on parkas of marten fur, and on dentalium shell necklaces. Considering the many shiftings of residence in the ordinary Dena year and the fact that almost all possessions had to be transported, it is hardly surprising that wealth to the Dena consisted of fine clothing and ornaments. This wealth, like prepared food, was made and distributed by women, men being responsible only for the raw materials (meat, skins, dentalia). One's wealth in clothing and decoration was worn when visiting or entertaining others, when hunting, and when facing death.

While "clothes make the women" in Tale 1, they also define the rich man in other stories. Thus, fine clothes win Raven entrée into the best houses, because only the wealthy are fit to entertain him. And it is because of his fine apparel that young women "fall in love" with him. Raven, therefore, who seems to lack such things, goes to great pains to manufacture finery out of trash. If there is a moral here, it is that such false finery is liable to revert to its original condition, and when it does—there go hopes of wedded bliss!

Raven takes advantage of this liability of his magical creations to revert to worthless origins when he trades his weapons and canoe with Foggy Man, who is thus left without defenses. And he employs the same technique in Attla's story of how he fooled the Bear who owned the fish trap (1989: esp. 119–27).

The rich man is the great man, the leader of the settlement, a position he often combines with that of shaman. Perhaps envy of his position, or a desire "to get even" with him by making fun of him, inspire the incidents in which Raven, as the rich one arriving at the home of the Willow Grouse girl, cannot be expected to walk on the bare earth and will not step ashore until her mother has paved his path with the furs from the family's beds. And when Raven's false finery reverts to trash, and his wife has left him and taken his canoe, he must return, naked and all scratched up from the bushes, to receive his grandmother's scoldings and ministrations—a fine end for the high and mighty aristocrat. In a despicable act, Raven retaliates by killing Willow Grouse girl when she comes to a potlatch at his village (Tale 17).

Sex and Marriage

Although both the coastal and interior versions of how Raven made women evidently contain explicit sexual references, neither in Tlingit nor in Dena myths is as much made of sexual motivation as in our popular stories. In fact, too great a sexual urge is characteristic of the man-eating Otter women (Tale 5). When Raven courts Willow Grouse woman, this is not so much because he is "stuck on her" (in love), as because she presents a challenge, the beautiful girl who refuses to marry anyone, and this braggart wants to succeed where others have failed. And he marries the Sun Owner's daughter not for love, but because he is plotting to get the Sun.

As for stories that show him with an interest in other women, I can cite only that about Raven and Hawk, in which Raven covets his nephew's wife so much that he tries to kill Hawk to get her, and one by Attla (1983:127–38), in which Raven wants one of the human women he has just created and is angry when the men will not let him have her. In Tale 29, the man with two young wives is so jealous that he tries to kill his own nephew because he suspects the latter of having "fooled" with them. But the Traveler, who is attracted to the Fox girl, conscientiously puts his "business" before marriage. On the other hand, the husband whose wife has been kidnapped by Eagle-Man (Attla 1989:85–109) is so pitiful that an old woman's spirit helps him on his perilous quest to regain her, and this tale comes very close to what we understand as a love story. But as for the many other captured women who have become the Eagle-Man's wives, their great concern is over who will take the place of their slain husband and get food for them. The Dena are too realistic in outlook to entertain seriously the notion of romantic love, even for good-looking girls or youths, and though in actual life marriages may seem to be casually entered into, they also seem to last (see above, McGinty's Autobiography).

Marriages could be forced, I suspect, among the Dena in ways similar to those of the Ahtna, who mixed the girl's bedding with that of her suitor. At least, that is how I interpret the way in which the girl who went to Sky Land was made to marry the youngest and best son of the woman: she was put in his sack and hidden under his pillow. In this story we may also note that, while his older brothers were sorry they didn't get the girl, there is no hint of any bad feeling between them—perhaps because "she stayed with all the brothers." We do not meet in Dena folklore any indication that the elder siblings were resented by their juniors, as they are apt to be in Ahtna life and stories. Rather than being the "boss" of his younger brother, the Dena older brother is simply more responsible and cares for his junior.

Among the Athabaskans, brothers-in-law become special partners through the marriage of one to the sister of the other, even though they may be cross-cousins. Since this new relationship is an important one, formally indicated by a change in kin terminology in some cases, the girl's brother has a personal concern in her marriage—note the happy excitement of Willow Grouse girl's brother, who exclaims: "Oh, Mother, someone is coming to be my brother-in-law!" (Tale 4), or "Mama, I found a brother-in-law!" (Tale 17). The brother-in-law is something like a "best friend," and it would be a terrible act to injure him, as nearly happened when the man was about to kill his sister's Caribou husbands, thinking they were only caribou.

One very serious motivation for marriage forms the basis for Tale 15, in which the brothers and their sister search the world for a husband to marry her. Indeed, as she asks, "When we get old, who is going to take care of us?" Children were expected to care for aged parents, and a single grandparent often adopted a grandchild of the opposite sex as helper. Fear of destitution in old age must have been real, since eventually the accompanying infirmities would prevent the elderly from keeping up with the seasonal movements demanded by the food quest, and for some the only solution would be an "easy death" by suffocation. This fear seems to have motivated Mosquito's grandmother (Tale 39), who tried to take out the wrinkles of her face by stretching and pinning back her skin (a face lift) in order to attract one of the young hunters as a husband.

Human Relations

We have noticed the bonds of friendship linking certain characters: i.e., partners in hunting and fighting, brothers-in-law, and, as with Raven and Foggy Man, the bond between namesakes. And such friends should give each other valuable gifts, even to exchanging what each has.

Personal remarks, criticisms, or complaints are never directed to the person at fault. That would be too insulting. Instead they are mentioned to a third party, but in such a way that the person for whom they are intended can hear them.

When a girl reaches puberty, she is secluded for a long period because she is dangerous not only to the powers of men but also to herself. To control her powers, she eats out of her own dishes, uses a bone scratcher (not her fingernails) when she itches, and sucks water through a drinking tube (not directly from a cup), so it will not touch her lips. This is a time during which her mother, or an older female relative, teaches her the skills of the housewife—especially sewing and working on skins. The Wolverine girl who escaped the massacre of her family, "all alone back in the woods," was such an adolescent. Since she was "about sixteen years old," we may infer that Athabaskan girls matured later at that time than they do now, no doubt owing to the difference in manner of life. We may also infer that her ability to prevent the Traveler from killing her was due to her special adolescent powers that rendered ineffective his strategies and weapons.

Things that every boy and girl should know appear at the beginning of the Traveler Cycle, and because the young protagonist is a bungler, he is made to leave home. He puts the fish trap in the water wrong end up, and it catches no fish; he throws the rabbit snares on the bushes, instead of setting them, and they catch no rabbits; instead of bringing home some porcupines, "crooked things from the trees," he gathers a sack full of bent twigs. And lastly, he cannot bear to chop trees because he thinks they are bleeding, and one cried "Ouch!"

Wrestling matches seem to be a way of sizing up strangers, as is the custom among some Eskimo groups. Thunder employs the wrestling match as a way of killing people, by throwing them onto the sharp rocks in his house, but the older of the two brothers kills Thunder instead. The Giant in Tale 9 has a similar ploy.

The common illusion of hearing noises in the woods when nothing is there began with the Traveler's experience (Tale 9).

The stingy husband and his wife's revenge are the subject of a story about an Owl (Tale 7). The woman is starved, but she gets even by stuffing her niggardly mate with the grease from a bear she killed herself. Such a tale would certainly represent the dream of the more ordinary docile wife, living with a husband far from her own people. Yet I suspect that there were far more valiant Amazons in Dena society than the men would admit (see Altona Brown, for example). This story only hints at what the relationships between husband and wife might be. We should note that, despite the moral of Willow Grouse woman, a girl did have the right to refuse a suitor. I do not know if pegging the bottom of her dress to the ground was a recognized way of exercising it (Tale 17).

315

The love between grandparent and grandchild is commonly accepted in many Native societies as greater than that between parents and their children, and it plays an important role in the story of how Raven got the Sun. The Sun Owner simply *has* to give this treasure to his wailing grandson. The Giants that steal little boys indicate their affection for them by asking the boys to call them "Grandfather." In contrast, aged and infirm parents may be too often neglected by their children.

Also relevant, perhaps, is the story of the pathologically jealous uncle who is sure that his sister's son is "fooling with" his wives (Tale 29; see Attla 1983:139–70, "The One Whose Uncle Put Him in the Water in a Log"). It is interesting that in Attla's version the uncle is identified as Great Raven. On the coast, the uncle is the Controller of High Water, and Raven is the nephew that the uncle tries to kill. In our version, however, "Crow" (Raven) is not mentioned. Even though the jealousy is certainly exaggerated, it suggests that among the Dena, as among the Tlingit, the sororal nephew (who would belong to the same clan as his maternal uncle) did at one time have access to the latter's wife. Tale 29 certainly suggests tensions within the close family.

The family, or household, may consist of a man, two wives, their children, and a mother-in-law, judging by Raven's household in some stories. In other tales, he lives alone with his grandmother.

At death, the bereaved relatives make songs about the dead, eulogizing the deceased and expressing their longing for the departed.

Weather and Shelter

Curiously enough, for a country where the thermometer can register seventy degrees below Zero Fahrenheit, and where the "Spirit of Cold" is one of the most powerful supernaturals, there seems to be no emphasis in the tales on the bitter cold of winter, although its darkness on moonless nights motivates the quest for the Sun and Moon. Nor is concern expressed about finding a house each night in which to sleep, or in building snug, warm shelters. Only in Tale 6 is the house of the two brothers purposely built strong enough to withstand the attack of Thunder. Is the cold so constant and extreme that it need not be mentioned? Or, are not the Athabaskan Indians confident of

their ability to shut out the cold anywhere, given a fire-making kit
and an axe? Some of the early explorers on the Yukon found that the
Natives' screen of brush (or a stretched canvas) with a fire in front
made a better winter shelter when on the trail than did the canvas
tent, and so adopted it. In some of the Ingalik stories from Anvik,
as well as in the Koyukon tales of the Traveler, the protagonist (like
the traveler today) is likely to find a house or a camp at the end of
a day's journey where he will be offered food and shelter. It is when
this expectation is unrealized, as when the host is the cannibal and
the Traveler is the anticipated meal, that the adventure enters.

The Gnawing Fear: Eating and Being Eaten

The dominant, overriding concern in all the Dena tales is food. There
is a very strong emphasis on eating and on the fear of being eaten,
clear evidence that the struggle for food in this harsh environment
has been a constant one, and that the specter of starvation is never
remote. And the end of every human being is to be eaten at last by
the Disease-Spreader or one of his assistant demons, the devourers of
human souls. Death is inevitable, though delayed, when the shadow
soul (*yega*) is eaten, but immediate when the human animating soul
(*nʉkk'ʉbedze*) is eaten.

Almost inevitably, every tale mentions some aspect of the food
quest—hardly surprising, since in reality this occupied most of aboriginal Native life in the seasonal round. The Traveler in Tale 38 asks
the Giant to kill caribou for him, so that he will have enough food to
last through the winter until spring. Later in the same tale, the Traveler plays dead in order to lure Raven and a Seagull, so that he can
seize their "knives" (bills) and, with these, bribe them into hunting
for him. We notice how food, when available, is generously shared
(except by Raven). And Tale 30 about the two little boys is surely a
lesson against stealing food.

Many stories involve cannibals or man-eating monsters, like
Foggy Man, and tell how the protagonist kills them or escapes from
them. (See especially Attla 1983:179–93, the section on a girl's escape
from a cannibal in "She's Dragging Her Bag.") The point of several
episodes of the Traveler Cycle is that the food of the animals is not

for human beings; so when the Traveler is entertained, the food he is offered may be either inadequate in amount, or unfit for a human being because it cannot nourish him. (See the Traveler's visits to Mink, Mouse, and Frog; see also Attla [1990:5–22] on the Traveler's visits to the Canada Jay, Rabbit, Chickadees, and the Ptarmigan and Grouse.) The food of the dead is unfit for the living and for the recently deceased.

Raven manifests a desire for food to an insatiable degree. In his gluttony, he not only titillates the audience with visions of enviable abundance which they can never achieve, but he also warns that the abundance to satisfy such gluttony is secured at too high a price. He is particularly fond of dog's eyes—food that any Dena would reject, unless dying of want. He has to be bribed with food to help others and, as on the coast, Raven is a greedy cheat. Not only does he betray his partner (nephew, cousin, or brother-in-law?), which is something that men have often wanted to do when the demands of kinship became onerous, but he sacrifices ordinary human decency as he becomes virtually a cannibal. The Dena Raven is disgusting, bringing his own intestines as food that he pretends was obtained on the hunt and, in order to share in the soup made from it, being obliged to plug himself with a mitten! I cannot call to mind any coastal tale to match this.

XII
RAVEN
AND TRAVELER

THE RAVEN CYCLE

THE RAVEN CYCLE, OR RATHER THE LOOSE CONNECTION OF
tales about Raven as represented in the stories we recorded in 1935,
can be broken down into the following incidents:

1. Raven makes land: 8a, 8d
2. Raven gets fire: 1, 8d
3. Raven makes women from men: 1
4. Raven meets and kills Foggy Man: 2, 32, 34 (see Attla
   1989:133–47, "Great Raven Who Killed a Water Monster")
   A. And kills Foggy Man's mother: 32
5. Raven courts Willow Grouse woman: 4, 17 (see Attla
   1983:31–40, "Willow Grouse")
   A. In false finery: 17
   B. She escapes with toilet ruse: 17
   C. He betrays self by eating dog flesh: 4
   D. Loses and regains beak through ruse of "war" of spruce
   cones: 4, 8e
6. Raven marries the Goose woman: 8a
   A. Is unable to cross ocean and falls: 8a
   B. Makes a canoe: 8b
   C. Is captured by Fish People and rescued by
   medicine-man Raven: 8c
7. Raven tricks Brown Bear at the fish weir: 3 (see Attla
   1989:115–31, "The Baby Who . . . Resembled His Uncle")
8. Raven becomes the Moon: 13 (This is a curious tale, very

different in tone from other Raven stories, and may be
foreign to the Cycle.)
9. Raven recovers Marten girl's arm: 16
   A. Makes self pitiable to fool the Bears: 16
   B. Makes islands with paddle: 16 (Jetté 1908–9:313, Raven
      makes the Khotol Range and Dinale the High One with
      his harpoon; Chapman 1914: 26, Raven makes only a
      little hill at Anvik, instead of a high mountain)
10. Raven and the seesaw: 18 (see Attla 1983:243–56, "The Ones
    Who Used to Say 'Adiyee Hughłkinh' ")
11. Raven maroons Hawk to take his wife: 19
    A. Makes mannikin of his dirt to warn him, but is
       marooned in turn: 19
    B. Chokes to death on Mouse bones: 19
12. Raven betrays Seal and eats him: 20, 35
    A. Is killed by arrow: 20; by magic arrow: 35
13. Raven betrays Whale and eats him: 21, 27 (see Attla
    1989:149–69, "Great Raven Killed a Whale")
    A. Raven drowns in soup (of own guts?), 21
    B. Willow Grouse cries for Raven's feathers: 21
    C. Raven fails test of feathers, but escapes into air: 27
14. Raven brings home his own guts: 20, 21, 36 (see Attla
    1989:149–69, "Great Raven Killed a Whale")
15. Raven bursts with soup of his own guts: 36a
16. Raven pretends to die: 37

The story of Raven making a raft and saving the animals during the Flood, Attla's (1983:127–38) "Great Raven Who Shaped the
World," while reflecting actual experiences of river rafts and floods,
also evokes the biblical tale of Noah and the Ark, for the animals go
aboard two by two, and later Raven and a Seagull fly out in a vain
search for land. But it also includes the Indian Earth-Diver motif of
making the land out of the mud brought up by Muskrat and Beaver
from the bottom of the ocean, and ends with Raven's creation of one-
way rivers, mortal men and women, and mosquitoes to bite them.
It serves to explain why the present world is different from that de-

stroyed by the Flood in Distant Time, including the extinction of the Pleistocene mega-fauna.

The best-known, most widely told, and most enjoyed story of the Raven Cycle is about how he brought the Sun and Daylight to his people who were living in the dark. The various incidents of this story are here analyzed:

Raven gets the Sun: 23, 25, 26
1. Raven originally made the Sun but lost it to rival medicine man: 25
2. Raven is bribed with food to get the Sun: 26
3. Raven goes in false finery: 23, 25; real finery: 26
4. Raven marries Sun-Holder's daughter: 23, 25, 26
    A. Spruce needle becomes Raven's son: 25 (reverts to spruce bough)
    B. Their baby cries for Sun: 23, 25, 26
5. Trouble with false finery, so Raven leaves during the night: 23
6. Sun and Moon are controlled by pictures of them: 25
7. Diversion of dog stealing a king salmon: 25, 26
8. Raven makes the Moon from a piece of the Sun: 26
9. Raven guards Sun and Moon from son of rival medicine man: 25

Jetté's version (1908–9:302–8) of Raven gets the Sun is almost the classic one. In this, the people discover that the Sun has disappeared, and they bribe Raven to recover it by offering him the flesh of two fat dogs. He flies to the village of the rich man who has the Sun and turns himself into a spruce needle, which the daughter of that man swallows when she drinks a cup of water. The woman thus becomes impregnated and gives birth to a baby who cries for the Sun. His mother gives it to him, and in his play he manages to get it outside the house. Then, turning into Raven once more, he flies home with the Sun. (His *mother* as giver of the Sun to the child is unusual. Miranda Wright informs me that her grandparents from Nulato tell almost the same version, except that the doting grandfather gives the Sun to his grandchild.)

Jetté (1908–9:308) writes: "The myth of the Raven is one of the most universally rehearsed among the Ten'a tribes." And he mentions the same story as told by narrators on the Koyukuk River and on the Yukon down to Kaltag. "The same wonderful feat of the Raven is related with many others by Ivan Petrof among the myths of the Thlinket tribes of South-east Alaska," citing the *Compilation of Narratives of Exploration in Alaska*, (1900:275–76, from Petrof 1884, the Tenth U.S. Census Report on Alaska of 1880).

Some interesting differences exist between Jetté's version and the story as told by the Tlingit. The Tlingit Raven threatens to bring the Sun and Daylight to men who are fishing by torchlight at night and who have refused to give him any fish. Daylight will spoil their fishing. The Sun Owner is the chief known as Raven-at-the-Head-of-Nass-River, and it is his daughter whom Raven impregnates by turning *himself* into a spruce needle, which she swallows. The baby (Raven) is born almost immediately, to his grandfather's delight, although a wise old woman notices that the child has the eye of a raven. It is the loving grandfather who cannot bear to hear his grandson cry, and who gives him in turn his treasures: the Stars, the Moon, and finally the Sun in the Box of Daylight. When Raven returns to the fishermen and opens the box, the people become so terrified that they scatter in all directions, becoming either land or water animals, according to the kinds of skins they are wearing. This turning into animals at the end reminds us of the Dena myths, from which, perhaps, the coastal tribes have adopted the idea.

Chapman (1914:22–26) also included the story of "How Raven Brought Light" in his small collection of the Raven tales. The Sun Owner is a wealthy man whose daughter refuses to marry. Raven decides to try his luck with her and travels, alternately flying and walking in the dark, to her village, recognizing her house by the pole beside it with wolf and wolverine skins tied to it, the tokens of wealth. He makes himself into a spruce needle and falls into the water that the girl drinks. She becomes pregnant, to the surprise of her mother, and soon gives birth to a son like a little raven with big eyes. He cries for the thing his grandfather has "that gives the light." When finally grown, he is allowed to wear the Sun on a string around his neck and so returns with it to his own village. This version is rather abbreviated. The wooing of the One-Who-Will-Not-Marry is not carried through, for Raven does not marry her; and there is no mention of what Raven does with the Sun.

The version of this story told by Catherine Attla (1983:87–106), "The One Who Took Back the Sun," is fuller than any of ours in describing how the people attempted to cope with life in the dark after the Sun disappeared. Raven is offered food to get the Sun. He outfits himself in false finery to arrive as a rich man, although the man holding the Sun suspects his real identity. Raven wishes that this man's daughter will fall in love with him, which she does, and they marry. Being hungry, he devises a means whereby he gets a chance to eat a dog. He narrowly escapes detection when he leaves a three-toed track at the carcass, and all have to show their feet. In order to get the Sun and Moon that were hanging on the wall, he decides that his wife should bear a child. He impregnates her with spruce needles that he drops into her drinking water. The baby is born, grows fast, and begins to cry incessantly for the Sun and Moon. His grandfather gives him the Sun. Raven creates the diversion of a dog stealing a king salmon from the cache, and in the confusion he grabs the Sun and Moon. He kicks the baby, who reverts to spruce needles. The nicest detail ending this story is Raven tearing off pieces of the Moon and naming the months as he does so, both in Koyukon and in English! The Sun Owner arrives before he can name December, so this month becomes the "One with No Name." Then Raven flies home with the Sun, again saving his people. This version has all the characteristic Koyukon motifs!

A number of episodes in the Raven stories, of Chapman, Jetté, Attla, and our informants, make no sense unless we know the classic Raven version of the coast. Thus, why should the spruce needle be mentioned at all, if Raven himself marries the Sun Owner's daughter, and if it is their child, conceived in the ordinary way, who cries for and gets the Sun? In the classic version, the spruce needle is a ruse for Raven *himself* to enter the Sun Owner's household as the child of the latter's daughter, and to conceal his identity until he gets the Sun and flies off with it. Most of the interior versions do not seem very close to an "original," or classic version.

On the whole, the interior Raven episodes appear to be much less closely integrated into a cycle than those of the Tlingit. There is no story of his birth, and of how the attempts of his jealous uncle to kill him led to the Flood, and so to the subsequent shaping, or reshaping, of the world. Of course, not all the Raven stories of the Tlingit are neatly fitted into a coherent narrative or chronological order, but there seem to be fewer loose ends than among the Dena versions. Furthermore, there is not just one Dena Raven, it would seem, but several. In Tale 8, for example, the Raven who married the Goose woman and had to be abandoned on the flight across the ocean is, as it were, reduplicated in the second half of the story. For the original Raven becomes simply *a* raven, from a village presumably of other ravens, who gets captured by the Fish people and has to be rescued by a medicine-man Raven. From there on, this medicine-man Raven gets fire, makes ground, and finally becomes so obnoxious that the people steal his beak, to recover which he has to fake a war, thus duplicating the exploits ascribed in other tales to just plain Raven or *the* Raven. Instead of Raven losing his beak when he steals the fisherman's bait, as the Tlingit tell the story, we have the Traveler playing a comparable role among the Dena (Attla 1990:89–93; our Tales 9 and 22).

Ann Chowning's study (1962) of Raven myths in North America and Siberia has successfully disproved the theory of a Siberian origin for these tales, first propounded by members of the Jesup North Pacific Expedition (Waldemar Bogoras in 1902; Waldemar Jochelson in 1908), or that of an origin on the Northwest Coast (Boas 1916). These and later scholars tended to dismiss the Raven stories of the Alaskan Eskimo as late manifestations of Northwest Coast Indian influences, and the Alaskan Eskimo themselves were seen as a recent "wedge, which split apart the trunk of the common mythological tree" (Jochelson 1908:358–59, quoted by Chowning 1962:2). Archaeological investigations, however, have shown that the Eskimo are no recent arrivals at Bering Strait, but have flourished there for at least three or four millennia, and Chowning's re-examination of their folklore, especially of its not inconsiderable body of Raven tales, finds the Alaskan Eskimo to have been more of a bridge than a break in the distribution of these tales. Raven, with his part-avian, part-human attributes and his character that combines the trickster-transformer, the dupe, and even occasionally the creator or benevolent culture-

hero, is quite at home among western North American mythic characters like Coyote, Blue Jay, and Mink. But in Siberia such a Raven character appears as an alien immigrant from North America. Although
we should not assume that the Raven stories necessarily originated
on the Northwest Coast, there is evidence to suggest that they were
probably most systematized by the Tlingit, in all probability con-
siderably before Swanton (1909) made the first systematic collection
of their myths in 1904.

Chowning has argued that "the distribution and content of the
cycle suggests that Raven myths originally formed a basic part of the
folklore of a group of tribes extending from the Koyukon to the Tsimshian, but not including the latter. Contact between the interior Atha-
bascans and the Alaskan Eskimo seems to have been intensive . . ."
(p. 4). "The Eskimo not only transmitted Raven myths, but may
have contributed elements of their own to the concept that reached
Siberia. . . . Of course, diffusion presumably proceeded in both directions," although the principal movement was from the New World to
Siberia (Chowning 1962:3). That the Raven cycle did not originate on
the Northwest Coast is suggested by significant facts cited by Chowning: that these stories spread only a short distance east and south of
the coast; and that, except among the Tlingit and the Bella Coola,
Raven is commonly known by some other name, like the Tsimshian
"Giant" or the Bella Bella "Real Chief," characters that seem to be
amalgams of Raven and a human culture hero. While the Siberian
Chukchee Raven is like his neighboring Alaskan Eskimo counterpart, the Siberian Koryak have mingled this character with others of
their own to produce Big-Raven the god and Raven-Man the rascal
(Chowning 1962:3–4).

It should be noted that the original speakers of both Tlingit and
Bella Coola seem to have been, at least in large part, migrants from
the interior to salt water, and their languages have retained clear ties
to largely inland linguistic stocks: Tlingit to Athabaskan-Eyak, or Na-
Déné, to which Haida makes a dubious claim, and from which Tlingit
separated about five millennia ago, while Bella Coola is a Salish language, although one geographically isolated from the block of its
many upriver and tidewater relatives in the south. Are Raven stories
part of their inland cultural and linguistic heritage? If so, the Tlingit

at least have, in organizing the myths into a Raven Cycle, successfully adapted them to the coastal locale, with its salt-water creatures — Seal, Whale, Petrel that once owned all fresh water, and the Controller of the Tides — just as the interior groups who are known to have come down the rivers to the sea adapted themselves successfully to the coast and to the people they found already living on the shores of Southeastern Alaska. The "classic" version of Raven stealing the Sun bears such a coastal polish, and the Dena versions we know may represent coastal forms of the story, (re-?)introduced to the interior and somewhat misinterpreted in the process.

Yet even this Tlingit story has two Raven characters: the familiar trickster-transformer and Raven-at-the-Head-of-Nass (who was the Sun Owner). And, especially as told at Wrangell (Swanton 1909), Raven-at-the-Head-of-Nass was also (?) Raven's jealous uncle, as well as the Creator, an all-powerful deity and/or a culture hero. Since the Nass is a river in Tsimshian country, I suspect that this proliferation of Ravens is the result of Tsimshian influences felt most strongly by the southern Tlingit.

THE TRAVELER CYCLE

We have six versions, or rather partial versions, of the stories about the "Man Who Went Through Everything," or "The One Who Traveled Among All the Animals and People," a story cycle that clearly belongs to the Athabaskan interior rather than the coast. Of these, two are from Nenana, with one each from Tanana Mission, Ruby, Koyukuk Station, and Nulato. It would thus seem to be as popular as the Raven stories. Only four of our versions start at what might be considered the beginning, that is, from the protagonist leaving home, and none reaches the end of the story. Catherine Attla's third volume (1990) of recorded and translated tales is devoted entirely to a Koyukuk version. In this, we learn that his name was *Betohoh* (Betoxox), and that when he died he became a Pine Grosbeak, both items of trivia having little to do with the major themes of the dramatic cycle. Titus Bedes at Nenana told us that it would take eight days (nights) to tell the whole story. Since we never heard what was supposed to be a complete version of the story, and since our six different narrators gave different emphases to the various episodes (elaborating, barely mentioning, omitting, or adding ones not mentioned by others), it is impossible to determine how many episodes there "should" be. Probably no version is "complete" in the sense of being exhaustive or all-inclusive. Attla's version has twenty-five episodes, but these are on the whole more inclusive units than those which I have used. C. Thompson (1990:60–61) has pointed out that Attla's episodes fall into a winter series of fifteen and a summer series of nine, with the canoe-making and Fox-wife episode as a spring transition. He also notes differences in the Traveler's actions or character (more deceitful and cruel in summer than in winter), differences in the characters met (only animals in winter, both humans and animals in summer), and in summer greater dangers to be overcome, from each of which he gains medicine power. Although I have attempted to arrange the incidents in our stories according to season, they fail to show a comparable pattern.

While two of our versions of the Traveler Cycle slight this episode, the canoe-making is always mentioned. It seems to be so important that *Ch'eteetaalkane*, the Traveler, was called "Noah" by John Silas of Nenana, not because he saved animals and people during a Flood, but because he was a canoe-maker. The careful testing of spruce bark, cottonwood bark, and birchbark to see which would float best, and the search for the correct bird breastbone or jaw as model for the bow, suggest what is not, to my knowledge, openly stated: that the Traveler was the builder of the first canoe (See Attla 1990:75–79; and C. Thompson 1990:40). Another canoe-maker who experimented, in this case to make the fastest possible craft, was the young man in Jetté's tale of "The Canoe" (1908–9:347–54). In this swift craft he was able to pass unscathed between the great knives that crossed the river like enormous scissors, and thus escaped the Man of Fire who had evidently killed so many others. In our Tale 6, the two brothers who were planning to "tackle" the Thunder, modeled their canoe on the fastest bird they knew, using a duck's breastbone — in this respect resembling the Traveler.

The versions of the Traveler Cycle that we recorded may be analyzed as follows:

327

I. Winter

   1. Leaves home: 9, 14, 31, 38 (omitted, 5, 22)

      A. Thinks his wives told sons to give him dirty water; lets wife who follows him with baby be eaten by wolves: 9

      B. Says will return as Coyote when his hair turns white with age: 14

      C. As a bungler, is sent away till he can prove self: 31 (Attla 1989:29–69, "The One Who Secured His Ax to the Sky," begins with almost the same incidents)

      D. As bungler, gets sick and acquires medicine power; his spirit goes on journey: 38

   2. Visits animals: (mention only, 31)

   3. Visits Wolverines and Wolves, other animals: 38

      A. Animal father angered by Traveler's words: 38

      B. In night they turn to animals, abandoning him; girl mourns: 38

   4. Meets helpful Giant who kills Caribou for his winter food: 38

   5. Hears robin, strangled on toboggan line: 9

II. Spring

   1. Makes a canoe: 5, 22, 31, 38, (no details, 9; brief mention, 14)

      A. Tests bark: 22, 31 (no test of bark, 5)

      B. Tests bird's jaws: 22

      C. Uses Spruce Chicken breastbone: 5 (as pattern for bow, 22)

      D. Gets girls to sew: 5, 14, 22, 31, 38 (frame is made when he wakes, 31)

   2. Fails to get Fox girl as wife: 5, 22

      A. Wishes her to lose awl: 14, 31

   3. Gets Fox girl wife but can't keep her: 14, 31 (story ends before she becomes a Fox, 22) (narrator doesn't know what happened, 38)

      A. Rejects offer of little Hawk, grabs Weasel's braid: 14

      B. Rejects offer of Mouse, 22

      C. Promises Fox girl's father to care for her, 22

III. Summer

   1. Visits Mink and Mice: 5; Frog and Mouse: 9

      A. Mouse food good: 5, 9

   2. Deceives Brown Bear father, who wants his daughter to kill Traveler: 14

A. Substitutes sharp arrow for blunt when shooting at Bear
daughter: 14

B. Escapes into lake as an Otter: 14

C. Bear gets Frog to drink lake, man gets Snipe to puncture
Frog: 14

D. Man puts dummy in Bear's trap while he escapes: 14

E. His canoe waits for him: 14

3. Becomes Fish to steal Bear's fish spear: 9; to steal fisherman's
hook: 22

4. Visits rabbit: 5, 9

A. It breaks its sharp tail on flat rock: 5, 9

5. Visits Otters, clubs Otter girl: 5

6. Visits (cannibal) man who is scraping human skin; kills him
and he becomes Otter; Weasel gets burned tail in the fire: 9

7. Hears noises in the woods, but finds nothing: 9

8. Wolverine's trap: 5, 9

A. Shoots arrow through as test, is caught by shirt: 5, 9

B. Wolverine kid sees he's not dead: 5; girl sees he is not
dead: 9

C. Wills Wolverine to lose his knife: 9

D. Kills Wolverine man with axe: 5, 9

E. Can't kill girl in tree: 5, 9

9. Visits Spruce Chicken women (cannibals?), who break his
canoe; he escapes: 9

10. Visits Gnats: 5

11. Eludes cannibal Giant, Giant's wife feeds him; he escapes as
Insect: 31

12. Gets a Raven and Sea Gull to help him kill Caribou; leaves
one for them: 38

IV. Beginning to freeze up

1. Meets and cheats Fox out of Ducks: 9

2. He and Fox chase away Giant, and defeat Giant in
wrestling: 9

On his journey the Traveler overcomes several man-eating animals and transforms them into their present-day innocuous or less dangerous forms. These are Rabbit, whose knife-sharp tail is broken and who now becomes food for men, and Wolverine, who is not

completely overcome, since the Wolverine girl survives and her descendents will plague men by stealing from their caches and fouling
what they don't eat. Otters were formerly man-eaters, but are rendered harmless when the Otter girl is killed (Tale 5), or Otter man is
slain and his body burned (Tale 9). Lastly, Spruce Chicken woman,
who was also suspected of eating men, was simply left behind, un-
changed, in the Traveler's flight (Tale 9). I do not know whether there
is any significance to the fact that all of these incidents were told only
at Nenana.

Both Miranda Wright and Eliza Jones have generously helped
me to understand these stories better. The latter explained that the
Traveler had dreamed in advance of all the places he would visit and
of the adventures he would encounter, and that he had the mission
of correcting the things in the world that were wrong. In this respect,
he offers a contrast with Raven, who certainly on occasion acted as
a marplot, as when he made the rivers run only one way so people
would have to paddle when going upstream, who fashioned men of
clay instead of stone so that they would be mortal, and who released
clouds of mosquitoes to plague them (Attla 1983:133–37). Of course,
Raven also helped people when it suited him or when they bribed him
with food. Yet, the Traveler, especially in some incidents in Attla's version, acts in a very cruel way, or is thoughtless of another's feelings, so
that the difference between him and Raven should not be exaggerated.

Because the individual episodes of the Traveler Cycle are loosely
strung together, and because the theme of traveling suggests additional adventures of like kind, we suspect that the Traveler Saga has
been built up by accretions from other tales, accounting for the Traveler's character being somewhat inconsistent. Yet it is interesting that
Attla's version of the Traveler Cycle should have incidents so different from the ones in our versions. We note that some incidents in
ours are duplicated in stories which she ascribes to other characters.
Thus, "The One Who Drank Water with Dog Droppings in It" is not
the beginning of Attla's (1990) version of the Traveler Cycle, but is
the initial episode of a different story (1989:379–405), which may be
summarized as follows:

After the husband leaves in anger, both of his wives try to follow
him, but one is frightened off by the head of a black bear he had put

in his trail. The other wife, however, with her baby, who soon dies, succeeds in catching up with him, and they join a group of people on an extended caribou hunt. That wife is killed or taken by a monster, a tailed man. Her husband finally kills the monster by chopping it into little bits. He then marries the creature's two wives. While out hunting for his new family, he is swallowed by a giant lynx, but because of his great magical power he comes back to life and, in turn, kills the animal. Then he begins killing people, and he becomes an old man because of this. Eventually, all alone, he wanders back to his first home, to his younger wife who had been afraid of the bear's head. She is now an old woman, but they marry again, and both are very happy.

Despite the happy ending, this story is not told often, and only then with the magical precaution of burning a bone, because of the "bad" (great) power of the protagonist. In some ways, this is a mini-Traveler tale.

The behavior of the man who is to become the Traveler, as described in Tale 9, can be taken as a typical of the paranoid shaman, sure that his wives had instructed their sons to bring him water with dirt in it. He leaves home in anger, to the exclusion of other feelings, and so is unmoved when the wife, who followed him because she loved him, and her baby, are killed by wolves.

Rabbits in Attla's version are completely innocuous, and the sharp tail that Rabbit used to kill his human victims in our stories from Nenana appears in Attla's version (1990:119–25) as a knife attached somehow to the buttocks of the cannibal woman, but the Traveler protects himself in both incidents by putting a rock on his chest when he sleeps.

The incident of stealing the fisherman's hook is found in the "Fishhook" episode of Attla's story (1990:89–93), and that of feigning death to kill Wolverine and his family is, with its details, in Attla's version (1990:95–101), which is another story, titled "How Unlikely to Be Hanging By the Neck from That." This, however, is simply about killing a man, presumably a cannibal, who is not identified as any animal. Attla's "When He Grabbed the Raven's Beak" (1990:111–17) is only partially paralleled by the incident in our Nulato version, in which the Traveler grabs Raven's and Seagull's "knives" (beaks) in order to pressure them to help him kill caribou. And none of our

331

versions contains anything about finding his older brothers who had
come to such miserable ends on their journeys, when they reached
the limits of their medicine powers (Attla 1990:119–25, 133–37), or
about his cruelty in how "He Made a Grave for the Girl Who Had
Been Given to Him" (1990:127–33). On the other hand, almost all of
the winter half of Attla's version is missing from our collection.

I was surprised to realize how much information on the Traveler's motivations and purpose had been included in the tales we had
recorded. I had not noticed this until my later analysis.

The Traveler "was a brave man and a great man." He had a mission. He wanted to have a wife, yet reluctantly had to let go the (Fox)
girl he had chosen. "Well," he said, "I'm no good for women anyway.
I'll get through my business first." When he came to Wolverine's trap
of the two crashing rocks, he knew he could avoid it by portaging
around, "But I couldn't get rid of that thing that way. That wouldn't
do." He was here recognizing an obligation to other river travelers.
On leaving the tiny Gnat people (surrogates for mankind?), he told
them, "Now I'm going to go. You remember me, my Old Testament,
when I leave you people." He had saved them. And "Before he died
Ch'eteetaalkane told the people, 'My story has got to be a long story.
It has to take eight days' time. When you start you have to tell the
whole thing. You can't pick around.'" (Tale 5)

"In the beginning, one man made the earth. All the birds and
animals were like men. All were talking." He left home after drinking the dirty water, and when one of his wives came after him with
their baby, half frozen, he simply told her, "I will never stop. I will
go through the country." Even though he saw the two wolves lying in
front of the next village, he did nothing to save his wife, but went on
alone. When he came to Wolverine's trap he thought, "This is the time
I'm going to get killed." But he permitted it to catch him. (Tale 9)

In Blind Joe's version of "The Man Who Went Down the River,"
the man says good-by to his father and mother, and to his brothers
and sisters. "I'm going to leave you now. When my hair gets gray and
as white as a rabbit skin (in winter), I'll come back to you people.
When I come back, I'll be (a?) Coyote. My hair will be white." He
was then a young man, and was starting from the head of the Yukon
River. While nothing here points to his purpose, we can see that he

is not abandoning his family altogether, even though he knows he is destined to leave them for many years. (Tale 14)

Our Koyukuk version of the story begins with a long account of the bungler's stupidity. He puts a fish trap in the water wrong end up, he scatters rabbit snares on the willows, he does not understand the allusion to porcupines and brings instead bent twigs, and lastly he can't cut wood because the trees bleed. So he is driven from home. But he is not really stupid. Rather, is he not thinking so hard about arcane matters and acquiring shamanistic powers that he fails to pay attention to his mother's instructions? What a pity that Ella Vernetti did not write down more of this version. (Tale 31)

In the Nulato tale the youth was also a bungler. But he became sick, and while lying half dead in a big wooden bowl, fell into a trance. And "his spirit went out and started to travel. His parents didn't know he had gone." This illness was certainly that associated with his acquisition of shamanistic powers. Whereas in other stories, the transition from human to animal happens sometimes almost mechanically, the most dramatic episodes of this kind occur when the Traveler visits the camps of the Wolverines and Wolves. At first, he angers the father in each case by referring to the animal (wolverine or wolf) by its common (vulgar) name, and by outwitting the father in the little test he'd devised. Then he is accepted. But after an evening of eating a good supper and making love with the young girl in the family, the "people" resume their animal forms and leave the Traveler to wake, alone on the bare snow, the house and all vanished. He sees them climbing the hills far away, while one hangs back and howls her grief at their parting. (Tale 38)

SOURCES

Allen, Lieutenant Henry T.
1887 *Report of an Expedition to the Copper, Tanana, and Koyukuk Rivers, in the Territory of Alaska, in the Year 1885.* U.S. Congress. Senate: 49th Cong., 2d session, S. Doc. 125. Washington, D.C.: Government Printing Office.

Attla, Catherine
1983 *Sitsiy Yugh Noholnik Ts'in': As My Grandfather Told It.* Traditional stories from the Koyukuk, told by Catherine Attla. Transcribed by Eliza Jones. Translated by Eliza Jones and Melissa Axelrod. Fairbanks: Yukon-Koyukuk School District and Alaska Native Language Center.

1989 *Bakk'aatugh Ts'uhuniy: Stories We Live By.* Traditional Koyukon Athabaskan stories told by Catherine Attla, with an introduction by Chad Thompson with Eliza Jones. Transcribed by Eliza Jones. Translated by Eliza Jones and Chad Thompson. Fairbanks: Yukon-Koyukuk School District and Alaska Native Language Center.

1990 *K'etetaalkkaanee: The One Who Paddled Among the People and Animals.* The story of an Ancient Traveler, told by Catherine Attla, with a Foreword by James Ruppert. Transcribed and translated by Eliza Jones. Fairbanks: Yukon-Koyukuk School District and Alaska Native Language Center.

Bancroft, Hubert H.
1886 *The Works of Hubert Howe Bancroft.* Vol. 33: *History of Alaska, 1730–1885.* San Francisco: A. L. Bancroft and Company.

Birket-Smith, Kaj
1953 *The Chugach Eskimo.* National Museets Skrifter, Etnografisk Raekke, vol. 6. Copenhagen: The National Museum Publication Fund.

Boas, Franz
1916 *Tsimshian Mythology.* Bureau of American Ethnology, Thirty-First Annual Report, Washington, D.C.: Smithsonian Institution.

Bogoras, Waldemar

1902 The Folklore of Northeastern Asia, as Compared with That of Northwestern America. *American Anthropologist* 4:577–683.

Brown, Altona

1983 *Altona Brown, Ruby.* [Autobiography]. Fairbanks: Spirit Mountain Press, for the Yukon-Koyukuk School District.

Chapman, John W.

1903 Athapascan Traditions from the Lower Yukon. *Journal of American Folk-Lore* 16, no. 62:180–85.

1907 Notes on the Tinneh Tribe of Anvik, Alaska. *Congrès International des Américanistes, 15th Session, Quebec* (1906)2:7–38.

1912 The Happy Hunting-ground of the Ten'a. *Journal of American Folk-Lore* 25, no. 95:66–71.

1914 *Ten'a Texts and Tales from Anvik, Alaska.* With Vocabulary by Pliny Earle Goddard. Publication of the American Ethnological Society, no. 6. Edited by Franz Boas. Leiden, Netherlands: E. S. Brill.

1921 Tinneh Animism. *American Anthropologist* 23 (3):298–310.

1948 *A Camp on the Yukon.* Cornwall-on-Hudson, New York: Idle-wild Press.

Chapman, John W., and James M. Kari

1981 *Athabaskan Stories from Anvik.* [Rev. John W. Chapman's "Ten'a Texts and Tales"] Retranscribed and edited by James M. Kari. Fairbanks: Alaska Native Language Center, University of Alaska.

Chowning, Ann

1962 Raven Myths of Northwestern North America and Northeastern Asia. *Arctic Anthropology* 1 (1):1–5. Madison, Wisconsin: University of Wisconsin Press.

Clark, Annette McFadyen

1970 Koyukon Athabascan Ceremonialism. *Athabascan Studies, The Western Canadian Journal of Anthropology* 2 (1):80–88. Special editor, Regna Darnell.

1974 *Koyukuk River Culture.* Mercury Series, Ethnology Service Paper no. 18. Ottawa: National Museum of Man.

1975 Upper Koyukuk River Koyukon Athapaskan Social Culture: An Overview. In *Proceedings, Northern Athapaskan Conference, 1971,* vol. 1:146–80. Edited by A. McFadyen Clark. Mercury Series, Ethnology Service Paper no. 27 (2 vols). Ottawa: National Museum of Man.

1981 Koyukon. In *Handbook of North American Indians* (general editor, William C. Sturtevant), vol. 6, *Subarctic* (volume editor, June Helm): 582–601. Washington, D.C.: Smithsonian Institution.

Dall, William Healey

1870 *Alaska and Its Resources.* Boston: Lee and Shepard.

Fitzhugh, William W., and Aron Crowell, editors

1988 *Crossroads of Continents: Cultures of Siberia and Alaska.* Washington, D.C.: Smithsonian Institution Press.

Fortuine, Robert

1992 *Chills and Fever: Health and Disease in the Early History of Alaska.* Fairbanks: University of Alaska Press.

Giddings, Louis

1941 Rock Paintings in Central Alaska. *American Antiquity* 7 (1):69–70, pl. 9.

Hallowell, A. Irving

1926 Bear Ceremonialism in the Northern Hemisphere. *American Anthropologist* 28:1–175.

Hosley, Edward H.

1981a Environment and Culture in the Alaska Plateau. In *Handbook of North American Indians* (general editor, William C. Sturtevant), vol. 6, *Subarctic* (volume editor, June Helm): 533–45. Washington, D.C.: Smithsonian Institution.

1981b Intercultural Relations and Cultural Change in the Alaska Plateau. In *Handbook of North American Indians*, vol. 6, *Subarctic*: 546–55.

1981c Kolchan. In *Handbook of North American Indians*, vol. 6, *Subarctic*: 618–22.

Hrdlička, Aleš

1930 *Anthropological Survey in Alaska.* Bureau of American Ethnology, 46th Annual Report. Washington, D.C.

Jetté, Jules

1906–07 L'Organisation sociale des Ten'as. *Congrès International des Américanistes, 15th Session, Quebec* (1906)1:395–409.

1907 On the Medicine-men of the Ten'as. *Journal of the Royal Anthropological Institute* 37:157–88. London.

1908–09 On Ten'a Folk-Lore. *Journal of the Royal Anthropological Institute* 38 (11):298–367; and 39 (12):460–505. London.

1911 On the Superstitions of the Ten'a Indians (Middle Part of the Yukon Valley, Alaska). *Anthropos* 16:95–108, 241–59, 602–15, 699–723.

1913 Riddles of the Ten'a Indians. *Anthropos* 8:181–201, 630–51.

Jochelson, Waldemar

1908 *The Koryak.* Jesup North Pacific Expedition, vol. 6. Leiden and New York: American Museum of Natural History.

de Laguna, Frederica

1934 *The Archaeology of Cook Inlet, Alaska.* Philadelphia: University of Pennsylvania Press. (See second revised edition, Anchorage, Alaska, 1975).

1935 Expedition to the Yukon. *The University Museum Bulletin* (December) 7:50–57. Philadelphia: University of Pennsylvania Press.

1936a An Archaeological Reconnaissance of the Middle and Lower Yukon Valley, Alaska. *American Antiquity* 2 (1):6–12.

1936b Preliminary Report of an Archaeological and Geological Reconnaissance of the Middle and Lower Yukon Valley. *Miscellanea* 1(2):31–40. Philadelphia: American Philosophical Society.

1936c Indian Masks from the Lower Yukon. *American Anthropologist* 38(4):569–85, pls. 17–20, figs. 1–3.

1947 *The Prehistory of Northern North America As Seen from the Yukon.* Memoirs of the Society for American Archaeology, no. 3. Menasha, Wisconsin.

1956 *Chugach Prehistory: The Archaeology of Prince William Sound, Alaska.* Anthropological Publications of the University of Washington, no. 13. Seattle: University of Washington Press.

1975a *The Archaeology of Cook Inlet, Alaska.* Second revised edition, with a Foreword by Karen W. Workman and William B. Workman, and a Preface to the second edition by the author. Anchorage: Alaska Historical Society.

1975b Matrilineal Kin Groups in Northwestern North America. In *Proceedings, Northern Athapaskan Conference, 1971,* vol. 1:19–145. Edited by A. McFadyen Clark. Mercury Series, Ethnology Service Paper 27 (2 vols). Ottawa: National Museum of Man.

de Laguna, Frederica, and Catharine McClellan

1981 Ahtna [Atna]. In *Handbook of North American Indians* (general editor, William C. Sturtevant), vol. 6, *Subarctic* (volume editor, June Helm): 641–63. Washington, D.C.: Smithsonian Institution.

Loyens, William J.

1964 The Koyukon Feast for the Dead. *Arctic Anthropology* 2(2):133–48. Madison, Wisconsin: University of Wisconsin Press.

McClellan, Catharine

1975 *My Old People Say: An Ethnographic Survey of Southern Yukon Territory.* Publications in Ethnology, no. 6. (2 vols). Ottawa: National Museum of Man.

McKennan, Robert A.

1981 Tanana. In *Handbook of North American Indians* (general editor, William C. Sturtevant), vol. 6, *Subarctic* (volume editor, June Helm): 562–76. Washington, D.C.: Smithsonian Institution.

Nelson, Edward W.

1899 *The Eskimo About Bering Strait.* Bureau of American Ethnology,

Eighteenth Annual Report (part 1). Washington, D.C.: Smithsonian Institution.

Nelson, Richard K.

1983 *Make Prayers to the Raven: A Koyukon View of the Northern Forest.* Chicago and London: University of Chicago Press.

Olson, Wallace M.

1981 Minto, Alaska. In *Handbook of North American Indians* (general editor, William C. Sturtevant), vol. 6, *Subarctic* (volume editor, June Helm):704–11. Washington, D.C.: Smithsonian Institution.

Osgood, Cornelius

1936a *The Distribution of the Northern Athapaskan Indians.* Yale University Publications in Anthropology, no. 7. New Haven: Yale University Press.

1936b *Contributions to the Ethnography of the Kutchin.* Yale University Publications in Anthropology, no. 14. New Haven: Yale University Press.

1940 *Ingalik Material Culture.* Yale University Publications in Anthropology, no. 22. New Haven: Yale University Press.

1958 *Ingalik Social Culture.* Yale University Publications in Anthropology, no. 53. New Haven: Yale University Press.

1959 *Ingalik Mental Culture.* Yale University Publications in Anthropology, no. 56. New Haven: Yale University Press.

Parsons, Elsie Clews

1921–22 A Narrative of the Ten'a of Anvik, Alaska. *Anthropos* 16–17:51–71.

Petroff, Ivan

1884 *Alaska. U.S. Tenth Census, 1880.* Washington, D.C.: Government Printing Office.

Renner, Louis L., S.J.

1993 The Koyukon Athapaskan Stickdance and the Changed Attitude of the Jesuit Missionaries Toward It. *Alaska History* 8(1):1–13. Anchorage: Alaska Historical Society.

Savishinsky, Joel S.

1975 The Dog and the Hare [Indians]: Canine Culture in an Athapaskan Band. In *Proceedings: Northern Athapaskan Conference, 1971*, vol. 2:462–515. Edited by A. McFadyen Clark. Mercury Series, Ethnology Service Paper no. 27 (2 vols.) Ottawa: National Museum of Man.

Snow, Jeanne H.

1981 Ingalik. In *Handbook of North American Indians* (general editor, William C. Sturtevant), vol. 6, *Subarctic* (volume editor, June Helm):602–17. Washington, D.C.: Smithsonian Institution.

Solomon, Madeline

1981 *Madeline Solomon, Koyukuk.* [Autobiography]. Blaine, WA, and Surrey, BC: Hancock House, for the Yukon-Koyukuk School District.

Stevens, Edward T.

1974 *Alaskan Petroglyphs and Pictographs.* Rasmuson Library, University of Alaska, Fairbanks. MS and microform.

Sullivan, Robert J., S.J.

1942 *The Ten'a Food Quest.* Catholic University of America. Anthropological Series, no. 11. Washington, D.C.: Catholic University of America Press.

Swanton, John R.

1908 *Social Condition, Beliefs, and Linguistic Relationship of the Tlingit Indians.* Bureau of American Ethnology. Twenty-sixth Annual Report, pp. 391–485, pls. 48–58. Washington, D.C.: Smithsonian Institution.

1909 *Tlingit Myths and Texts.* Bureau of American Ethnology. Bulletin 39. Washington, D.C.: Smithsonian Institution.

Thompson, Chad

1990 *K'etetaalkkaanee, The One Who Paddled Among the People and Animals: An Analytical Companion Volume* [to Attla 1990]. Fairbanks: The Yukon-Koyukuk School District and the Alaska Native Language Center.

Thompson, Judy

1990 *Pride of the Indian Wardrobe: Native Athapaskan Foot Wear.* Published for the Bata Shoe Museum. Toronto, Buffalo, London: University of Toronto Press.

VanStone, James W., and Ives Goddard

1981 Territorial Groups of West-Central Alaska Before 1898. In *Handbook of North American Indians* (general editor, William C. Sturtevant), vol. 6, *Subarctic* (volume editor, June Helm): 556–61. Washington, D.C.: Smithsonian Institution.

Whymper, Frederick

1869 *Travel and Adventure in the Territory of Alaska.* New York: Harper & Brothers.

Zagoskin, Lavrentiy Alekseyevich

1967 *Lieutenant Zagoskin's Travels in Russian America, 1842–1844.* (The 1847–48 text.) Edited by Henry N. Michael. Translated by Penelope Rainey. Toronto: University of Toronto Press, for the Arctic Institute of North America.

INDEX

adaptability, Native, 45
adze and axe, 11, 38, 101
afterbirth, 61
aged: care for, 161
Ahtna (Atna) Copper River Athabaskans, xviii; fish-smoking, 9;
  clans, 22, 25; doorway as profane, 38; starvation deaths, 40;
  cremation, 52; ritual cannibalism,
  56; riddles, 285; historical traditions of, 289; taboo on killing
  dogs, 294; attitude to bear, 295
Air, People (Spirits) of the, 57
airplane, 6, 13
Alaska Native Language Center,
  Fairbanks (ANLC), xvii, xviii, 13,
  78
alphabets, Native, 13, 78–79
amulets: bags or boxes, 52, 62; as
  animal songs (Ingalik), 59
animals: once human, 47–48, 58,
  154, 292; names of, 48, 59, 60, 61,
  235–36, 271; souls, loss of (Koyukon), 58; disposal of remains of,
  59–60, 61, 68; important, 59, 294–
  96; in myths, 75, 292–98; tame,
  229–30, 293; food for, 317–18;
  human change to, 333
Animals' Ceremony (Ingalik), 59
animal spirits (yega), 38, 58–61;
  songs of (Ingalik), 59; homes of,
  in hills, 106

animate world (animism), 48
Anvik (Yukon River): mission at,
  xvii, 47
Anvik monster, 58
arrow: and bow, 10, 101; head, 156;
  magical, 309
Attla, Charlotte (Koyukuk River),
  xix, 285; on myths, 76; on storytelling, 290; classification of tales
  by, 291. Tales mentioned: Foggy
  Man, 88, 243, 300; Brown Bear,
  90, 312; Seesaw, 175; Raven and
  Whale, 219; Jealous Uncle, 229,
  316; Beaver and Porcupine, 246;
  clan war story, 289; stingy Woodpecker, 293; Wolverine, 297; Eagle
  Man, 308, 309, 313; descent from
  Sky Land, 308; Traveler, 309–10,
  324, 327, 330–32; Raven, 313, 319–
  20, 323; escape from cannibals,
  317
audience for storytelling, 73–74
autobiography: of Native elders, 13;
  of Francis McGinty, 249–53
awls: aboriginal bone, 11
axe and adze, 11, 31, 101, 317

backrest, 109
bags, skin toboggan, 7, 317
Baker (Tanana River) Indians, 15
ball playing, 172
band (subtribal unit), 20

341